Contents

List of Illustrations

Acknowledgments

I have dedicated this book to a special and wonderful teacher, Joseph Campbell, and quoted him often in its pages. However, I take full responsibility for my own approach, and the philosophical world view presented herein. I learned much from twenty-three years of study and association with Campbell; but he always encouraged his students not only to follow the creative spirit that pulled us most strongly—our "bliss"—but to think for ourselves. Even more than for his vast knowledge and personal kindness, I thank him for that.

Although myth beckons me always to make pilgrimage to its storied temples and groves, it is in my ongoing work as a psychotherapist that I feel I have done my own deepest explorations. It is precisely the dialogue between myth and psyche that has provided the inspiration—and the substance—for this book. I gratefully acknowledge the contribution of my clients, whose luminous words, dreams, and images fill these pages. From Joseph I learned to look for great things in the small, the minutiae of life, and to read images as full of potential meaning; I also learned never to devalue another perspective, person, or tradition. But my clients and students have also been my teachers in a very real way, and I owe them a debt of gratitude. Wounded in life (as we all are) they took the dare of an inner journey with me and my own very human limitations as a guide—to find the healing path. In the process they deepened their, and my own, sense of life's mystery, wonder, and somehow hopefulness.

Now, through giving permission for pieces of their journeys—I call them mythogems—to appear in this book, they have empowered a still larger community to deepen and extend their own vision, sense of inquiry into the deep things of life, and hope.

Special thanks are due to my wife, Robin, for her own dreams, drawings, and substantial editing and archival work. My analysis and training with Dr. Edward Whitmont and Dr. Stanislav Grof provided insights of extraordinary depth and importance that subsequently inspired my own therapeutic style.

Barbara Zucker worked long hours on word processors, reading my cryptic notes and helping with details. Roger and Jennifer Woolger, Julie Garrison, and George Dole read my manuscript and provided helpful commentary. Jonathan Fox helped my explorations in psychodrama, and clowning; Arya Maloney and Lucy Barbera helped with pictures, dialogue, and stories about sandplay. William and James Thorpe contributed lore and experience in living mythology. The sapient word processor *Nota Bene*—and our household R2D2s—also helped with scholarly detail; and in Leslie Meredith, this book finally managed to find just the editor it wanted.

Foreword

≋

In 1980 I chaired a symposium on personal mythology at the American Psychological Association's annual convention, held in New York City. One of the speakers was Dr. Stephen Larsen, who described how his studies of shamanism had led to his conceptualization of personal mythology, and his use of that concept in education, counseling, and psychotherapy.

Myths have not enjoyed great currency in recent years. The very word is used as a synonym for falsehood. Yet Stephen Larsen realized that mythic narratives are patterns of meaning that state and restate universal human activities. As such, their accounts of creation, conflict, and achievement are metaphors for concerns common to all those who participate in the human adventure.

Cultural myths served several vital purposes. They explained the workings of the world to those bewildered by natural phenomena. They assisted people's transitions through life's developmental stages. They helped members of a society find meaning in their social position, economic status, and ethical constraints. They enabled human beings to participate in the mysteries of the cosmos and to worship an entity or process deemed worthy of supreme importance.[1] However, cultural myths became fragmented when science and technology produced dependable ways to understand and control nature; when pluralism seeped into monolithic societies; and when religious doctrine, national laws, and social customs provided frameworks—often sterile—by which people's behavior could be directed.

Yet the deep need for underlying symbols and metaphors remained; personal existence without myth was unsatisfying and stultifying. As a result, myths became personalized, albeit on an unconscious level.[2] Portions of these personal myths surfaced during dreams; reveries; bodily feelings; play;

passion; slips of the tongue; ritualistic behavior; and spontaneous music making, dance, writing, drawing, and painting. From these sources one can discern what Larsen calls
the psychomythology of everyday life.

The Mythic Imagination is an engrossing account of personal mythmaking that draws on Larsen's extensive experience as an educator, counselor, and psychotherapist. He
demonstrates how rigid personal myths warp an individual's
experience and distort one's perception of the world. Moreover, a paucity of myths in a person's mythology may
impair flexibility, openness, and those coping mechanisms
that allow behavior to alter as life circumstances change.
Larsen points out the shortcomings of those myths held by
the cynic as well as the dogmatic believer; neither glimpses
the "hero with a thousand faces,"[3] the myriad of options
available to all recipients of humankind's legacy.

STANLEY KRIPPNER, PH.D.

THE MYTHIC IMAGINATION

Our Fortunes and Lives seem Chaotic when they are looked at as facts. There is order and meaning only in the great truths believed by everybody in that older wiser time of the world when things were less well known but better understood.

—RODERICK MACLEISH

I believe that the mythic revival that is now under way is no mere fad. In modern times myths have been thought of as illusions, but if so, they are the kind that still retain the power, as Joseph Campbell put it, "to carry the human spirit forward." Psychologist Jean Houston identified myth as the cognitive and emotional DNA of the psyche—somehow ever new, always generative, yet as old as the hills that hide the ancient secrets of our race.

The fresh and open mind of the child creates and understands myths intuitively, whereas the psychotherapist, the creative writer, and the scholar labor long to mine myth's rich veins of wisdom and creative inspiration. Yet even now, mythology emerges as the legacy of a whole planet. To understand other people and other cultures and the images we share—and fail to share—with our fellows, we must relearn an aboriginal language: the universal tongue of the human imagination. With its inexhaustible vocabulary of symbol and story, it is at once our ancestral birthright and the ever-brimming well of dreams into which we look to find our future. I call this innate resource of ours "the mythic imagination."

THE BRIGHT WORLD

As I am writing this introduction, I interrupt my solitary work to teach a college class titled "The Psychology of Consciousness." In it the students keep dream journals, and I ask for a recent dream, to demonstrate a method of dream interpretation we have been discussing. A woman artist in her forties presents the following dream.

I dream that there is a world next to this one. It's similar but different, bright, colorful, beautiful. The people are more like royalty, kings, queens, noble persons. But there's something going on between that world and this. Though it's beautiful there, they need something from this world. I think it's children, they need to marry them. They're pledged from a very early age. If the parents know it's all right, they're honored, but if not . . . I don't know. There's something about the age of eighteen, at that age they have to make the contact. I see the doorways between the worlds: They are like great arches.

Dreams are wild things, as I have found from years of meeting with them in all sorts of strange places, and they do not always lend themselves to our interpretations. At times, we may get the feeling that dreams allow us to peer into another world. My student had no personal associations whatever to her intriguing dream, so I inquired further. I first asked her if she had ever read the magical Welsh epic, *The Mabinogion.* She had not, nor had she any familiarity with Celtic mythology, where the "bright world" lies so close to this, that heroes such as Pwyll or the wizard Gwydion are always back and forth through those mysterious doors glimpsed by my dreamer. Nor did she know any stories of the Sidhe, the fair folk, with their age-old affection for earthly children and history of child theft.[1]

As my questions brought up the topic of the fair folk and the hollow hills, her eyes lit up in a wonderful way. She somewhat shyly admitted she was of Welsh background and had been having powerful dreams and visions like the one presented here for years. She asked if I thought such things could "travel in the blood." I told her that most scientists would probably say no, but she would do best to trust her own experience. The dream was to have an empowering effect on her creativity, as she told me sometime later. Just as in the final image of her dream, new doorways were opened for her.

I have often seen the enlivening effect of the revelation of a "big" dream such as this one in a communal space, and our classroom was no exception. The students in the class asked the dreamer questions about her other dreams and visions and retold some of their own. As in the long-ago campfire or longhouse ceremonies of our ancestors, when the dream breaks into this world from that unknown one, it brings with it another kind of illumination: the light of the mythic imagination. Seeing into the other world, using our imagination, requires a different kind of seeing—with the inner eye, the mind's eye—that we have almost, it seems, forgotten how to do. And that is why, as the legends tell us, that other world is "the bright world." Its images, the myth forms, are lit from within, "self-luminous." Simply to contemplate them kindles the imagination, and they are contagious, they may illumine other human minds. That is why the native Americans referred to certain dreams as "big dreams": They show us how large our mind truly is.

The dream, as I heard it, was exactly suited to introducing the subject of this book, even prickling my scalp as I considered how appropriate it was. Such an event seems remarkable, but shows how dreams and myths slip from one human imagination to another, even without our conscious awareness.

"There is another world," this dream says. "Right next to our own." It is a bright world, a world of colorful and memorable images, royalty, pageants, and great stories being enacted. And there are doorways between the worlds, for each world needs something from the other. Something even as intimate as marriages may be going on. The other world needs children from this one. That is to say, the other world requires the imagination that is alive in us as children, which seems to wither away for most of us after the age of eighteen, as the dream implies. What would it take to keep those doorways open? I hope that this book will help you to open doors in your own mind.

This current world of ours would appear to be physical, sociopolitical, and economic. But our sixth sense—the imagination—discerns another, which shines and streams through cracks in our visible universe. But let us peek, for a moment, back into the imaginal world of our origins. . . .

CHILDHOOD MYTHOLOGIES

The children are playing. "I am a princess, and you are ugly goblins," says one. Suddenly the room is full of ugly goblins, hopping and capering, scratching their sides and making weird cries, while the princess recoils in mock revulsion. They are still children, and yet they are indeed goblins and a princess, in some immemorial drama. With the conspiracy of the imagination, somehow our child mind knows we can fill the world with wonders.

Do you remember how, in that time before the time when we all grew up, there were monsters and magicians everywhere? How a single phrase or image could set us off into a delirium of storytelling and mythmaking? And a darkened basement could so swarm with mind-created images that we fled in terror? Cartoonist Gary Larson has told us of the ultimate torture of the childhood mythic imagination: His older brother would lock him in the basement and, as little Gary stood pleading at the door above that well of darkness, intone, "They're coming, Gary, *they're coming . . .*" The cruelly clever lad knew he needn't even specify what "they" were; his younger brother's mind would do the rest.[2]

But there are other aspects to this proximity of the child mind and the world of myth. When I was growing up, in our neighborhood, as in many others, there was an unfortunate boy (I shall call him Johnnie), who was overweight. The children would follow him around, celebrating this one trait of his—ignoring all the others—he was fat, Fat, FAT! He could crush chairs, eat a mountain of pies, and if he fell down he would never rise again. This time may have seen my own dawning recognition of, indeed, the power of myth. In this case, sensing also the potential cruelty of that power, my cousin (fellow collaborator and mythmaker) and I tried to carry the mythmaking beyond the level of personal cruelty into insane humor: Johnnie could fly like a dirigible, but when he chose to descend, squash legions of his enemies; raise the levels of the oceans by going swimming; even affect the gravitational field of the earth. As I think back on those days, I realize that profound currents were moving beneath the surface of our child minds. Embarrassed by the cruelty and secretly sympathetic with Johnnie (who was funny and smart as well as fat), we sought to liberate his personal defect by hypermythologizing it to the transpersonal level—a fatness that lost its individual reference as it became cosmic.

Once we got the idea, we were a virtually unstoppable myth-and-comedy team. There was Arthur, who was big and strong and not very smart. We mythologized raw elemental power without cognition: Arthur could overturn cars, throw teachers out the window, walk through walls without stopping. (I know now we were creating Heracles,

Paul Bunyan, or perhaps Godzilla.) One neighborhood boy was excessively vain and self-important, but in our mythology he could stun crowds, merely by his presence; they would be so impressed they could not move. The only way to neutralize him was with a mirror, which he could not resist (I did not yet know the Narcissus story, nor how Perseus approached Medusa with a mirror-shield). Another fellow was quite nosy, but his nose, far outstripping Pinocchio's, became so long it could knock over roomsful of people or allow him to sit on the bottom of the sea, while his periscopic nose cruised the surface like some impossible sea serpent.[3]

In addition to keeping us entertained for hours, our myth-making showed me a number of things about life and the human imagination. These began to crystallize into psychological insights for me as an adult. Mythmaking, I saw, in fact goes on every day, all the time; and these bright, large images fit so well into our perceptions that we grow unused to seeing without them. Undigested myths are cruel and full of childish prejudice, but how many of them indeed persist into adulthood? Stereotypes may well grow out of archetypes.[4] We all have an intuitive idea of how stereotypes work: a fixed set of unexamined inner images and values substitutes for an ongoing open-ended experience of reality. Archie Bunker's world makes us laugh because its simplifying solution to reality is so familiar and easy to grasp. We have understood his mythscape. We know how he regards women, minorities, and certain political issues and laugh when he confirms our worst expectations. His myth has deformed his world into a caricature of the real one—filled with stereotypical images of mindless housewives, shiftless blacks, or "the yellow peril."

Of myths then, it might be asked, how do we "head them off at the pass"—before they move in a painfully self-limiting way into the stereotyping mind of the child within the adult? The immediate corollary to this question might be: How do we, at the same time, preserve the creativity and the wonder of the mythmaking mind of the child? The last part of this book particularly addresses this question.

MYTHS IN THE WORLD OF ADULTHOOD

In college, dissatisfied with the unadorned psychology of behaviorism, I began to study myth and comparative religion, and found them to add an important dimension to understanding the human mind. In graduate school I went on to the psychology of language (psycholinguistics) and anthropology, which deepened my conviction that mythological ideas permeate human consciousness.[5] Can there be *personal* mythologies, I wondered, as well as the traditional kinds that belong to a whole culture? (This is the issue that I take up in Chapter 1.) Is it possible for people to be caught up in myths unaware, so that they find themselves enacting a mythic drama whose plot we would understand if we had access to the mythic key? (This poignant issue is taken up in Chapter 2.)

What of people willing to live and die for a myth? As our questions grow in size, the very well-being of humanity seems implicated. The areas of research they lead to extend past the boundaries of psychology into philosophy, religion, and sociology. People with fanatical or fundamentalist myths, for example, may behave in ways that violate common sense or a spirit of compromise. Religious differences have often been the cause of wars: Christian against Moslem, Hindu against Buddhist. But even subtle differences in theology can cause rifts *within* religions: Catholic against Protestant, Shiite against Sunni. Mythology is obviously implicated in many thorny controversies of the day: creationism versus evolutionary theory, pro-choice versus right to life, and equal rights issues in a traditionally patriarchal culture.

If you overhear different camps arguing, they may sound as if they were speaking different languages, but actually, their underlying mythologies are fundamentally different.

These deeper mythic structures give rise to different values, points of view, and emotions. Myths affect social units as small as families and as large as nations.

Carl Jung thought that the best instruction in the language of archetypes (primordial patterns of meaning that influence our psychology) were the grand old texts of mythology. If we can learn to recognize the heroes, demonic or shadow figures, and godlike images that occur over and again throughout the history of the human imagination, we may fare better when they beset us personally. Recognizing the archetypes might save us from succumbing to stereotypes. This is why it is useful to compare dream and myth. We may look to our dreams, or daydreams, and find a deed-performing figure resembling Heracles, thus we come to suspect a heroic element in our personal psychology. We might encounter seductive Aphrodite or warlike Ares and learn that the classic gods and goddesses are not dead, but very much alive in our individual psyches. Can we learn from the strong contrasts and high relief their stories display?

While working as a psychotherapist for the New York State Department of Mental Hygiene in the early 1960s, I saw how often the dreams of naive and uneducated people contained mythological symbols. The imagination need not be specially tutored to be swarming with myths. My patients were in and out of the state hospital system and led bleak and usually depressing lives. Those who were not tranquilized into stupor, however, often had vivid imaginations, as if to compensate for that outer barrenness. The patients spoke of voices and visions, strange delusions, and carnivalesque fantasies.

The confrontation with this world was disturbing to my own psyche. It is one thing, I found, to romanticize the mythic imagination but another actually to swim between Scylla and Charybdis, to risk the terror of drowning in the fathomless unconscious. I entered Jungian analysis myself to help me recognize and develop my own relation to archetypal patterns within. From in-depth work on my own dreams I learned to work with others.

THE VITALITY OF MYTH

In Joseph Campbell, whom I first met in 1963, I found a long-term teacher and friend who had swum in those same seas for decades. Although not a therapist himself, Campbell knew beyond doubt that myths contained a wisdom for life, and he was at home with the inexhaustible variety of world myths.

In addition to a very valuable internship with him, which I began in 1971, Campbell was to set my wife, Robin, and me on an extraordinary series of mythological journeys around the world to cultures whose mythologies were still alive and well: On an initial trip we lived in India, Sri Lanka, and Nepal. While my wife, who is an artist and art historian, focused on art, temple architecture, and rituals, I studied myths and spiritual psychologies such as yoga and meditation. Later we visited the ruined palaces of Crete, the amphitheaters and sacred sites of Greece, the paleolithic caves of France, and the megalithic sites throughout Europe and Great Britain. One more recent trip included research in Scandinavia, as visiting scholars under the auspices of the Swedish Institute, and another focused on the rituals and spiritual systems of Japan.

Our journeys to other cultures showed me that living mythologies play a profound role in the lives of their participants. I saw further how important it is for modern people to find their mythic roots and regain their lost sense of spiritual connectedness to the universe. During a visit to the Parthenon in Athens, our seven-year-old son, Merlin, who had just been to Asia with us, said, "These places aren't alive; no one takes off their shoes, or lights candles." He knew the difference. When we went to Chartres Cathedral,

FIGURE 1. *Joseph Campbell at Esalen Institute, 1982.* (PHOTO © KATH-LEEN THORMOD CARR.)

on its lovely hill in rural France, however, and visited the very moving shrine of the Black Madonna and saw the candles lit, we knew that Western mythology was not dead, but alive in the root, and quietly awaiting another spiritual renaissance.

In my first book, *The Shaman's Doorway,* I introduced the term *mythic imagination,* showing how modern people could use age-old shamanic wisdom to reconnect with their mytho-logical roots. The book expressed my deep belief that we must not only learn from history but, in part, reclaim it: especially our inherent powers of vision and creativity, magic and healing. Hence I relied on material from traditional societies: Iroquois and Senoi dream psychologies, ancient and modern tales of shamans, Patanjali's venerable *Yoga Sutras,* and more modern styles of *sādhana,* or spiritual practice—"something old and something new," as in the required ritual for wedding gifts. (Maybe something old in psyche is always marrying something new; something from this world—as in my student's dream—marrying something from the timeless world.)

In this book my focus is more on the psyches of contemporary people and their personal mythologies. I am increasingly convinced we need not necessarily go to places and eras that are strange and exotic, but may find what we are looking for close at home: wisdom and power to make our lives wonder-full, interior decorations for our souls.

Sigmund Freud's office was full of art, especially Greek and Egyptian archaeological artifacts. His work was full of antiquities as well: myths of "the primal horde," the endlessly enacted tragedy of Oedipus, and later, the great contest of the gods of life and death, Eros and Thanatos. He felt acutely the closeness of myth, dream, and psyche. Carl Jung hand painted the archaic-looking frescoes in the rooms of his "medieval" stone tower—his retreat from all modern haste and its disconnectedness from psyche. He carved the stones inside and out with dwarves, mandalas, and symbols of all kinds. His psychological concepts abound with themes from mythology: wise old men, sapient serpents, witchlike animas. Both psychologists obviously felt the necessity of a richly furnished chamber of the psyche.

As a practicing psychotherapist I have come to understand Freud's office furnishings. Every psychotherapist must be prepared to be a kind of archaeologist of the spirit, willing to look at archaic fragments that arise in people. We would

FIGURE 2. *Sigmund Freud at his desk, with sculpture from his collection of primitive and ancient art. Portrait by Max Pollack (etching and drypoint, 18⅞ x 18⅞", 1914).* (PHOTO COURTESY OF SIGMUND FREUD COPYRIGHTS, LONDON.)

not always wish for these to be there, as, for example, when we find ourselves behaving atavistically, or like a "primitive." But there they are, as even some shallow, but sincere, digging will reveal: mythic fragments, the pieces of the gods.

My dual profession of college psychology teacher and psychotherapist has offered me unique opportunities for research. Students in my classes are trained to keep psychological journals, in which they regularly record dreams and fantasies. Over the years I have read (and saved, with the students' permission) hundreds of these journals. In my psychotherapy practice, people from many walks of life and various backgrounds present their dreams to me on an almost daily basis.

In the following chapters, when I quote from people's dreams, I stay close to their own words and images. This has been necessary not only because the demons of scientific objectivity are glowering over my shoulder, but also out of respect for the dream itself, which possesses its own native integrity and deserves to be rendered accurately. I see this aspect of the work I do as in no way different from that of an anthropologist or ethnologist who records verbatim the words of his native informant.

FIGURE 3. *Carl Gustav Jung in his tower at Bollingen.* (PHOTO COURTESY OF THE C. G. JUNG INSTITUTE, NEW YORK CITY.)

FIGURE 4. *Jung's tower at Bollingen on the Zurichsee. Jung built the tower with his own hands, aided by two Italian masons. "I learnt to split stones in the Bollingen quarries, and the masons also taught me a lot and I learned their art relatively quickly with a certain innate intelligence." (C. G. Jung:* Word and Image, *ed. by A. Jaffe Princeton, 1979, p. 189.) (*PHOTO BY AUTHOR.)

It is important for the reader to know that these dreams, which may sometimes seem exotic and extraordinary, come from very ordinary people in our own culture. The sample of dreams on which I have drawn numbers about 3,000, collected over a period of twenty years of teaching, clinical work, and private practice. A few are from myself or members of my family. My goal has not been to do a statistical content analysis of large numbers of dreams (as for example in Calvin Hall's famous study),[6] but to look for particular thematic elements related to the mythic imagination. In addition, because I already know much about certain dreamers' lives, I have information on how the dream may interact with life issues. I have found not only illustrations of mythic themes, but individual dreams powerful enough to speak for themselves, to retell our ancient mythologies, and to help us find the creative ones born always anew in the sometimes fiery cauldron of the here-and-now encounter with existence.

You will find that I usually identify a dreamer only as "a thirty-year-old businessman," "a forty-five-year-old woman in a 'change of life,' " and so on. My intention in this book is not really to give anything like case histories, or any kind of analytic exegeses of particular psyches. I want, rather, to show the structure of mythological ideas as they pertain to human psychology in a general sense and as they illustrate themes that are clearly alive for us today. Ultimately, you may find, as I have, that simply contemplating these dreams can change your life, opening your own mythic imagination

FIGURE 5. *The Stone, with homunculus, at Jung's tower at Bollingen on the Zurichsee. Jung carved the image and Greek inscription, which reads "Time is a child—playing like a child— playing a board game—the kingdom of the child. This is Telesphoros, who roams through the dark regions of this cosmos and glows like a star out of the depths. He points the way to the gates of the sun and to the land of dreams." (Translation from Jaffe, ed., C. G.* Jung: Word and Image, *Princeton, 1979, p. 201; and* Memories, Dreams, Reflections, *New York, 1963, p. 227.)* (PHOTO BY AUTHOR.)

in subtle ways. I feel we are entitled to learn the maps of the "living landscape" of psyche and the stations and passages on our mutual great journey. But I also wish to protect the privacy and sanctity of the personal lives who have lent their soul images to this study. As the poet W. B. Yeats put it, "The greater energies of the mind seldom break forth but when the deeps are loosed. They break forth amid events too private or too sacred for public speech, or seem themselves, I know not why, to belong to hidden things."[7]

MYTHOGEMS

I have chosen dreams as the principal source for my examples of mythic imagination, because their imagery is relatively pure, uncontaminated by our conscious ideas and theories. My concern is less the fabrication of new myths than our awakening to the presence of mythic themes in our lives—those "fragments of the gods." The mythic elements of psyche (I like the term *mythogems*) may be encountered either in the individual—say, through a dream—or a collective mythology. Campbell, using an architectural metaphor, referred to them as "bricks" in his essay "Mythogenesis."[8] We may find these structural components in a great edifice, such as a world religion, or in a far more personal dwelling, such as an individual human psyche.

The anthropologist Clyde Kluckhohn cataloged a number of recurrent mythic themes that were transcultural. These include incest, hero motifs, monster slaying, magic wielding, and a number of others.[9] Surely we must recognize the transpersonal to be an even larger category than the transcultural.

From my own dream inventory I have cataloged the following elements: the earthly paradise or garden of delights; deluge/world-catastrophe myths; undisguised incest and Oedipal themes; divine or angelic beings; elementals of nature (devas), elves, dwarves, and sprites of various sorts; the "living-landscape" quality, which is the subject of Chapter 4 (magic mountains to be ascended in stages, mysterious caves, enchanted gardens); the wounded-animal/helping-animal motif; use and abuse of magical power, magicians, shamans, witches; monsters of both bestial and superhuman varieties; people changing into beast form (theriomorphism); and rituals of all sorts, including initiations, absolutions, and transformations.

Although not myths in themselves, mythogems are the threads from which the whole cloth of a life myth might be woven. The psychoanalytically oriented reader will see that I often stay with the surface of the dream (which Freud called "manifest content"). Sometimes, but not that often, it seems necessary to penetrate layers of complex disguise or transformations of the dream material from repressed problems (which Freud called the "latent dream"). Because of a certain respect for the "material," however, I usually look first to its own patterns, as if observing the grain of wood or the spiral patterns of a shell. I believe the "deep structure" behind the dream is also the big picture of Vishnu's dream, the dream of universal mind, in which we are all the characters and images. That is why it is legitimate to compare the dreams of people who have never met and have nothing apparent to do with one another. They dream alike, however, and the dream mechanism works the same way in them, although it is handling their different personal materials. The personality of the archetypal Great Man, the Universal Human, seems to be reflected in each of us, yet wonderfully subdued and attuned to an individual human psyche.[10] We are afloat in a sea of symbols, awash in elementary forms, and we are like fish, who are the last creatures to ask, "What is a sea?"

The patterned energy of which our neurons and genes partake is the elemental force indwelling all life. Just as we find that stars, no matter how unique, strange, isolated, or how many million light-years away, are constituted of hydrogen and helium, oxygen, and carbon, so too all human beings partake of the "elementary forms" of consciousness.[11]

Noam Chomsky, the M.I.T. linguist, has postulated an inherited "deep structure" for human language learning. This he describes as the underlying, genetically transmitted pattern code for a human being to internalize and use any language from Swahili to Sanskrit. If this structure constitutes the organizing matrix for language behavior (left hemisphere), what is the corresponding organizing matrix for the right hemisphere, which specializes in more holistic activity: pattern recognition, places and faces, and emotional behavior?[12]

Only through mythmaking, Plato observed, can certain profound truths be understood, or conveyed to others. (Plato used the term *mythos* to describe storytelling: orally transmitted fables and folktales.) Philosophy was developed by the ancient Greeks, as the language of the mind, or cognition. But they knew that myths made soul talk, evoking the passions and the sense of meaning. Aristotle used *mythos* for the events or plots enacted by masked actors (see Chapter 10). The masks resonate with right-hemisphere meanings, as do gestures and tone of voice (but not content of speech). The left hemisphere tracks the plot, paying attention to sequences of things, as it likes to do. When the meaning of a sequence of actions or a pattern of behavior becomes evident, it is once again the right hemisphere that has made sense of the whole gestalt, especially its feeling implications. Myths involve us, grab us emotionally. By so doing they also reveal our emotional deep structure. Myths, dreams, and dramas are life simulators; they involve us *in vivo*.

In conscious mythmaking, the mind may be opened creatively to new possibilities and instructed with luminous images. I believe the real value of this book is to aid the reader in transforming unconscious and, therefore, potentially hurtful mythologizing—holdovers from the child mind—into mature, vibrant, and healing affirmations of life.

What I am proposing is really a kind of "awakening" to myths, because, although mythic symbols are universal and perennial (embedded not only in all the traditions of world culture, but in the human psyche as well), on the whole, we have been asleep to their potential—and what to do with them. But once they have begun to speak to consciousness, we can never return to sleep in the same way. The myths we have come to know consciously, live ever after in our creative imaginations, as well as our dreams.

The chapters that follow each move in their own way between psychology and myth. I do not think that I am marshaling scientific evidence to bolster my points, but simply detailing *human experience,* which, if truth be told, is what life is really about.

Part One

～～～

PSYCHOLOGY, MYTHS, AND MAPS

Chapter 1

THE ROOTS
OF PERSONAL
MYTHOLOGY

The latest incarnation of Oedipus, the continued romance of Beauty and the Beast, stand this afternoon on the corner of Forty-second Street and Fifth Avenue, waiting for the light to change.

—JOSEPH CAMPBELL

The term *personal mythology* contains an inner contradiction. Myths are by nature transpersonal—beyond individuals—and their elements are universal themes. How then can they be "personal"? Whenever any of us becomes a hero, a dragon, a princess, or any of the other dramatis personae of the mythological world, we are dissolved in an archetype—an identity larger than ourselves. Our personal uniqueness perishes as we enter an eternal role. And yet it is only through entering this paradoxical zone that we truly find our individuality, as I hope to show herein. Ephemeral as we human beings are, the myths seem to be our windows to eternity.

For some, *personal mythology* may immediately summon the world of psychiatry, madness, and asocial individualism—and those curious patients whose minds and lives seem to hold the carnival mirror up to classic mythology: self-appointed world saviors, the delusion of magical powers such as mind reading or a gaze that can destroy. And mythological language has long been familiar to psychology. Narcissus has lent his myth to a great many successors, and Oedipus as well. Modern people still partake of mythic themes, but in very singular ways.

Group behavior looks for its validation to the collective myths we call religions, so time-honored and familiar we forget "fantastic facts" on which they are based. Joseph Campbell has defined myths (lightly) as "other people's religions." And we shall see this may be true in the personal as well as the collective sense of *religion*. As I was working on earlier versions of this manuscript, my typist kept rendering the term "personal my theology," throughout. After I got over my annoyance, I thought, "Not bad," seeing the message in the mistake. No matter how collective and ancient—or, in contrast, unique and novel—the belief system is still held to be valid by an individual person.[1]

The further from our own world view such a system is, the more we tend to read its imagery and significance as "myth" or as a peculiar delusion that probably has some kind of psychological significance to its adherent, but little or no positive value and more likely a negative one. By this definition, a person living in a myth is wearing blinders, or a filter woven of habitual credulity and indoctrinated dogma, which distorts a clear view of the world.

Campbell's deeper reading of myth takes us closer to the sense in which I want to introduce the concept of personal mythology in this chapter. As he put it, "Mythological symbols touch and exhilarate centers of life beyond the reach of vocabularies of reason and coercion."[2] Nowadays, it seems, this exhilaration is missing from our lives, as many of us try to find a meaningful path through life in a universe rendered secular, stark, and inhuman somehow by the revelations of science. We might feel at times a nostalgia for our old illusions, perhaps a longing to return to a vision of the universe ensouled, in which the isolated human adventure participates somehow, in a larger, spiritual ecology.

PSYCHOLOGY AND MYTH

Carl Jung completed a revolutionary book on myths in mental illness, *The Psychology of the Unconscious,* in 1911. Some years later, he wrote,

> Hardly had I finished the manuscript when it struck me what it means to live with a myth and what it means to live without one. Myth, says a Church Father, is "what is believed always, everywhere, by everybody"; hence the man who thinks he can live without myth, or outside it, is an exception. He is like one uprooted, having no true link either with past, or with the ancestral life which continues within him, or yet with contemporary human society.[3]

Jung made it his life's work to show that only by understanding myths can one truly understand psychology, and vice versa. Mythology provided the basis for understanding the dreams and symbolic images of modern people. This approach appealed to his older mentor of the time, Sigmund Freud, who wrote back to Jung, "One thing and another have turned my thoughts toward mythology and I am beginning to suspect that myth and neurosis have a common core."[4]

Later Jung wrote to him, "Now to better things—mythology. For me there is no longer any doubt what the oldest and most natural myths are trying to say. They speak quite 'naturally' of the nuclear complex of neurosis."[5]

Right at the turn of this century, then, these two great psychologists of abnormal behavior hypothesized that the neglected myths of our long, myth-filled history, which had gone underground during the European Enlightenment, were now to be found in the subterranean space of the psyche, the unconscious. Cultural historians as well as psychologists and therapists of all kinds are still encountering the impact of this revelatory notion, which itself constitutes a myth—a pattern of meaning—for our time.

But Freud and Jung, the two torchbearers who offered to conduct twentieth-century culture into this uncharted zone of the shadows, found different paths in the labyrinth and different meanings for myth, and went their separate ways.[6] They who hoped to illuminate one place—*the* unconscious— by the brilliance of their revelatory theories, found themselves in separate realities. Freud came to see myths as neurotic distortions, illusions without much future,[7] except for the psychoanalyst, who would find them, perforce, in his consulting room and in the psychopathology of everyday life (the title of one of his books). Jung, in marked contrast, felt myths contain the creative wellsprings of personality and invite humanity to contemplate a spiritual reality within our own nature, a grail to the quest of modern man in search of a soul (the title of one of his books). In these two perspectives we may sense a great division of values that is abroad in our time—and perhaps will be for some time to come.[8]

"I have a few objections to your method of dealing with mythology," Freud wrote to Jung in 1911, toward the end of their friendship.[9] Jung was "above" the material, not in it, he complained. Jung had just written to him, "the outlook for me is very gloomy if you get into the psychology of religion. You are a dangerous rival—if one has to speak of rivalry. . . . Our personal differences will make our work different."[10] This last was prophetic, although at the time Jung did not know *how* different.

Throughout the following chapters I return to this mythic split in the two psychologists a number of times, as a kind of leitmotiv, invoking the words of these masters often on a particular subject or theme of myth and psyche. Freud is always veering toward the personal and the historical, and

Jung toward the transpersonal and mythological. I feel that they both illustrate personal mythology in a fascinating way and at the same time speak for principal factions in modern thought.

LITERARY PERSONAL MYTHOLOGIES

Psychologists were not the only minds arrested by this paradox of collective image and personal life. Another root of modern personal mythology begins in eighteenth-century literature with the visionary poet William Blake. Blake's personal mythology was so richly elaborated that it overflowed constantly into his art, forming, in fact, a living tissue of creative imagination. Reason became personified as Urizen, an old man ruled by his own calculations; the creative imagination was the fiery Los, who transforms what he touches; the rebellious human spirit as wicked Orc, whose fate is to be bound and chained; and Oothoon, the lovely and vulnerable feminine eros, whose fate is to be violated. For Blake, the human soul and the world were in constant symbolic interpenetration.

> For all are Men in Eternity: Rivers, Mountains, Cities,
>   Villages,
> All are Human, & when you enter into their Bosoms you
>   walk
> In Heavens & Earths, as in your own Bosom you bear
>   your Heaven
> And Earth & all you behold; tho' it appears Without,
>   it is Within,
> In your Imagination, of which this World of Mortality is
>   but a shadow.[11]

Blake could well be the first herald of the awakening of mythic imagination in modern Western civilization, and may have understood it better than anyone since the Platonists, whose tradition is probably the deepest historical taproot of mythic imagination in the West.[12] For Plato, the human mind was always losing its primordial spiritual awareness. Blake believed the remedy lay in the human imagination. "To the Eyes of the Man of Imagination, Nature is Imagination itself," Blake said. And apropos of personal mythology: "As a man is, so he sees. As the eye is formed, so are its powers."[13]

FIGURE 6. *Los, creative-heroic "Blake-smith" and counterplayer to Urizen, the controlling creator, "misguided Demon of Heaven," in* The (First) Book of Urizen *(detail, relief-etching, 1794) by William Blake (1757-1827). (Lessing J. Rosenwald Collection, Library of Congress, Washington, D.C.)*

FIGURE 7. *Yeats's tower, Thoor Ballylee, near Coole in County Galway in the west of Ireland. The tower was built in the thirteenth century and restored for Yeats under the direction of his neighbor, Lady Gregory.* (PHOTO BY ROBIN LARSEN.)

Perhaps an archetype related to myth was germinating at the end of the eighteenth century (even as at the end of the nineteenth—and now, the twentieth). The poet Samuel Taylor Coleridge, Blake's contemporary, also formulated a concept that he called the *primary imagination*, which he defined as "the living power and prime agent of all human perception."[14] The poet's relationship to this faculty informs his creativity, and his aesthetic. When Coleridge awakened from a state of dream (probably enhanced by an opium sedative) and found the extraordinary mythical poem "Kubla Khan" already formed in his mind intact, it confirmed for him how autonomous his primary imagination could be.[15]

Moving to the late nineteenth to early twentieth centuries, the great Irish poet W. B. Yeats, who studied Blake intensively, knew that in order for his own poetry to find its richness and its true voice, he must not only steep himself in the myths and folklore of his native land, but allow a personal mythology to form within him. Those who study Yeats know that the inner key to the haunting images that grace his poems—the tower with its winding stair, the mysterious influence on the soul of the waxing and waning of the moon, the figures of "The Song of the Wandering Aengus" and "Crazy Jane Talks with the Bishop"—are to be found in his inner mythology, at once personal, and yet profoundly archetypal.[16]

Yeats wrote, "the images of the gods can pass from mind to mind, our closed eyes may look upon a world shared, as the physical world is shared, though difference in degree of purity has been substituted for difference of place."[17]

Yeats acknowledged his inspiration, as did Blake, from the eighteenth-century Swedish visionary Emanuel Swedenborg's translucent vision of reality, in which the imaginal or spiritual world hovers close to this one, with ourselves between the two. Earlier than Coleridge, Swedenborg had said that the human imagination is a symbol-discerning organ, which can really make sense of the forms of this world only by intuiting their spiritual correspondence (see Chapter 3 for a fuller exploration of the concept of an imaginal world within us).

Yeats said, "literature dwindles to a mere chronicle of circumstances . . . unless it is constantly flooded with the passions and beliefs of ancient times." But then he added a mysterious footnote that brings us back to our main theme:

"I should have added as an alternative that the supernatural may at any moment create new myths, but I was timid."[18] The great twentieth-century novelists James Joyce and Thomas Mann seem to have shared this same perspective; their influential novels *Ulysses* and *The Magic Mountain* showed the daily life of everyman to recapitulate ancient myths in the ever-present moment. For example, Leopold Bloom, who lives in Joyce's modern Dublin, is not much of an external hero at all, but on the inner plane is nonetheless living out Ulysses's great adventure.

It is an open question, then, whether the true meaning of personal mythology is simply to discover that we are repeating a traditional mythic pattern or, as Yeats suggested, that we are in touch with a still-alive "supernatural," which requires us to create new mythologies with the very stuff of our lives. If we are searching for patterns, we must rely on our reading of myths. If we must create new myths to live by, however, knowing traditional myths may be helpful, but not enough. What new thing may be required of us is as

FIGURE 8. *"Someday, my son, all this will be part of your personal mythology."* (Drawing by Lorenz, © 1981 The New Yorker Magazine, Inc.)

yet unknown; but we may find that the answer lies only in the living.[19]

MODERN MYTHS

A fifty-year-old professional woman wrote in her dream journal:

> Mother is dressing to go to an appointment. She is totally in red; velour pants, shirt, and a wraparound turban on her head. She has a bright yellow turtleneck dickey at her throat . . . almost psychedelic, which I suggest she change and put on a soft blue one. She pays no mind to my suggestion, and is self-absorbed. I see her sturdy sensible shoes and practical utilitarian pocketbook. I want to talk to her about Dad but she hasn't the time. I am in a long patchwork quilt skirt and white long-sleeved blouse. Quilt is light blue, rose, green on white ground. She turns to look in a mirror and I say to her "What is my myth?"

Although her mother had died many years before the dream, her symbolic presence still works strongly on the dreamer. The women are in front of a mirror (the dream itself is a mirror; see Chapter 3) trying on what is, transparently, "soul clothing." The dreamer herself is in patchwork; she must assemble her "costume" from a greater complexity and a polychromatic emotional style, as symbolized by all the colors. Even though she admired aspects of her mother's (monochromatic) style, the dream shows what very different people they are.

One task of psychotherapy is often to help in the disentanglement of personal from parental myths. The dream here directly addresses and clarifies this issue and shows how active personal mythology is in the private inner worlds of many people. "What is my myth?" she asks. This is not quite the old question "Who am I?" Her language is very specific and reminds us that the makeup of our soul goes beyond biological selfhood and social role. Myths are made of the ancient images and stories of our race and it is of this timeless—yet ever-present—zone her soul is questioning.

Jung's insight, mentioned earlier, talked about the cultural and psychological "vertigo" of living without a myth. He came to the same impasse as my client:

> I was driven to ask myself in all seriousness: "What is the myth you are living?" . . . I took it upon myself to get to know "my" myth, and I regarded this as the task of tasks, for—so I told myself—how could I, when treating my patients, make due allowance for the personal factor, for my personal equation, which is yet so necessary for a knowledge of the other person, if I was unconscious of it? I simply had to know what unconscious or preconscious myth was forming me, from what rhizome I sprang.[20]

Jung searched all his life in the mythic depths. His question also brings up the "personal equation." Jung here was assuming that myth has a prior and seemingly causal relation to human (his own) existence. The "rhizome," he implied, is the meaning-creating root of our being in the world. The mythic pattern originates from behind and beneath us, as it were, in the "transpersonal" realm, yet is the key to our personal existence.

In psychotherapy, everybody from Freud and Jung to Bruno Bettelheim to Eric Berne has been certain that if they could explain and raise to consciousness the mythic script on which a particular dysfunctional bit of human behavior was based, they could eliminate it—or cure it—through demythologizing. The myths by which we live are empowering structures that affect our health, vitality, and psychological well-being. They can have positive and negative effects on our lives.

Not until Jung, and then later Maslow, did psychology

emphasize the positive as well as negative effects of myth on life. Kraeplin had cataloged the grand (psychotic) megalomanias of mythic identity, and Freud our endlessly botched Oedipal and Electra dilemmas. But Jung showed that while our (normal) sense of personal identity is forever threatening to dissolve at its deepest boundary into the mythic archetypes of the collective unconscious, once a person has accepted this (essential unreality of one's own nature), he or she is for the first time in a position to construct an authentic selfhood (*individuation,* the creative, integrated psyche).

Individuation is to normal as normal is to neurotic, and neurotic is to psychotic. And this hierarchical model of integration–disintegration suggests that it is not the presence or absence of mythic themes in personal psychology that determines sanity, but how the ego relates to these. The "cards" we have been dealt by fate are a hand from a recognizable deck, which, like the Tarot, is made up of a finite number of archetypal forms (fools, magicians, priestesses, hanged men, and so forth). Whether one is simply possessed by these recurring archetypes or may learn to relate to them in a creative dialogue would seem to make all the difference. Jung said, "Man must not dissolve into a whirl of warring possibilities and tendencies imposed upon him by the unconscious, but must become the unity that embraces them all."[21]

At the meeting mentioned by Stanley Krippner in his foreword I was able to meet with many other psychologists who felt that myth was vitally related to our field. A number of key concepts each of us had identified were known to the others. I began to feel that the subject we were addressing was a coherent field with an already partly established subject matter: myths in psychology, the psychology of myth, and myths in and of psychotherapy.[22]

The terrain of personal mythology, as I came to see it, has its near boundaries in academic and clinical psychology and its far boundaries in ancient cultures, in storytelling, and fable, in visionary processes. The nearest, yet least-visible, zone is the mythology (not necessarily psychopathology) of everyday life, perhaps its most personal dimension. Myth is plastic grafted to a thousand cultures and deployed in furthering the unique social objectives of each one. But modern people are perhaps less bound to a specific social tradition than our ancestors.

Herein may be found our justification for a personal mythology: If individual cultures have always developed a unique integrity through myth, why not the individual person, who also seeks to give coherence to his or her internal parts? Social psychology has helped us verify the existence of an "internal cast of characters," and psychoanalysis as well (see Chapter 8). Myth addresses the coherence of divisive forces in the self as well as society. The modern individual can choose to attempt to create his or her own meaning in life, rather than participate in a traditional, historically continuous, meaning-bestowing system. And if we are indeed like T. S. Eliot's "hollow men," we must choose our own ways of filling our emptied-out psyches.

"For in the history of our still youthful species," wrote Campbell in his seminal book *Creative Mythology,* "a profound respect for inherited forms has generally suppressed innovation."[23] Mythology was, perforce, collective mythology. But in our modern times these forms have relaxed their collective grip on the psyche, placing the burden for a meaningful experience of the universe on the individual person, whose creative relation to mythology, Campbell said, "springs not, like theology, from the dicta of authority, but from the insights, sentiments, thought, and vision of an adequate individual, loyal to his own experience of value. Thus it corrects the authority holding to the shell of forms produced and left behind by lives once lived."[24]

Once we have recognized the validity of Campbell's deeper definition of myth—as a compendium of soul-vitalizing forms—the next immediate question concerns our "adequacy" as individuals to relate to this wealth of images and meanings in a creative and life-enhancing way. What do we do when we no longer feel that our souls may find shelter beneath the umbrella of a single historical orthodoxy, which has already answered long ago—and to its satisfaction—certain annoying perennial questions: What is the meaning of life? How shall we conduct it? To what basic values shall we hold? Some of us may experience metaphysical vertigo, or the "nausea" Jean-Paul Sartre and the existentialists have described. A disorienting passage through "the cloud of unknowing" may well be the initial test of our adequacy as individuals.

But there are other tasks that lie before us, as the many ordeals of the hero's journey reveal: battles with inner monsters, seductions, and labyrinths in which to lose our way. Are all myths equal? Or are some wiser than others? Are different mythologies appropriate to different stages of the life process? I enter some of these questions more deeply in Chapter 3, in the section "Seeing through Myths."

The mythic revival that is under way and has been at least in part occasioned by the Campbell-Moyers television interviews, and the popular book based on the interviews, *The Power of Myth,* has received criticism from two quarters: first, the more conservative factions in organized religion who do not like the "leveling tendency" of comparative mythology, in which the doctrines and beliefs of *their* religion are compared (heaven forbid) to the myths (which originally were religions) of all ages. (Why does the comparison make them so insecure? we might ask.) The second type of objection is from the other end of the spectrum, from the secular and "scientifically socialized" quarter, who feel that myths are simply a fuzzy impediment to clear cognition. This group may have failed to see that science itself operates like a mythology when it shapes our world view, and that as an "explanation for everything" it generates its own problems of depression and alienation.

Others have questioned the very feasibility of personal mythmaking: "We may wonder whether any single person— even so intense a poet as William Blake—can fabricate and promulgate his own mythology? Must not a private myth, rather, be labelled a pseudomyth?"[25]

Harry Levin is a literary critic, and in his essay "Some Meanings of Myth," from which the passage above is quoted, he complains about the *myth of myths,* using the term in the negative sense: that we may get carried away, not only by the word, but by its imprecise and yet evocative atmosphere, which induces us to imbue *myth* with more meaning than we should. There is, indeed, some validity to this point, and it may be wise at this juncture to warn ourselves ahead of time against the potential of "mythic fundamentalism," in which we may assume that because something is mythic it is good, or necessarily contains wisdom, losing precision to the magic of the power that surrounds the mythic realm. But don't these problems arise precisely because in modern times myth is so "fallen," dismembered, and dispersed?

"The modern myth is no longer sung by bards in the halls of kings, nor told by grandmother in the glow of the fireplace. It has to be pieced together from the jottings of news commentators and editorial writers, social ideologists, and political candidates."[26] Contemporary Jungian analyst Edward Whitmont does not agree with Levin that it is intellectually futile to look for this ephemeral thing, the personal myth, but suggests that it is fragmented into our lives in almost unrecognizable ways. Our personal schizophrenia is echoed in the broken mythology of our culture.

Between the religious fundamentalists and the "scientific fundamentalists" lies a vast population of seekers, eager simply to enrich their experience of being alive and for whom neither philosophical extreme is a satisfactory approach. For the more open-minded in religious circles, the Campbell-Moyers television series has been a blessing and a herald that frees them from parochialism—opening the way to a universality of religious symbols and the possibility of a planetary spiritual vision that transcends cultural boundaries. For those who have been convinced, yet at the same time frightened, by the impersonal vision of science, the very universality of the mythological world offers a new vantage, based simply on the human experience, and thus without the daunting necessity of living only by objective truth. Members of both these groups are eligible to apply for membership to that thousand-faced heroes' society of which Campbell wrote so eloquently.

I will cite just a few other views on personal mythology from varied intellectual perspectives, but united by theme. French literary critic Roland Barthes has found the source materials for his modern *Mythologies* in the bold and tawdry rituals of professional wrestling, in advertisements, in striptease, films, plastics, even detergents—which are thought to have magical powers to affect matter, or (as in Mr. Clean) inhabited by genies. "I had . . . acquired the conviction," he said in regard to myths, "that one might go further than the pious show of unmasking them and account in detail for the mystification which transforms petit-bourgeois culture into a universal nature."[27] The French postmodernist school, to which the neo-Freudians Jacques Lacan and Barthes belong, believes that consciously evoked myths enrich experience, adding a texture and depth that is transformative to the experiencer.

Stanley Keleman is a modern bioenergetic therapist who for years had been doing seminars with Campbell, in which he would evoke images from the energetic fields of a person's body and Campbell would interpret and amplify them mythologically.[28] Keleman wrote,

Experience is connected to myth. Being immersed in self-experience is living one's own myth, one's own life story. . . . As our connectedness to living deepens, we learn that experience is the teacher. And experience cannot be programmed. We are our own mythmakers, knowingly or unknowingly.[29]

Keleman insists that myths arise in and from the body, as if all our history and our stories were recorded in our muscles, connective tissue, and viscera. Simply to partake of the physical condition, if Keleman is right, is the precondition for a personal mythology (see Chapter 3 for a discussion of the notion of an imaginal body whose organs are feelings, fantasies, and images).

Personal mythology begins with an individual's awareness of timelessness. With it comes the sense that our own individual lives, although they take place in an eternal now, are connected through that still point to people of all times and places. While we are alive, we tread the same earth on which the ancient shamans danced and sang their spirit songs, and King Arthur's men rode in quest of the Holy Grail. Can it be that our journey through life is to be no less wonder-filled than theirs?

Having looked at personal mythology from many sides now, we are ready to move on to my next concern, which is how we relate to myths in our lives.

Chapter 2

THE RELEVANCE OF MYTH TO EVERYDAY LIFE

Unless we prefer to be made fools of by our illusions, we shall, by carefully analysing every fascination, extract from it a portion of our own personality, like a quintessence, and slowly come to recognize that we meet ourselves time and time again in a thousand disguises on the path of life. This, however, is a truth which only profits the man who is temperamentally convinced of the individual and irreducible reality of his fellow men.

—CARL JUNG

MYTH AND CONSCIOUSNESS

In what ways may we come to experience the relevance of myth to everyday life? The perennial solution seems to be: through the exercise of consciousness. Early students of psychology were taught how to be introspective in a systematic way. In philosophy, the mind learned ways to discover its own contents through the practice of "phenomenology."[1] More recently, psychologists have begun to study the profoundly introspective psychologies of the East, such as Yoga and Zen; and self-awareness techniques of all kinds, for example, G. I. Gurdjieff's self-remembering, and Frederick Perls's gestalt awareness. And biofeedback provides an electronic form, even, of self-surveillance.[2]

In each of these systems, mind is asked to separate itself into a witness or observer but also remain a behaver. We think of ourselves as a consciousness as well as a stream of experiences (notice we need both self-awareness and experiences to have a "stream of consciousness"). Introspective writers, such as James Joyce, and modern poets, such as Ezra Pound and T. S. Eliot, have probably done as much to aid our understanding of the stream of consciousness as psychologists. They have shown how deep currents move among the seemingly ordinary affairs of life. The secret of apprehending those depths is an extra awareness—beyond that required to execute our daily affairs. The awareness of the creative artist or the sensitive person exercising a mindfulness of the everyday is not far from that of the yogi or the Zen master.[3]

Lacking the formal context of traditional mythologies, our psyche still is responsive to mythogems—the "bricks" of which mythologies are built. These elements, being of the stuff of psyche, are far from inert building materials, rather, like RNA and DNA, they structure the living processes in which they participate. And herein lies the urgency to our conscious rapprochement with the mythic world. If they are not monitored, myths can seize on behavior, as well as consciousness itself, in inadvertent or compulsive ways. If we wish to avoid "being made fools of by our illusions," there is no substitute for becoming conscious of them.[4]

Here is an example from psychotherapy: A middle-aged man who I have counseled dreamed,

I am swimming far out to sea. As I notice where I am, I become frightened and try to return, but there are sharks everywhere. I make it to shore in terror and with extreme difficulty.

I start by asking him if he ever used to do in real life what he did in the dream. After a few moments of thought he nods. "When I was young and foolish and lived near Coney Island I would swim way out into the Atlantic. I don't know why, except it made me feel daring and impressed my friends. But I would never do anything so foolish now."

As the session unfolds, however, it begins to emerge that the dreamer still does indeed possess a youthfully heroic self-image. He has recently extended himself in a business venture, perhaps beyond the limits that prudence might dictate, but his feeling is blithe and optimistic. Another side of him knows full well how unforgiving certain economic and business conditions are. One could easily say, as people do, "There are sharks out there."

The dream by itself was not sufficient to provoke an insight until its images and their potential meaning were brought to consciousness. At such a moment, an "aha!" takes place; a mythogem has spoken to life.

Although we are often unconscious of our mythologizing, if we are willing to heighten our awareness, myths may appear to us in the following ways.

1. **Through a spontaneous mythmaking experience.** A spontaneous experience can occur when the intentional mind is "taking time off": a night dream, a daydream, or a hypnagogic fragment, such as a vividly perceived (eidetic) image at the threshold of sleep. These are what Freud called "primary process" events, experiences that I have elsewhere referred to as possessing "primary meaning."[5] The key here is that the experience happens without your own volition or effort; you are actually "carried along." This sometimes makes it difficult for you to "catch" such events; all your intentions, including your desire to be inwardly observant, are swept away by the process. The dream cited above is an example: it captures in an image form something of the person's life

predicament, yet he is unaware of its meaning until directed to it.

2. **In our feelings.** We are attracted to and fascinated by mythic forms. We don't know why some situation makes our guts roil or our palms sweat—it just happens.[6] (Remember Stanley Keleman's idea that myths are stored in the body.) One young woman client found herself recurrently anxious in the presence of a particular type of older woman: feminine, composed, and well-dressed, but not necessarily mean or authoritarian. Further analysis showed that these women embodied an ideal she felt she lacked—but one that her mother had tried to instill in her for years. When we find ourselves in a situation where we are reacting helplessly, it may help to make a mental note. Has this happened before? In what way is this typical of me? (Leave more profound analyses for later; answering this simple question may be enough for the time being.)

3. **Through a belief system.** These may vary from fairly familiar religious beliefs (often first presented to us in childhood, when the mythic imagination is wide open and receptive) to highly personal beliefs—sometimes peculiar delusional systems such as those held by paranoid schizophrenics.[7] We know that religions may contain both psychologically constructive, as well as destructive beliefs: respectively, "There is a loving God who cares for me," and "My sexual feelings are from the Devil." Likewise personal myths may tell us we have a special divine endowment or a crippling moral weakness passed down by generations. Two simple questions to ask about any belief system (particularly ones we think may have a destructive aspect) are "How does it affect my life?" and "Is it open to change?" (especially in the face of new information).

4. In a relationship problem. Mythology has given us many examples of how a mythogem might rule a relationship—the stronger feelings that emerge between two people seldom seem to be fully in their control. There are relationships based on "my hero" and ones that embody the idea of a personal nemesis. Henry Higgins in *My Fair Lady* is not the only modern Pygmalion; we all seem to have the urge somehow to transform, improve, and render beautiful our partner (so easily do we project our own inner potential for transformation). As is often the nature of myth-driven behavior, even when our efforts are unsuccessful, we go on trying. Another example is the starting situation of many fairy tales: "Everyone else has gone off to seek their fortune, but our hero (heroine) is still at home with mother." When we are deprived, fantasy comes to rule the imagination, and only an extraordinary person like a princess or a prince, can end our loneliness. Even if we find our prince or princess, though, we will not necessarily live happily ever after. At this point, a new kind of trouble often begins—especially if we fail to become aware of how mythologized our expectations are. Questions to ask yourself might be "What are the compulsive aspects of this relationship?" and "What never seems to change no matter how hard I try?"

5. In unconsciously ritualized or repetitive behavior patterns. This is what we call, appropriately, "acting out." We may find ourselves behaving in a primitive manner; we may feel driven to do certain things, unable to resist, even when we would like to. At the rare or extreme end, are stubborn irresistible psychopathologies with ritualized overtones. ("I don't know why," the person says, "but I cannot get sexually aroused unless someone heaps abuse on me and beats me.") More common examples would be the things we find ourselves saying and doing during arguments with lovers, even when we tell ourselves not to! Or the little superstitions of everyday life. Here we come close to a subject I return to in just a few pages: the ways in which myths make us dramatize, even melodramatize, and the special relationship of myth and ritual.[8]

6. **Through conscious mythmaking.** I will develop this theme further in Part Three of this book. The reader will see I am partial to this approach, because here we try to encounter our own nemesis—the unconscious tendency to get caught in mythmaking—to achieve our own redemption. If I have described what seems like pathology in some of the previous patterns, here too is healing, as in the original "medicine" of Asclepius, the healing god. (In the wonderful ancient Greek tradition of dream incubation, the ill or afflicted patient and his temple-priest guide, the *therapeutes*—the original "therapist"—would wait together for a dream or vision. This would be shared, discussed, perhaps acted out to accomplish the healing.) A human affliction can be mythologized, brought to the realm of the gods. And the answer of the healing god can be humanized, rendered into a form relevant to the sufferer's personal predicament. Vision quests, such as those of native Americans; dream theater or psychodrama; and the mask-making rituals, described later, are also examples of conscious mythmaking. A symbolic structure or container is made in which myth and consciousness are aligned in a special way.[9]

Of these six patterns of relationship between myth and consciousness, we may experience several in a given day. For example, we hear a story of a burning building and imagine how we might have rescued that child in it. Our eyes cloud over and our heart beats faster as we imagine the virtual enactment. (Our companion may wonder where we have gone for a moment.) Our inner hero has come forward in a fantasy, without our even noticing. Sometime later, in an argument with our spouse, we find ourselves unbearably hurt that he or she has not noticed all the heroic sacrifices we have been making, day after day, week after week (we may exaggerate, but it feels so good to be dramatic like this). We are unconsciously caught up in martyrdom (sometimes the other side of the hero fantasy). Later, without even knowing why, we take too many drinks; the alcohol helps the martyr to drown his feeling of being unappreciated. That night we dream—was it *Demetrius and the Gladiators,* that funny old movie about Christian martyrs in the Roman arena? (Am I the martyr or the cruel emperor Caligula in his box at the stadium?) Wherever did that one come from?

Myths appear interwoven with our feelings and our behavior—and our dreams. We think we know how we feel most of the time, but we may not take the time in daily life to notice all the connections; how our soul life does in fact hang together. By exercising both a little extra conscious-ness and a knowledge of how myths operate, we can help ourselves make sense—to ourselves.

Psychologists found out only about thirty years ago that human beings may not be able to survive mentally and emotionally without dreaming. The now-famous dream de-privation studies of William Dement showed that, after a couple of nights without dreams, we become highly irrita-ble, anxious, and unable to concentrate; and eventually we are inundated with hallucinations and delusions. Even our daydreams are compensations for life's bleakness, or boredom.

Spontaneous mythmaking, then, is a natural and unavoid-able type of mythologizing that has a healthy function. With a little conscious effort, though, as I have suggested, these myths may be highly instructive to us: keep a dream jour-nal, share your dreams with therapists or friends, catch yourself in a daydream.

It's not easy to react to events as we do every day, and watch ourselves doing it at the same time. Likewise we would usually rather hold our beliefs than examine them. Some of the creative mythology exercises given in Chapter

12 are designed to separate dysfunctional myths from useful ones. But the remainder of this chapter is really addressed to the relationship between myths and acting out.

MYTH AND DRAMATIC ENACTMENT

When the great bard asserted "all the world's a stage," he did not say "like a stage." Apparently he saw the dramatic arts, which was his profession, not just as a mirror of life, but as an intensified piece of it. The nature of life itself is dramatic.[10] "Not always, thank God," we may say; it is true that the dramatic mask life wears is not necessarily visible except on certain occasions. We do not respond well to people who summon the dramatic mode too frequently.

There are two psychological clues to the appearance of the dramatic mode in daily life: a strong feeling or emotional tone and the presence of onlookers. The actor on the stage of life, like his theatrical counterpart, is an artist whose medium is the human emotional life. And curiously, modern psychologists who have studied facial expressions find that as in the classic theater, each basic human emotion has a mask. These masks of love or rapture, pain, aggression, disgust, and curiosity are recognizable across cultural boundaries.[11] The spectrum of masks and their complex interrelationships are the concern of theater (see Chapter 10).

We are not only cerebral and calculating creatures, we are dramatic ones. Human emotions are incomprehensible without a sense of drama. The symbolic vocabulary of drama is far more than words, although language is an important aspect. But until we add the gesture, the tone of voice, posture, facial expression, and, most important, the context and story or plot, we are not fully involved. Emotional behavior is made meaningful by recognizing the story surrounding it. In life as in theater we may never understand fully either a person or behavior until we know the context in which it is embedded. This provides us with another way of understanding the relevance of myth to everyday life. Drama looks to nuances of behavior, especially incongruities, disparities between fair word and foul intent, to subtleties of facial expression or gesture that indicate insincerity or the concealed motive. We are especially sensitive to this notion of the hidden versus the revealed in human affairs. (I think of the Northwest Coast Indian masks that open to reveal another, different, mask hidden within.)

The audience (those who hear) and spectators (those who watch), as a drama unfolds, go through a kind of Platonic regression to the world of ideal forms as the plot crystallizes or resolves itself. We are ever—yet never—surprised to see the presence of an eternal cast of characters beneath the merely personal mask. We learn again of the secret workings, in ordinary life, of gods, heroes, and daemonic beings. The unclarity and mystery that has prevailed, as the story works itself through, reveals its hidden structure, becomes discernible and intelligible at last. But the psychological organ capable of this understanding is not the intellectual mind, but the mythic imagination.[12]

We may find the mythological "deep structure" (like Chomsky's linguistic "generative grammar") in our (emotional) insistence that the drama must unfold in certain ways, and our discomfort when it fails to do so. What is it in us that becomes so instinctively uncomfortable when the hero succumbs to self-congratulation or braggadocio? Did we learn it from our Judeo-Christian heritage or from Aeschylus or Sophocles? But examination of cross-cultural mythology shows the theme of hubris to be of world-class, hence archetypal, status, rather than culture specific. This element of drama, which warns ordinary people to beware of inflation, or taking the prerogatives of the gods, belongs to Adolph Bastian's *Elementargedanke* (elementary ideas) rather than *Völkergedanke* (ethnic ideas).[13]

It is easy for us to see life in larger-than-life images; simpler, yet more colorful and clear, they fit easily into the mind's eye. Myth and drama show us life in bold outline, and speak to our feeling as well as our seeing. They have roots in our autonomic and limbic nervous systems. We feel more deeply about what we see when archetypes are involved.

Jungian analyst Whitmont observed,

> Life as a dramatic play, as theater (*theatron* in Greek meant a place for seeing, but especially "a showplace for divine onlookers"), is an archetypal motif recurring over and over in dreams and poetry. The profoundly moving cathartic effect which dramatic art continues to exert through all the ages may well be based upon its presenting us with a mirror of soul and life in the theme of men and women against their destinies. [14]

Does Whitmont here imply that gods are not only the real dramatis personae of the theater, but the audience, as well, whether invisible or visible to our eyes? Or may we ourselves become "divine" in the role of onlookers at theater?

When we find, as we so often do, that we say or do much more than was ever intended by our willing and conscious selves, that our behavior outdoes our consciousness, we are in the perilous zone of "acting out." Then all the world becomes a stage, indeed, and we don't know how we got there. Dreams often take up this theme. The following is a prototypic or skeletal version of a universal dream: *"I suddenly find myself onstage. A play is going on. I don't know my part, but find I am acting anyway."* Sometimes a dreamer will find himself or herself hopelessly and uncontrollably acting out a part. Or, sometimes, the setting or an audience that expects something becomes the agent of compulsion. This loss of self-control is frightening. We are used to thinking of ourselves as consciously directing our own behavior, and become anxious when we find that we are seized by a role, a logic inside ourselves, outside ourselves, or, usually, both.

"I don't know what got into me," we often say, implying both personal hollowness and an inadvertent mediumship. As in the dream, we have acted a part with an unknown or secret script. And people the world over having a marital argument or a lovers' quarrel act a recognizable pattern with gestures, looks, tones of voice, even phases of the process. We all may become Zeus and Hera, it seems, and if we feel godlike to ourselves, we are demonic to each other. We ought to get along (but we don't). She storms jealously, imitating his divine wrath; he throws thunderbolts. The outcome will not always be the same, from couple to couple, but the sense of helpless participation in a timeless drama is universal.

When consciousness is in the power of myth, we may not control our feelings or our behavior directly; our intentions are ineffectual. We need to construct a special container or ritual form to hold the mythic energy and regain our balance. As Whitmont put it, "[A] ritual, then, is a deliberate play or enacting within a formalized context, or affect-charged impulses, feelings, and archetypal visions or fantasies. By virtue of seeking and creating a formalized context these energies are safely contained; they can be propitiated, invoked, and confronted."[15]

I don't think that I understood the deep reality of the rapport between actor and audience until I was fortunate enough to see *Oedipus at Colonus* done in the classic mode at Epidaurus, on the Greek Peloponnisos. When we read these dramas in college, they often seem to be more intellectual than emotional events. In the live performance, as the community of several thousand people groans viscerally and weeps aloud with blind Oedipus' agonies, there is a palpable emotional bond. This original version of catharsis, recognized as one of the most important elements in modern therapy, unites the participants in the commonality of human emotional experience.

The theater at Epidaurus was integrated into one of the greatest healing centers of the classic world. Body, mind, and spirit were included in their regimens. In this legendary-sounding, yet historically very real (fifth century B.C. to fifth century A.D.) "holistic health center," diet, massage, personal hygiene, and exercise strengthened the body; philosophy, the reasonable mind; and the theater on the hill ministered to the soul.

The gods and heroes of Greece embody the qualities of soul in their emotional behavior (*thymos*): above, Aphrodite is seductive; Hera, jealous; and Zeus, in a rage; and down below, Helen is seductive; Menelaus, jealous; Achilles, in a rage. If Greek philosophy, like Eastern religion, shows us a more spiritual dispassion (and Christianity shows us spiritual compassion), the classic theater shows us, simply, passion at work in the world, the errant, turbulent adventures of soul.

When you next find yourself in the grip of passion, or perhaps in a "theatrical" mood, ask yourself, "Who are my 'divine onlookers'? For whom am I acting out this drama? To what god or goddess is this passion sacred?" The illusions that make fools of us are perennial themes and persons, alive in psyche and in the world. Coming to know them in the drama of life sets us on the labyrinthine path toward wisdom.

THE PSYCHOLOGY OF MYTH AND RITUAL

Myths emerge from, or are contained by, rituals. Rituals are the embodiment of myths. If we aren't conscious of our myths, they may turn into inadvertent rituals. Rituals often repeated become or induce mythic beliefs, which is why they are used to perpetuate religious systems. Campbell wrote, "Myths are the mental support of rites, rites the physical enactment of myths."[16]

Jean Piaget's cognitive stages of mental development, which many consider one of the most important contributions to twentieth-century psychology, constitute a mythic morphology of consciousness, with the egocentric (magical) world of everyone's childhood, yielding year by year in (now) fully recognizable stages through the first decade of life to the operational (logical-causal) mind of adulthood. Piaget asked children how they interpreted commonplace events. His techniques were simple rituals: "I am going to pour the water from this jar [tall, thin] to this [short, fat] one; which has more water?" In another exercise he showed the children a model of two mountains and asked, "If I am on this mountain, what do I see? If I move over to this other one, what do I see?" Children's initial view of the world shows themselves at its center (egocentrism), all things to be alive (animism), and their parents to be as infallible as deities (mythologizing).[17]

However, I agree with Jung and Maslow that it is an error to imagine that these developmental processes finish at "childhood's end." For adults we have needed more subtle and evocative tests to show the persistence of the mythic substructure; the Rorschach test and Henry Murray's Thematic Apperception Test (T.A.T.) are two examples. These are called "projective techniques," because they evaluate the personality on the basis of the illusions that mind adds to an ambiguous stimulus (ink blot). Through the ritual of the structured test the psychologist "tricks" the adult mind into betraying its own covert mythologizing.[18]

Even more open-ended are the mandalas into which Jung invited his patients' psyches. He would ask them to draw in or around the circle in any way they wanted. The circle ritually structures whatever takes place in the psyche into an image referring to its own wholeness. Jung also used clay modeling and painting as more free-form evocative modes. Modern art therapy, in part following Jung's lead, has further refined these rituals of revelation.[19]

In traditional societies the relation of myth to life stage is evidenced by the clusters of mythological themes that appear at the points or nodes of life development. From womb to tomb the inner stages of maturation are marked by corresponding rites—puberty, marriage, and childbirth among them. Our ancestors, long before Piaget, knew about developmental stages and just what ritual was needed to provide a mythic tissue of transformation to the growing psyche.

Precisely because our society does not schedule these outer rites of passage adequately, psychological problems tend to arise at the traditional nodes of transition (examples of which will follow). For the past several years I have made a special study of people's passages to adulthood in our society. In both individual and group therapeutic contexts, men and women have come to me to ask for what seem to be initiations. It is as if the depths of their psyches say to the therapist, "You are the closest thing to a shaman we have in this society. Please provide a safe space and some guidance, and the needed initiation will emerge."

The client may have no conscious model of what is happening, but is driven by anxiety, emotions that seem to get out of control, or by a situation—often a relationship problem—that is tearing one apart. Because of the stoicism about tender or painful feelings that is enjoined on them by our society, men, especially, are not always eager to enter therapy (but the psyche will often gear up to the threshold of stoicism, using that scourge we call a symptom). The frequent oblivion of the conscious ego to what is happening strikingly underlines the purposefulness of the unconscious in provoking these confrontations.

MEN'S MYSTERIES

Men's puberty rites worldwide are known for violence and torture (infallible for gaining the attention of adolescent boys, which is otherwise usually hard to get). I believe there is also something here in the archetypal structure that is sex differentiated. The real initiation into adulthood for a person of either sex means a coming to terms with mortality and the realities of human frailty, pain, and fear. Women are usually destined to come to a reckoning with these through the process of childbirth (as experienced through the millennia, without anesthetics, or surgical backup, a narrow, dangerous crossing indeed). Men's confrontation is rather through

FIGURE 9. *Hamatsa initiation ritual. The young warrior returns to the community in a feral state, possessed by the Cannibal Spirit. Depicted is a contemporary celebration of the ritual of the Cannibal Society of the Northwest Coast.* (PHOTO BY EBERHARD OTTO.)

the external field: the realities of battle and the hunt. Their initiation too must partake of blood and danger and must banish fear and tender-mindedness.

In modern society our closest approximation is hazing in fraternal organizations and the military. These provide the oppression and tortures by a senior cadre, which has previously survived initiation (and hence, they always think, become entitled to administer it). Failing these, young men in our society provide their own initiations in the following acting-out ways: participating in dangerous sports; driving cars or motorcycles at the very edge of control (why are their insurance rates so much higher than young women's? we ask); consuming mind-altering drugs, used in rites of transformation since time immemorial, but to the point of being "destroyed," or "blown away," to use current parlance; or joining a club or gang that may employ such symbols of transformation as skulls and cross-bones, daggers dripping blood, and names such as "The Hell's Angels," or "The Alien Nomads." Such a fraternal organization may also bestow experiences otherwise unavailable in modern life, for example, the chance to experience a battle initiation, like a knife fight with someone in a rival phratry. Because societies always discourage intragroup aggression, but encourage intergroup aggression, normally an American youth would have to go as far as Southeast Asia or Central America for an appropriate extracultural adversary.

Must we necessarily turn to an external school of hard knocks of some sort to achieve our initiations? We enter now a zone of experience and behavior that shows connections between personal myth and ritual. At the same time, implications for collective well-being are examined in the comparison of unconscious and conscious forms of myth-making. The following examples are from the more interior, symbolic level as experienced through psychotherapy. One male therapy client told the following dream:

We were supposed to shake all the men's hands, as if we were
at a bachelor party. Two men killed somebody . . . hanging
him over the bar. Then they began to drink his blood as it
dripped over his body. We participated like some kind of
Holy Grail ceremony.

The thirty-three-year-old dreamer had been feeling childlike
and unable to enter the adult world. Following his work
with this dream, and especially facing up to the feelings of
fear and repugnance it occasioned, he felt a fundamental
change had taken place in his maturation. The initiation was
from within. It is important to note here that the shocking
quality of the imagery is necessary to the symbolic rite of
transformation. Later we discuss the importance of exaggerated, grotesque, and repugnant imagery in dreams. It calls
attention to, alerts, attracts, and repels us all at once.

Another male dreamer in a mid-life crisis had all sorts of
meetings with cruel initiators over a period of several months.
In his dreams he was confronted with harsh realities, including a curious ritual in which he must let his finger be
painfully scraped by a sadist with a knife (an overt reference
to symbolic circumcision or subincision?). In a different
dream he was *"spread-eagled naked in a tunnel."* This image
reminded me of the myth of Ixion or any of the many other
crucified hero-victims.[20]

Another male client in search of his manhood dreamed,
"State troopers crucified on telephone poles with their cocked guns
strapped to their chests." He thought this image referred to the
psychological torture that was thrust on these officers in
their training ordeal (which he had earlier passed through
himself, with considerable trauma), which presumably was
meant to weed out the weak and unprepared candidates. We
think of the psychological ordeals of soldiers and Marines
trained for battle, and how later they are asked to go back to
a peaceful civilian society. (How does the veteran of Viet-
nam or other military aggressions integrate that initiatory
violence?) The second dreamer is accompanied by his son, a

theme that appears in a number of men's initiatory dreams, as if in a definite reference to the fact that these are male mysteries.

The following clearly archetypal dream also has a younger companion, whom the dreamer must heal:

> *I am going along through an area I've been to before—old desiccated villages—now replaced by one long row of buildings. Not much room in front so I have to go underneath. I am accompanied by an inexperienced young warrior, a Galahad figure. Now it gets portentous. We are attacked. He is hit by three arrows in the throat, they point to his chest. He is in pain but gallant, he is bleeding a milky substance. I go for help, but what needs to happen is not medical—it's shamanistic. Gods are involved in this society. I flag down a huge conveyance with a god and goddess in it. They know me, somehow I'm their footman. The young hero will be taken to the sea. He's not cured, but it will arrest the course of his injury.*

The reader's attention may have already been drawn to Authurian lore by the mention of Galahad, who is the "pure in heart" knight who finds the Holy Grail, in one version of the story. In an earlier version it is Parzival, not only inexperienced, but downright foolish, who is the Grail knight. He is brought into the Grail Castle, which exists in a wasteland, not unlike the desiccated landscape in this dream. He beholds a mysterious ritual involving the Grail, a spear, and the wounded Fisher King and fails his test because he does not ask about the obvious wound of the suffering king.[21] In this dream, however, it is the young hero who is wounded and the dreamer who is in the role of an older savior figure. It is clear from the dream's own logic that the healing is to come from the gods, to whom the dreamer is to render service somehow. Also the sea, source realm of all life and often the symbol of the unconscious, is involved. It offers to offset the "desiccation" of the dreamers' inner wasteland.

Although the dream is enigmatic and oracular, quite simply
he is to open himself to the unconscious and the inner ocean
of feelings. He described his own dream as "portentous,"
and full of mystery.

Some dreams seem to speak openly about "the sacred," a
topic I take up in Chapter 4. Divine or spiritual beings may
appear. When the dream architect places such a ritual in a
church, as it did in several cases in my dream sample, we see
Jung's definition of the symbol as the "best approximation
of an unknown psychic fact." A church is a familiar setting
for rituals, but not usually ones like the foregoing examples
(except perhaps in the symbolic reference to dismemberment offered by the crucified man on the altar). The church
provides the only kind of "sacred space" we know, which
the ritual evidently requires.

Not all men's initiations are so violent. One dreamer
experienced an initiation that opened his sense of awe and
mystery.

> I am in my office, at a party, there is loud modern music. A
> kind of idiot is my guide. He is enormously powerful, and can
> throw me around. He takes me through a mirror door to
> another space, where quiet music is playing. We enter a
> Church-like place with a proscenium altar. I am dressed as a
> Lord of Power, with a white cloak with a high collar. I am
> wearing the most incredible hat or helmet, like the head of an
> eagle, all white. A solemn ceremony unfolds. Each person is
> to choose a talisman from a vaulted chest. The "idiot" is still
> with me, now seeming like a magical sort of being.

The mirror door, the other building "we didn't know was
there," the dream labyrinth we find in our clothes closet and
so easily enter with dreamlike logic, and the idiot who is
wise show our participation in a simultaneous and separate
reality. Do initiations come whether we provide a sacred
space for their unfoldment or not? This dream was so powerful for the dreamer that he "carried it around with him"

for several days. It had a special life-empowering quality; and although archetypal, like the quest-acquired visions of traditional societies, it bestowed an individual sense of meaning, a personal myth indeed.

The foregoing dreams give us just a glimpse of the inner world of growth awaiting men with the courage to attend to their inner lives. Although the imagery, especially its initial phases, can be shocking, this seems necessary to get our attention. The symbols that follow a breakthrough speak of higher phases of the initiation process, and contain the nobility and the beauty that is our true birthright.

WOMEN'S MYSTERIES

The following dream initiations came to women and seem just as congruent with their traditional mysteries as the men's dreams. Men's and women's dreams have many things in common. The woman, no less than the man, is confronted with something from so deep in her nature it seems totally other and is often encountered with a sense of astonishment.

One woman in her fifties dreamed:

A large high-ceilinged room in a house, filled with women. There is a tall leader with dark hair. As she is speaking, fires break out in parts of the room. The women are making a sound together like oooh! and aaah! There's something in a square glass case in the center of the room. I think, "That can't be!" There is a phallus in there, ringed about with smoke. (I am making a funny noise in my throat, my body is red hot, and a pain in my navel.)

The mythological reference here would seem to be to the Dionysian mysteries, which were especially for women and which indeed celebrated the erect phallus (and through this male symbol, introduced woman to the dark and wild zones of her own nature). Here there is an overt reference to "heat."

It is difficult to avoid the comparison with Jung's early big dream in which he saw in an underground chamber, a great phallus like a tree trunk with a single jeweled eye sitting on a throne. A dream voice told him: "That is the man-eater!" Jung connected the dream to his mother and her dark side, related to magic and nature.[22]

Another woman dreamer in her thirties wrote:

I was watching an Indian ritual . . . an initiation of sorts. The oldest woman-grandmother of the tribe was there. She pierced a foot of a young woman with a pin. . . . Then I was seated behind the old woman, with my legs wrapped around her. She was piercing my feet as she had done the girl's. My feet were crossed and on the left instep she kept pushing the pin in hard knowing that it was probably painful, but she did it with a determined strength. The last time she put a glass tube to the spot and let some blood flow partway up it. Then she hugged me for having gone through a difficult ordeal.

The figure of the wise old man has gotten adequate coverage from Jungian authors. But as psychologist Jean Houston has observed, the figure of the wise old woman is reemergent in our time. Women, no less than men, need a same-sex wisdom figure to which to relate. The transpersonal figure serves as a window to this wisdom within the individual personality. But if only a wise old man is available to both sexes, there is an implication that wisdom chooses only male spokesmen.[23]

The initiation ceremony evokes the birth position, with the old woman in the position of the child, who brings pain in asking to be born. Notice also the role of blood, as in the men's rituals. Later in the same dream the dreamer has to face and fight a lynx with sharp teeth that draws blood (the theme of the animal as initiator is discussed in more detail later). Initiations from within like these (particularly with the aid of the psychotherapeutic situation to help bring insight and establish context) serve as powerful transformers of psyche. They "grow it up" from inside; or as Stanley Hall said of analysis, "It speeds up the process of maturation."[24] After this dream the dreamer wrote in her journal,

> Dreams are the stuff that creeds are made of. If we are ever to have a new workable religion—one that encourages immediate experience, that helps people when they are on the brink of discovering themselves but are frightened by the unleashed forces and their vulnerability, we must be brave enough to stand before God and listen to the voice within . . . to take down the safe walls of external authority and face the fear within ourselves.

This statement is quintessential for our modern search for meaning, and the dreamer shows through her conscious formulation, her adequacy as an individual (in Campbell's sense) to undertake her own mythic quest.

But what about the general instance? Do we tell each dreamer that he or she is in mythic territory? Might that not just be a kind of elite intellectualizing, which avoids feelings? My own sense is that this criticism is often true for psychological theories, which must be told to clients cautiously (lest they fall into the "psychosexual doldrums": "I must be oral," or anal or phallic). But it is much less true for myths, which embody and relate to primary meaning, which is the very connection we need to make sense to ourselves. As the Jungian scholar and analyst M.-L. von Franz said of myths elucidated in the process of psychotherapy:

> One may perhaps tell the myth . . . [the] person then feels that his problem is not unique and insoluble, but that it has been solved dozens of times in certain ways; it also reduces conceit, because one feels that one is in a general situation and not a unique neurosis. The myth

has a magical impact on layers [of the psyche] which cannot be reached by intellectual talk; it imparts the feeling of déjà entendu, yet is always new and awakening.[25]

The myth moves us to a universal human community, which also transcends time in the historical sense, and culture. The reference is to a perennial field of inner validation. My preference as a psychologist is to see psyche as the primary mythogenic source, rather than culture (which the anthropologists, of course, emphasize). Culture, indeed, can provide the rituals for our growth and transformation, but it is the human psyche that fills out the patterns of our cultures with living myths and symbols.

To encounter the relevance of myth to our everyday life in today's secular society requires, as Campbell said, "an adequate individual," whose real adequacy is ultimately to be tested by our willingness to dare the adventure of life without fixed guidance and to open ourselves to recovering the depths of meaning that lie around us and within us. Chapter 3 offers some guidance on seeing our way through to that potential.

Chapter 3

SEEING THROUGH THE IMAGINATION

Imagination is the star in man . . .

—Ruland, *Lexicon Alchemiae*

There is an intentional double entendre in the title of this chapter, because this chapter is both about using the imagination to see and about seeing through its images. There is evidence that in the initial evolutionary stages of development of mental life, imagination and perception were an identical faculty.[1] We perceive the world through a system of internal imagery neatly evolved over years to mimic reality in certain ways. And yet our perception is never free from imagination (apperception, or the projective hypothesis in psychology).

IMAGINATION AND VISION

You can separate imagination from perception by putting a person in a sensory-deprivation chamber, devoid of any input from the outside world. After a while, the imagination begins to run wild, creating hallucinations (perceptions detached from outer reality) and delusions (ideas belonging to a belief system detached from outer reality).[2] Perhaps our vaunted "reality orientation" is simply imagination that has become geared to and reliant on external events? Imagination is a world-mimicking faculty, so that we may envision colors, shapes, people, places, and events. Other sense modalities also belong to imagination: we can hear mental music, sometimes the kind you can't turn off; voices and reconstructed conversations; and experience mental tastes, odors, and the texture of an object once touched.

Imagination may imitate life as we have experienced it, or help prepare us for likely events that have not yet unfolded; and all these functions seem reasonable and necessary to our existence. But then there is imagination's darker, wilder side; we are capable of imagining things that were never seen or heard in outer reality. Mythologies abound with mythical beasts that never walked the earth, and humans lie, and go mad, largely because they are capable of imagining creatively.[3]

The mind, we are told by the Eastern mystics, makes a good servant, but a poor master. The same holds for the mythic imagination, because it enables us not only to model the world accurately, but also to fabricate fancifully and to imagine things wildly that never can or should come to pass. Thus we are often chagrined to find our carefully imagined plans foiled or that we have grossly "misrepresented" reality—in myth this is sometimes represented by a lying adviser or corrupt soothsayer. At such times we are likely to discover the imagination really has been responding to the internal dynamics of the personality, rather than approximating the outer world. Psychology becomes all mixed up in our perceptions.

Our wondrous world-building faculty, then, may act as a reality facsimile generator or (following its own inner laws) delusion generator. Like omniscience, imagination is free to "know" or to model itself on anything in the universe. But

unlike divine omniscience, human imagination never knows
how accurate its model is. Our human vision seems envel-
oped in a "cloud of unknowing." We need, then, to learn a
new art of vision.

THE WORLD OF SELF-LUMINOUS FORMS

In this section I consider the metaphorical relationship between outer and inner light. Traditionally, the world of the
imagination is the starlike "astral" or spirit world. It is
called in some Yoga texts the world of "self-luminous forms."
(Perhaps this is why daytime consciousness is so easily lost
in the world of dreams. The light of consciousness, which
seeks to illuminate the objects of our thoughts, wavers when
confronted with self-luminous forms.) In general, vision
gives us the richest metaphors for consciousness and introduces us to a world characterized by surfaces, contours,
textures, colors, and more. It also brings transparency, dimensionality, and depth—as well as opposites in the form of
opacity, obscurity, and shadow. Above all, vision as a metaphor for consciousness empowers with the qualities of its
own illuminating medium, light.

Everyday speech is full of our visionary metaphors: "I
see," "Could you shed a little light on this?" and "It has
begun to dawn on me that . . ." And we envision the most
complete breakthroughs in human consciousness as being
filled with illumination: enlightenment. The soul of the mystic resembles the eye in its capacity to perceive the living
illumination of the spiritual experience. The soul sees through
the *māyā,* the illusory surface of things. And at the moment
of death, for Tibetan Buddhists, there is a face-to-face meeting with the clear, white light, the Buddha consciousness.
Failing that recognition, the soul begins to sink further and
further into deep, hypnotic illusion, and finally into rebirth.

In the metaphor of light for consciousness, we have the
important notion that "seeing with the mind's eye" may

include its own kind of lucidity, rather than always illusion or delusion, as when our dreams mask "reality."[4] Images of the imagination are not always "imaginary" or untrue, but "imaginal," presenting truths of a different, inner kind. In the modern tradition of archetypal psychology, writers such as James Hillman (originally trained as a Jungian analyst, he has since developed his own approach to psyche and myth) and Roberts Avens (a philosopher and the author of *Imaginal Body*) have helped remind us of an ancient tradition pertaining to the realm of the imaginal and how its luminous revelations should be treated. The psyche or soul *is* the imagination.[5] Jung, though, said it most elegantly:

> The protean mythologem and the shimmering symbol express the processes of the psyche far more trenchantly, and in the end, far more clearly than the clearest concept; for the symbol not only conveys a visualization of the process but—and this is perhaps just as important—it brings a re-experiencing of that twilight which we can learn to understand only through inoffensive empathy, but which too much clarity only dispels.[6]

The "too much clarity" of which Jung spoke is the light of daytime consciousness that expects hard-and-fast boundaries between things—and ideas; this is quite different from the protean, poetic, and yet symbolically rich world of the dream. The Neoplatonic thinkers of the Renaissance, in fact, identified the imaginal soul with the Greek figure of the sea deity Proteus, who could change into all things, human, beast, or monster. He would only take his true form and bestow a blessing, however—as the legends tell us—if you catch and hold him. Likewise the anima (Latin, "soul") often is shown in the ancient fairy-tale lore as a shape-changing nixie, who reverts to true form only if captured and held.

In the *Yoga Sutras of Patanjali* is an ancient formulation of the ambivalent nature of the imagination: "The psychic nature, taking on the color of the Seer and of things seen, leads to the perception of all objects."[7] The yogi's task, through his discipline, is to hold Proteus—"the psychic nature," the living organism of imagination—still.

"When the perturbations of the psychic nature have all been stilled, then the consciousness, like a pure crystal, takes the colour of what it rests on, whether that be the perceiver, perceiving, or the thing perceived."[8] This simple-seeming principle is the root metaphor for all the meditative practices of the East, the pathway to true seeing, self-knowledge, even cosmic consciousness. Is there one of equivalent profundity and efficacy for the spiritual tradition of the West? Visualize this: On your next hero venture you have caught magical Proteus (our Neoplatonic metaphor for the soul), but if your grip is too tight, you may never get to see his legendary and spectacular transformations. You relax your grip a bit to take a kind of "magical mystery tour." (You tighten up when he threatens to carry you away totally, as in the legends, on the back of a dragon or tiger.) With a combination of mental control and mental permissiveness, the mythic imagination is conduced to reveal its hidden workings. This is the essence of what Jung called the transcendent function and what I outlined in *The Shaman's Doorway,* as the highest (fifth) stage of mythic engagement.

The poet Blake sought to restore to imagination its divine origins:

The eternal Body of Man is The Imagination, that is,
    God himself
The Divine Body: Jesus: we are his Members.
    It manifests itself in his Works of Art (In Eternity
    All is Vision).[9]

Blake believed the artist was the priest of the imagination and that the artist was closer to true spiritual vision than the philosopher. We remember his personal mythological figure for the creative life was Los, the fiery blacksmith artist with his rage and passion, the opponent of Urizen—personification of "your reason" (see *The Four Zoas*).

Coleridge, too, as I described earlier, envisioned a primary form of imagination, not based on objects from the external world—its merely "mirroring function"—but on the creative and visionary power of life itself.[10] The poet or creative artist is the yogi of the West, who connects with this deeper function of the imagination. Unlike the yogi, he does not seek to banish all illusion to find the one truth; rather like the shaman, he finds truths in the illusions, and shares the visions.

Yeats said, years later, but still in the same tradition,

The arts are, I believe, about to take upon their shoulders the burdens that have fallen from the shoulders of priests, and to lead us back upon our journey by filling our thoughts with the essences of things, and not with things. We are to substitute once more the distillation of alchemy for the analyses of chemistry, and for some of the other sciences; and certain of us are looking everywhere for the perfect alembic, that no silver or golden drop may escape.[11]

Campbell has argued that the creative artist of today has inherited (and rendered yet more colorful) that priestly mantle. The art, literature, and cinematography of which Campbell was speaking was the same that Joyce has Steven Dedalus discover: the myth-infused vision, the aesthetic arrest that leads the mind to a new realization of its own depth.[12]

In his perceptive and synthesizing book *Imaginal Body*, Avens evokes archetypal psychology's colorful panoply of soul images: from the Greeks' *psyche*, literally "butterfly," to Jung and the alchemist's *cauda pavonis*, the "tail of the peacock," to those many-petaled symbols, the rose (West) and the lotus (East). Perhaps the soul's most translucent representation (Avens credits Owen Barfield for the image) is the rainbow:

Soul or imagination is not concerned either with mere matter or with pure spirit; to use a portmanteau term, it is a psychosomatic activity, which, like a rainbow, links these extremes harmoniously together and produces a "new level of being," a "third," which is none other than the soul itself. The soul creates itself by imagining itself and it exists only while it imagines. The truth and reality of the soul is created and exists in the created. Imagination is a self-originating, autonomous occurrence, sheer presencing, a "something" which, as a Buddhist would say, is "just so." In the strict sense of the word, it is a colorful experience.[13]

Hillman, who inspired much of Avens's thought, in his classic *Revisioning Psychology,* has suggested that the psyche has a fundamental need to see through itself, ever making transparent the ideas and images that always seem real (the Latin root of "real" is *res:* literally "thinglike") when they occur to us. The Greek *eidos* is the root of both "idea" (a thought by means of which one sees) and "image" (*eidolon,* "form or shape"). "The soul seems to suffer when its inner eye is occluded," Hillman wrote.

[And] psychological learning or psychologizing seems to represent the soul's desire for light, like the moth for the flame. The psyche wants to find itself by seeing through; even more it loves to be enlightened by *seeing through itself,* as if the very act of seeing through clarified and made the soul transparent.[14]

When we try to understand a dream we are making ideas about images. And when we dream, we find the images loaded with our ideas, as associations always reveal. Is the essential life—and growth—of the soul to be found in our ability to self-reflect: idea/image/idea? (I give examples of how this works in more detail below.) Certainly, we identify self-reflection with a higher level of consciousness. The ability to see into oneself and laugh at what we find there, we find winsome. Seeing through, like humor, resists all fixed and foregone conclusions, all rigidity and opacity of thought, and encourages the symbolic or analogical and the transparent.

Each time we acquire a new idea or system of ideas we begin to see things in new ways, as if ideas were eyes. After a few hours of study of the popular system Transactional Analysis, for example, we may come to see our own behavior or the behavior of others as variations on the theme of those three perennial characters: parent, child, and adult; the seeing will, indeed, show us things we didn't know were there. More mythically (and more colorfully) we might identify the tenebrous shadow lurking behind us; that spritelike thing, the anima; and the mask, the persona. It is the nature of any myth form, held in mind or operating beneath awareness, to form our experience in its mold.

To see mythically, then, is not just to fantasize richly or to dwell only on classic myths and fables. The mythically awake imagination would rather see through the ordinary-seeming surface of everyday life to discover the "secret cause," the mythic, archetypal patterns beneath. Above all, seeing through has shown us that mind is susceptible to myth forms and also produces them. The only cure is to continue seeing through, beyond, and within. We become skeptical of mythic ideas that seem opaque, that block seeing through. The mythic imagination is always on the lookout for mythological persons, such as heroes or messiahs. But when it finds them self-convinced, it is always suspicious, because they, more than other humans, are most dangerous when they fail to see through themselves.

When a person identifies too literally with a myth we are all eager to see through. We like to see a hero who is self-congratulatory, someone who pretends a godlike omniscience, fall from his mythic identity. Is this a reason for our collective fascination with the gossip columns, which specialize in all-too-human revelations about the rich and the famous? One of our principal "civilized" styles of mythmaking—especially evident in America—is to elevate our heroes—athletes, politicians, and movie stars—to an almost divine status and then expose their human weaknesses.

Myth forms light up our world; they are the self-luminous forms that arouse psychological motives and incite behavior. But perpetual work is required to see through them transparently. In our quest for self-knowledge, we need to study first the symbols, images, and ideas by which we know things. Then, through using our imperfect, yet infinitely perfectible, faculty, the imagination, we may come to create successively deeper approximations of the whole universe. We may learn to dream great Vishnu's dream and know it for reality.

SEEING THROUGH REFLECTIONS

What landmarks and symbols will we encounter on a journey into the living landscape of psyche? What sights do we see when we step "through the looking glass"? The looking glass itself, or magic mirror, or the surface of water, is often the initial image in which the unconscious discloses something about its nature. Its first function is to mirror consciousness. As Perls, the founder of Gestalt therapy, discovered, we find our own image in all the images of the dream. This quality is so consistent throughout the imaginal realm that very often the first image that you see in a fantasy or imagery experience is a condensed image of your immediate state of consciousness, a glimpse of your own face in a dewdrop.

Psychoanalyst Herbert Silberer was one of the first investigators to describe adequately this consciousness-mirroring function of the imagination, for which he devised the apt term *autosymbolic*. He studied twilight states of consciousness and mental imagery. Silberer noticed that whatever concern had been going on in consciousness was likely to be (unconsciously) represented in inner imagery: visual, auditory, or both.[15]

As we hover at the threshold of the unconscious, images flit by; there is a moment-by-moment reflecting going on. Settling in, a particular *Eigenlicht* (or "self-luminous form") may persist; this now may be taken to refer to a more permanent state of being. "One I've often seen is formed out of delicate fern leaves . . . which seem to go with a very peaceful languid state, the feeling suggested by ferns in shaded areas," said the psychologist Wilson Van Dusen, one of Silberer's students.[16] He noted that the appearance of abstract patterns seemed to correspond to an abstracted mental state. Our imagery declares the (temporary) qualities of mind by a precise kind of signature. Van Dusen said, "It is as though at our core is a process which cannot help but represent itself."[17] Jung said something very similar: "We know that the mask of the unconscious is not rigid—it reflects the face we turn toward it. Hostility lends it a threatening aspect, friendliness softens its features." Elsewhere Jung added, "It only becomes dangerous when our conscious attitude to it is hopelessly wrong. To the degree that we repress it, its danger increases."[18]

"Pass within to the living landscape," we seem to be told, "but beware your own inner state, for you are entering a psychic hall of mirrors." And if the portal region of the psyche is reflective of our immediate state, the deeper regions show the more permanent structures of psyche. Here too one enters a moral zone, where ego is allowed to behold not only its known self, but its (perhaps unknown) fundamental assumptions about life. With the aid of a psychological amplifier such as LSD, it is possible to observe this connection between image and personal meaning in more detail. One professional volunteer at the Maryland Psychiatric Center, after taking the psychedelic, saw the usual initial kaleidescopic show of brilliant colors and forms, then:

At one point the geometrical structures became stabilized and got organized into the shape of a rather complicated frame of a large baroque mirror. It represented a maze of branches with rich foliage carved in wood. The mirror was divided into five or six compartments of irregular size separated by ramified offshoots of the frame.

To my great surprise, when I looked into these compartments, various interesting scenes started unfolding in front of my eyes. . . . The persons participating in these scenes were highly stylized and slightly puppet-like. The general atmosphere was rather amusing and comical, but with a definite undertone of secrecy, mystery, and hypocrisy. I suddenly realized I was watching a symbolic satire on my childhood, that was spent in a little provincial town of "la petite bourgeoisie . . ." To my surprise all my emotions from that period of my life emerged from the deep unconscious and became real and vivid once again.[19]

As we develop a deeper rapport with our own imagery, it will "mirror" our concerns at ever-deeper levels, drawing from that forgotten past when certain crucial personality-shaping events happened that have since become unconscious. The image in the magic mirror, like the ones in fairy tales, gives you a true seeing about yourself, but not necessarily the one you expected or wished to see.

Patricia Garfield, a modern dream psychologist who has worked extensively on lucid (conscious) dreaming, noticed that when the image of a mirror appeared in one of her dreams, it often seemed to be a signal to "wake up" in the dream. She wrote,

For this reason, I have termed this type of image the Mirror Gazer. If I have not already become fully lucid by the time I see myself in a mirror in a dream, I will almost invariably, as I gaze into the dream mirror,

FIGURE 10. *Like the divine imagination, the human imagination mirrors creation.* The Days of Creation (the Sixth), *by Sir Edward Corey Burne-Jones (1833-1898). Painting in a series of seven, 1875-1876. (Fogg Art Museum, Harvard University.)*

realize that I am dreaming. . . . Many of my lucid dreams are preceded or triggered by the image of the Mirror Gazer.[20]

As if to confirm the gist of Garfield's observations, one of the most prolific and "lucid" dreamers in my sample, a woman in her forties, wrote, *"As I go out I see myself in a mirror. I have a scarf around my hair and my eyes look enormous."* The focus, as Garfield described, was on "seeing herself seeing herself." The dream, itself a reflection of yourself, shows you yourself in a reflection.

Sometimes inner imagery may be of deceptively simple appearance yet have profound and very helpful bridging qualities to feeling. Martha Crampton, a psychologist with a strong interest in the use of mental imagery in therapy, wrote of her work with a middle-aged man whom she asked to experience an image about a tightness he felt in his chest. He saw himself, like the fabled Dutch boy, "with his finger in a dike, holding back a mighty sea." Recognition of the meaning of the image initiated a cathartic release through crying, and, as Crampton described, his subsequent freeing from a smoking habit of thirty years.[21] If psyche's magic mirror seems to trick us with a mere reflection, it can also, when looked into more deeply, have psychological value. This seems an almost textbook illustration of Jung's concept of "the self-liberating power of the introverted mind." In Crampton's example, the pattern was from sensation (tightness) to image (Dutch boy) to idea (understanding the image) to catharsis (healing release of affect).

When psyche itself wishes to bring up seeing through, its imagery includes reflections on its own transparency. Dreamers often describe windows, water, or even the atmosphere, in ways that show this metaphoric property. One woman dreamer portrayed her dream mood: *"Windows are sparkling clear, beautiful early dusk sky, can see the mountains in the distance."* But sometimes dream windows have glass so thick you can hardly see through them. Glass may be clouded, cracked, colored, or opaque. Dreamers lose or break, or get new glasses or contact lenses; use—or lose—telescopes, binoculars, and microscopes. One dreamer in search of clarity for her life wrote,

> *Two women (mentors and friends) were visiting me in my house. Upstairs the windows were so cloudy we could not see out. We were unable to "go outside" to clean them. Finally S. (the therapist) comes, and he is able to "go outside" to clean the windows.*

This dream was certainly therapeutically positive, because it indicated I was giving her the "outside help," or objectivity, needed for her personal perspective. The other women were positive figures, but so close to her, they too were caught in "her space."

A dream atmosphere may be cloudy or foggy, or it may be nighttime. In the dark, we need artificial aid to see, and we may have an adequate or inadequate source of illumination. We can't find the light switch or the flashlight, the candle keeps going out, or the only light source is a tiny crack. In all these situations, it is valuable to notice what factors relate to seeing through your or your dream figure's predicament. An interesting woman dreamer in her late twenties captured the gist of my theme in a dream worth exploring in some depth. She titled it, "John Lennon's Glasses":

> *I see a book about John Lennon. On the cover he is lying on his stomach on the floor. His glasses are off, and lying nearby. Then he is looking through them, and they are dark. (Now I am watching him actually.) As I (With a Camera?) am moving around to the right, he continues looking at me through his glasses. They are changing. At the far right I can see his eyes, and they are very big—looking almost vulnerable.*
>
> *Then it's like I'm watching or writing some documentary on him, focusing on his glasses, saying, "He wore them when he*

*was young, they changed, and they were what he found when
he died." Next they have big, black rubber frames.*

*The scene changes to when he was about 2–3 years old. He
was in a dance practice room. The instructor had beautiful
blond hair—she was running her hands through it as she
watched John. He turned his head sideways, and a black
thing (like a centipede) moved around and off his eyes. He
was doing [it] telepathically.*

You may have noticed that this dream almost "plays" with
the metaphoric structures I have introduced: its specific images include "seeing through" the cover of a book, glasses—
and frames, camera, and eyes. The dream itself "says" it's
about glasses. As I worked with the dreamer in a session, it
was obvious that an affliction lay in her perception—rather
than anywhere else—at least at the moment captured by the
dream. Like many people, she explained the wrenching blows
that culminated the sixties for her; the awful, balefully mythic
deaths of the Kennedys and John Lennon. Her view of the
world had begun to change; it darkened, like the glasses.
The dream introduces the "different perspective" offered by
the presence of death (see Part Two). The spectacles change
from wire-rimmed (association: the Aquarian world view of
the sixties) to black-rimmed (which she associated with Henry
Kissinger). The dreamer, who had never read this chapter,
wrote, "John's glasses: ability to see? Perspective changes
through changes in glasses?"

I wondered if the dream were talking about the "after-
death perspective" mentioned by Elisabeth Kübler-Ross and
Raymond Moody: many people have claimed that while
seeing "with the eyes of the spirit," the universe seems
somehow "right," as the mystics also report, as if everything were unfolding somehow in its proper way. However, to the saddened worldly eyes (of both John Lennon
and the dreamer), just the opposite was true.

In a way, the dream was transparently offering her an

alternative viewpoint to her depressed outlook—connected
with the strange black creature that crawls off his eye and
the image and meaning of the black-rimmed glasses. She is
to see through the depression, portrayed as an eldritch spirit
creature that was "wrapped around her eyes, as it were: a
perceptual affliction. John Lennon then reappears as a magical child—the child's view of the world—and a nurturing
maternal figure present, with golden hair in a movingly
poignant way running her fingers through the hair. (Golden
hair in fairy tales is often associated with a blessing or a
special anointing or destiny.) Even though Lennon's death
seems tragic and premature to us, did he fulfill his mission
in some important way?

With luminous images, the dream instructs, encouraging
us to see differently. We only have to get our eyes used to
the soft refulgence of the twilit world of dreams—the world
of self-luminous forms.

PARANOIA AND MYTH

When we lose our way in the dark, we are vulnerable to
whatever lights up the world for us. And "all that glitters is
not gold." We may follow the phosphorescent forms, or the
will-o'-the-wisp, only to end up deeper in the swamp. We
have often been accused as a species of living by our illusions, something understandable enough in the face of the
"hard fact" of ultimate mortality. To live by delusions is
less understandable; they steal time, rather than making it
bearable or enriching it. They are often dysfunctional and
uncomfortable, for ourselves and others. We must again
look to a theory of the archetypal to understand their ambivalent power.

A mind that is trying to personify or imagine the quality
of the universe in depth will find itself mythologizing. As it
enters further into a spiritual zone, the logic of the material
world drops away. Our main concern comes to be the

relationship to the totality of things, the big picture. Consciousness, in this mood, becomes suffused with primary meaning and all perception is numinous (Latin, "partaking of divinity"). The urge that compels us to find a meaning in life here becomes irresistible; the mind is drawn to closure with its own inner meanings. Jung described this state as "psychic inflation": to be filled with a spiritual atmosphere, possessed by an archetype. (I have used the term *mythic identity*.) Contact with the spiritual dimension in this mood is dangerous.

Emanuel Swedenborg, the eighteenth-century Swedish scientist-visionary, in his own spiritual diaries described this state well. He saw the soul as the recipient of spiritual energies and even beings that inhabit it. "Our true nature is that of receptacles," he said.[22]

Van Dusen, who acknowledged his debt to Swedenborg, in *The Presence of Spirits in Madness,* gave a modern clinical description of "entities" he felt to be inhabiting his patients. A "higher order" left the person in freedom, while a "lower order" sought to enslave them."[23] For this model, which is also consistent with the animistic world view, the hollow spaces in the human psyche may become filled with a volatile and intense energy or even a deluded "personality" (see also Chapter 8).

Chogyam Trungpa, the modern Tibetan Buddhist spokesman, described something similar in a discourse on paranoia, which he says comes from association with a realm of deluded spirits, the Asuras, who dwell on the Bardo plane.

If you are trying to help someone who has an Asura mentality, they interpret your action as an attempt to oppress them or infiltrate their territory. But if you decide not to help them, they interpret that as a selfish act: you are seeking comfort for yourself. If you present both alternatives to them they think you are playing games with them. The Asura mentality is quite intelligent, it sees all the hidden corners.[24]

The great mystics throughout the ages have sought to become conscious of everything—to "see all the hidden corners" —even the universe as a whole. But such an experience is a heady wine, and the mind unprepared for God intoxication may become mad. Meher Baba, an important mystic of recent times, worked in India with the *masts,* people halfway between conventional madness and spiritual enlightenment. (He told of his experiences in his book *Among the God-Intoxicated.*) The mind that steeps itself in psychospiritual realities must be trained to regard all its own experiences transparently. This is the only sure countermeasure to the (inflated) states of subjective certainty that arise. The paranoid, no less than the mystic, imagines a relationship to the totality of things, but the mythology is destructive. As William James put it,

> In delusional insanity, paranoia as they sometimes call it, we may have a diabolical mysticism, a sort of religious mysticism turned upside down. The same sense of ineffable importance in the smallest events, the same voices and visions and leading and missions, the same controlling by extraneous powers; only the emotion is pessimistic: instead of consolations we have desolations; the meanings are dreadful; and the powers are enemies of life.[25]

Paranoia means literally "to know what is beyond." When we imagine on a scale too large for our comprehension we become "as the gods," and mythologies agree on the terrible consequences of that psychological state the Greeks called hubris. What is the scale and proportion appropriate to "seeing"—human knowledge here in time and space? And are there unknown limits that when we lose or ignore them make us lose or absolutize the boundaries of the soul?

Paranoia and especially paranoid schizophrenia are interesting for a principal theme of this book, because they produce very intense personal mythologies. The relationship between self and world is magnified and dramatized. Our personal existence acquires enormous importance, and a relatedness to everything else in the universe is assumed; in raw form we see the intensity of the soul's quest for meaningful participation in All That Is. Above all, paranoia is a distortion of the scale and perspective that properly belong to vision.

We are chips off the old (uncarved) block, and it is in our natures to try to assume the prerogatives of deity. We all would like to be infallible, omniscient, and omnipotent. Piaget showed how we start life with this attitude in germ (egocentricity); and if we are unlucky and unconscious, we may end with it, reverting to our myth of origins in adult megalomania!

Unresolved personal problems and accompanying negative emotion bend the mythic vision into a baleful form. Major life crises and trauma are often generative of unconscious, destructive myths. Moments of crisis and strong affect provoke us psychologically to confront the nature of life itself. We may then assess everything in life as relative to an imagined "moment of truth," to which we ascribe great meaning and which nonetheless may be strongly configured by a particular affect: panic, remorse, or blame.

In traditional psychotherapy, the therapist often traces a destructive personal myth back to such an event and "exorcises" it through emotional release. But I believe that the myth must also be seen through and understood in terms of both its biographical origin and mythic meaning, to be truly transcended. This is not always an easy process, and people who fail to see through often lead much of life in the thrall of outmoded myths that they stubbornly cling to and that were appropriate only at the time when a life event brought that particular myth into being.

SEEING THROUGH MYTHS

In *The Shaman's Doorway*, I introduced the concept of "mythic assimilation". In cognitive *assimilation,* as described by Piaget, a person has an unchanging model or schema about reality that bends incoming data from the world to its own form. Its complementary and necessary counterprinciple is *accommodation,* which allows for modification of one's internal schema to "accommodate" new information.[26] The term describes the potentially destructive power of mythological thinking. Mythic ideas that are not amenable to change, such as rigid orthodoxies and fixed religious ideas, deform the world of experience into their own image. The myth is held to as literal and exclusive reality. Here, too, are "personal constructs" as described by psychologist George Kelly: unconsciously held personal beliefs, which may warp the individual's experience in certain directions.[27]

The cognitive balancing act, in which we must each engage to grow up mentally, requires both principles: assimilation and accommodation. Myths that cannot be seen through blind consciousness. Our psyches require both structure and flexibility, surface and transparency. This may be especially needed when myths collide or conflict with each other. Psychologist David Feinstein wrote,

> An individual's personal myths may also exist in dialectical tension with one another, since different cognitive structures within a single cognitive system may organize data in conflicting ways. Such conflicting personal myths also engage in a process of equilibration—assimilating and accommodating one another toward equilibrium and synthesis. The evolution of consciousness in the individual is a product of this unending dialectic between myths and among myths and their sources of input.[28]

Myths are not meant to be procrustean beds (even though "procrustean beds" are mythic—originated by a man on the Greek isthmus (Procrustes) who used to cut off parts of his houseguests if they were too tall or stretch them to fit the bed if they were too short). But they may, indeed, become that when they are literalized and rigidified. The venerable psychologist Jerome Bruner argued that mythology provides a library of mythic scripts from which to choose, not just a single fixed pattern. In their positive, life-guiding, or empowering form, they may see us through stages of our psychological growth. But our relationship to them must remain open to change.[29]

Psyche requires more than a single myth. Life, at its most challenging, may request of us great flexibility and openness. Full freedom implies the ability to choose our meaning, posture, and response to any given situation. To see through this universe in the depth and transparency it truly invites, we need all our wealth of religions, yes, and atheisms, philosophies, divergent schools of thought, orthodoxies, and heresies—perspectives from which to look at other perspectives.

You might expect that the practice of seeing through could lead to a kind of cynicism about life. But this attitude too must be seen through. The committed skeptic or cynic has engaged in a seeing through that stopped short, mistaking one of his own mythic ideas for "underlying reality"; and Freud, one of the great masters of seeing through every kind of disguise of the psyche, still stopped short on one of the many transparent levels that may be glimpsed within. Any clinical psychologist who tries the psychoanalytical filter will discern many of the phenomena described by Freud: the psychosexuality, the Oedipal dynamics, and the workings of those three mythic persons of the psyche—the id, ego, and superego. But the psychoanalytic literalism comes in the "nothing but" attitude. Yes, there is that, but there is also this . . . and this . . .

We have arrived at a point of paradox. If myths are always to be transparent, where do we find something solid on which to base our lives? Can we stand on the insubstantial? Campbell asks: "And why should it be that whenever men have looked for something solid on which to found their lives, they have chosen, not the facts in which the world abounds, but the myths of an immemorial imagination?"[30]

Campbell was much better equipped to answer his own question than anyone I know, having immersed himself profoundly in the world's great mythological traditions for more than fifty years, focusing especially on the ways in which myth speaks directly to life. Once in a conversation, I commented on how easily we moderns put on and take off soul clothing—membership in Vedantism one week, Buddhism the next, Sufism the third—especially considering the age and dignity of some of these religions. He said, "I think each of these traditions has something valuable to teach us, at different points in our life development." I looked at my own life process and saw it was true. Christianity teaches us about love and about sacrifice; Judaism, about spiritual loyalty and respect for the law; Islamic Sufism celebrates the spiritual wisdom of foolishness (as in the parables of Mullah Nasrudin); the Sanskrit traditions may initiate us into the warriorhood of detachment; Tibetan Buddhism invites us to hallucinate the world full of colorful symbolic deities and then to erase them as illusion in a *vajra* flash; Zen shows us the potency of paradox and of simplicity.

Every now and then, soul falls in love with spirit, and we may have a romance with a spiritual tradition. We would make our way, slowly or quickly, to its living heart, all the while playing our feelings and thoughts against its images and ideas. And as with lovers finding each other, there are parts that fit well and less well. What forms of ecstasy may we share; what meanings, values, or dreams; will we have soul children?

Our ancestors lived and died within a monomyth, a single great tradition, received at birth, membership automatic. It may seem to us now like an arranged marriage (they also liked those) rather than a love affair, which flows from the spontaneous movement of the heart (as Campbell would say, "following the recommendation of the eyes," in the language of the troubadors of the medieval courts of love).[31] But our modern task may be to find the sense of the One in the many and the reflections of all traditions, each in the other, as in a hologram.[32]

People who have been transformed within the embrace of a spiritual tradition may have a luminous quality; they may seem to have become a window to the transpersonal. We see through the surface to a living spirituality in them. They seem blessed—the normal inner conflicts or personal vices we all struggle with, seeming to have been swept away—enabling them to exemplify the potent simplicity of a life lived with spiritual meaning.

Whether or not we resonate with their specific religious system, it is difficult to avoid wishing such people well, as they embody our collective quest for meaning. The danger lies in our tendency to concretize in them the image of the avatar, one beyond the human condition. Because we have lost the images of the gods, as Hillman says, we are susceptible to the creating of cults around the charismatic human personality.[33] To worship such a person uncritically puts a burden on him no less than us. I believe Jim Jones to have been his people's victim in no less a sense than they were his. It is important for us to know that any of us fools is a potential avatar and any living avatar, a potential fool. We need awareness of the ways in which spirit relates to and leads soul. Do myths need people in no less a way than people need myths?

To learn the lore of shamanism, and recognize its inner coherence, was an important personal teacher for me. Shamanic lore is a primer of visionary psychology; and I have found its ancient symbols ever since, in virtually every religious tradition: the crisis, the soul journey, the transformation through death, the willing victim and the sacrificial feast, the savior-healer. The vocabulary of images and ideas in such a tradition teaches us a kind of living language, the vital essence of which carries us deeper into the experience of life. It also provides an initiation into a wisdom tradition, because the symbols educate us, drawing forth feelings and values, and recontexting them in a spiritual way (see Chapter 5).

In the early Castaneda books, Don Juan trained Carlos in the art of seeing through "visionary vegetables": the peyote cactus, the mushroom, the datura. The altered state is to replace secular seeing by spirit seeing, and from this, the power will flow. Psychiatrist Claudio Naranjo studied this same process in South America and found that modern people who consumed yagé, or ayahuasca (made from the hallucinogenic *Banisteriopsis caapi* vine), indeed *saw* some of the traditional mythic beings of Brazilian Indian shamanism: the spirit jaguars, anacondas, and even more mythical creatures like the feathered serpent.[34]

Some of Naranjo's subjects felt they had acquired the X-ray vision of the shamanic experience. This faculty is similar from South America to North America, from Siberia to Australia, and sometimes is attained with drugs, sometimes without. The shaman begins to *see* the metaphysical causes of the illness or other problem—whether sorcerer's dart, offended forest spirit, unpropitiated dead relative, or whatever.

Mircea Eliade wrote that the *angaqok,* the magical sight of the Eskimo, is

a mysterious light which the shaman suddenly feels in his body, inside his head within the brain, an inexplicable searchlight, a luminous fire, which enables him to see in the dark, both literally and metaphorically speaking, for he can now, even with closed eyes, see through darkness and perceive things and coming events which are hidden from others. Thus they look into the future and the secrets of others.[35]

The shaman-visionary functions as a kind of psychic telescope, then, empowered by the community to extend its vision and knowledge. The great visionaries of history are those whose vision extended beyond the little and personal purview; a notable example being the Sioux Black Elk, whose great vision pertained to the psychic predicament of his whole people.[36] Jungian analyst von Franz has speculated that a mystic like Nicholas von Flue—deeply steeped in contemplative practices,—was, more than any other person, able to see the best course for the whole Swiss nation at a time of travail.[37]

Ultimately our mythological seeing through should transform us, not into cynics, but into believers of a new kind—in the reality and ubiquity of spiritual experience and in the endless creativity of human beings in the face of it. For these beliefs may be verified any time we choose: the mysteries of this universe continually expand with our ability to symbolize them (and our ideas and images are seeing devices), a whole psyche perceives a wholesome universe, when one looks into any mythology one finds a wisdom tradition embedded among its images and the fundamental patterns of this tradition do not belong exclusively to any specific religious system, but are universal.

My personal belief is that the study of comparative mythology instills a respectful openness to spiritual experience. Furthermore, as we see that the hero really does have "a thousand faces," we experience a deeply felt humanitarianism. Most important, perhaps, we experience a growing openness to all sacred traditions and an ecumenicism that is willing to see through any surface set of beliefs and symbols to the inner sense. "We have not even to risk the adventure alone," said Campbell,

for the heroes of all time have gone before us; the labyrinth is thoroughly known; we have only to follow the thread of the hero-path. And where we had thought to find an abomination, we shall find a god; where we had thought to slay another, we shall slay ourselves;

where we had thought to travel outward we shall come
to the center of our own existence; where we had
thought to be alone, we shall be with all the world.[38]

It seems to me that it is in this symbolic and transparent
direction that the spiritual sensibilities of humanity must
turn, not to neoorthodoxies and literalistic fundamentalism,
which have ever-alienated and separated the traditions—as
well as the people—one from another.

Chapter 4

THE LIVING
LANDSCAPE

*Understand that thou art a second little world and that the
sun and moon are within thee, and also the stars.*

—ORIGEN, *Homilae in Leviticum*

As the mind finds itself through image making and image interpreting, through seeing, and seeing through, it seems natural to find our mental imagery full of landscapes, which give a breadth and spaciousness to our outer experience. There is room for things to be and things to happen. A flat landscape is two dimensional, but mountains and caves immediately imply a third dimension; landscapes in which there is history—ruins, moss growing on things, or geological forces at work—show us the action of time, a fourth. An ego encountering not only the world of time and space, but the world of the imagination, is often symbolized as a person having an adventure in a landscape. "Personifying is a way of being in the world and *experiencing the world as a psychological field,*" says archetypal psychologist Hillman.[1]

If life comes to imitate the imagination, as when a fantasy is played into reality, so too the imagination fills itself with images out of life. (Again we see our consciousness hovering between two principles that mirror each other.)

In Freud's model for the creation of dream or daydream, a

psychological impulse is overwhelming in its internal protean state and becomes projected into an external event that may be "managed": encountered, objectified, or confronted. Jerome Bruner believes this is true of both myth and dream, "where impulse is transduced into image and symbol, where an internal plight is converted into a story plot."[2]

Jung, von Franz, and other scholars have suggested that myths and fairy tales may have been generated in states very much like "active imagination."[3] The mind is to be attentive to its inner workings, as in meditation, but in active imagination, the goal is not to suspend the spontaneous movements of the mind. It is this mix of mental discipline and mental permissiveness that produces some of our most profound inner adventures.

Freud noted the "living" quality of dream landscapes, but identified them in his rather literalistic way with the body:

> We have recognized that *landscapes* represent the female sexual organs; mountains and rocks are symbols of the male organ; *gardens* a frequently occurring symbol of the female genitalia. *Fruit* stands for the breasts, not for a child. *Wild animals* denote human beings whose senses are excited. . . . The pubic hair in both sexes is indicated in dreams by *woods* and *thickets.*[4]

Thus the sensuous landscape. And the psychoanalytic tradition has confirmed the gist of Freud's observations. The dreaming and imagining human almost cannot help but represent himself or herself, body as well as soul, and this erotically toned mode is certainly one of the major ones. But is this level necessarily *more* real, say, than the psyche's symbolizing of its power struggles (Adler), or its spiritual yearnings (Jung)? In later sections of this chapter we see dream mountains as rather evident symbols of aspiration, and "sacred space" clearly set apart by the dream architect for inner rituals of transformation.

As discussed in the last chapter, the first encounter with

the unconscious reflects back an image of our mind, especially our skepticism, Aristotelian logic, or perhaps that dangerously naive mood von Franz calls frevel: a mocking, disbelieving attitude toward psyche.[5] Perhaps this is why some people never get past the initial encounter with the unconscious, the mirror just seems to reflect their own negative expectations. This may be why we have so many psychologies of the unconscious, all valid in their own way and likely to be confirmed by any investigator who holds that particular myth in mind.

In almost all premodern cultures it is the outer landscape that appears to be spiritually alive, so heavily does the mythological projection work. The sea and sky are the abode of supernatural forces; each tree, brook, and stone has its indwelling spirit; deities and demons hold sway over all natural phenomena. Human doings against this backdrop are mythologized and seen as intertwined with the doings of nature. Ritual sustains the coming and going of the seasons and even the rising of the sun and moon. The comparative religionist Ananda K. Coomaraswamy used the term *landnam* to define this universal tendency to mythologize the local landscape. Everywhere, and throughout history, images of psyche have become entangled with the physical environment.[6] These images, said philosopher Avens,

> confront man in the shapes of elemental spirits, in the rustling of leaves, the murmuring and roaring of the wind, in the voices of the forest. The world of the primitive is fully alive because it is neither purely subjective nor purely objective, neither spiritual nor material, but *ensouled.*[7]

If we contrast this older world view, which still persists in the *philosophia perennialis* and all nature mysticism in which the earth is seen as a living organism, with our modern "scientifically socialized" one, in which the sea is a saline solution (not the mother source of life) and the sun a mass of fiery gases (not a living being), we can see the extent of our modern dissociation. A demythologizing, and depersonification of nature has taken place. I am convinced this leaves us with a psyche swarming with the displaced myths. But I am most frightened of psychologies that try to carry the demythologizing powers of science even into the psyche: the "nothing-but," reductionist schools of behaviorism, biogenic neuropsychology, and purist psychoanalysis. These systems, employed literally—as they usually are—can be most destructive to our soul concept. They invite us to one and only one level of seeing through and then leave us eyeless in their opaque environment, out of touch with the psyche's native ability to move freely among mythological ideas and images, its ways of seeing in depth.

Recently however, the cognitive psychologists have been willing to peek into behaviorism's "black box," the inner vacuum John Watson felt necessary to postulate, to isolate and study observable behavior.[8] Yale psychologist Jerome Singer, UCLA's Marielle Fuller, and independent researchers and writers such as Akhter Ahsen have also begun to reestablish the presence of the imaginal in American psychology (long the stronghold of black boxes).[9]

Attention to the interior landscape has been increasing in some academic high places, which can be considered tribunals of a sort, helping to determine our reality orientation. But why is there so much resistance to these ideas? Have we failed to see through—as a modern myth—the scientific socialization we grew up with, hardening it into a literal dogma? Modern academic psychology is far more Cartesian–Newtonian in its outlook than physics, which entered the age of Einstein about sixty years ago.

THE LANDSCAPE OF FAERY

Recently we have seen the return of our old soul-permeated landscape, or "mindscape"; it shows up in art, record albums, and novels of the fantasy genre. Of the fantasists of this domain, none is now better known and beloved than J. R. R. Tolkien. But his work slumbered relatively unknown for several decades, until that strange phenomenon of the collective imagination we call the sixties called him forth.

Tolkien takes us effortlessly, and in style, to a place it seems we all have been before. Whether we are in The Shire; the dragon Smaug's mountain; or visit the cottage of that strange shape-changer who is both bear and human, Beorn the Berserker (a figure straight out of shamanic lore), we recognize the place.[10] Tolkien's personal mythology fills a whole world, and when we join him in it, we find, wonderfully, that somehow it is ours too. It is certainly archetypal, but that is not all. Our modern imagination dilates its nostrils wide, once again to breathe in the mythic atmosphere of Middle Earth, of the world itself alive, and full of magic.[11]

The living landscape should swarm with adventures. The very earth is to be porous, filled with caves and passages. The old willow tree opens to eat the little hobbit who snoozes against it (in the Fellowship of the Ring). Creatures disguise themselves, lay traps, and are full of surprises. One must open doors or magical chambers with unknown things beyond. And every good dungeonmaster in the game Dungeons and Dragons knows how to keep his party of warriors and magic users from being bored as he guides them through his private labyrinth (dungeon).[12]

It is the motif of the quest, however, that renders magical adventures coherent, rather than chaotic. The ring of The Lord of the Rings trilogy becomes, as for the Niebelung, a great symbol, a central motif to be enacted against the mythic backdrop. From the ordinary and everyday, we become aware of great powers and destinies abroad in the world. Gandalf the wizard raps on the door and prosaic hobbit-life transforms into the stuff of myth and legend.

The road leads ever on and on
    Down from the door where it began.
Now far ahead the Road has gone,
    And I must follow, if I can,
Pursuing it with weary feet,
    Until it joins some larger way,
Where many paths and errands meet.
And whither then? I cannot say.[13]

In the initial stages of the hero quest, as depicted in the worldwide tradition of the fairy tale, or wonder story, the hero adventurer usually meets with something that needs his help or attention. It may be a beggar, a hurt animal, or even a bug. This seems to be a crucial test. It provides the measure of the willingness of the consciousness principle to show its genuine concern or compassion for the instinctive side of life, even if it appears in an insignificant role. If he or she passes this test, makes the accepting or helpful gesture, the favor is always returned.

One dreamer in my sample dreamed of *"a wounded lion, and I must touch the awful wound on its thigh."* Von Franz, who has studied fairy tales extensively, says that this is the one stage of the hero journey that may not be omitted (see also Chapters 7 and 8).[14]

While all real initiations do require the hero to confront and overcome serious trials and ordeals, having completed this stage, he or she is now related to the hidden source of this landscape that lives. His own entelechal, or purposeful growth process may continue to unfold, but now on good terms with the secret cause, the instinctive inner principle of psychic growth, which is often represented as the lord (or mother) of animals, or "the Old One" (hence his or her interest in how you treat them). In Tolkien this figure is portrayed both in Beorn, part animal himself, and the forest power Tom Bombadil.

As we explore deeper into the geography, the very geology and ecology of the living landscape, we see that an unquestionable, but secret affinity exists between the conscious ego (explorer) and that which he or she encounters. There is not simply the active-passive relationship we, as physical beings, have come to expect from the landscape we tread on, or climb on, or swim in—a world of inert matter. Instead, with conspiratorial appropriateness, obstacles arise, adventures befall, and helpers come. When the hero needs a test of courage, a quest emerges: a glass mountain appears that must be climbed, a giant or ogre comes to be slain, the Grail appears to the knights of the Round Table, initiating their great quest.

The deeper levels of the living landscape are not necessarily obtained by all who take the adventure within. Rather there is convincing evidence that to do so, very definite requirements must be met. The hero should have an honest, open-ended attitude toward life and not too much savoir faire or sophistication, which seems to get in the way. This is often exemplified in the character of dummling, the "stupidest" or youngest brother of the traditional fairy tale, who nonetheless always gets through the ordeals the others have failed.[15] He is the one who talks to the ants or spiders. He befriends the ugly shaggy pony, takes the thorn out of the lion's paw, or asks the ingenuous question—the one Parzival should have asked the first time round in the Grail Castle—"Why is the old king wounded?" or "What is the meaning of the Grail?"[16] He must partake of the quality of the Fool, the zero card in the Tarot, and be open and receptive to what the visionary world has to teach.

One middle-aged man in my sample dreamed he entered a bar in a seaside area. In the bar he saw *the most beautiful woman in the world. Almost like a goddess,"* he thought. The dreamer was caught between worship and lust, but the latter feeling began to prevail. Suddenly a trapdoor opened in the floor beneath him and he was dropped into the sea. To his total astonishment, undersea beings came to him and began to teach him appropriate conduct for being in the presence of a goddess. He experienced a kinder treatment from

Aphrodite (goddess of beauty and love, whose place of origin is the sea) than poor Actaeon, who came upon the virginal goddess Artemis at her bath in the fountain of Parthenius. When he looked at her with disrespectful eyes, she transformed him into a stag, which was then torn apart by his own dogs.

In a Sioux legend, White Buffalo Calf Woman, an important and sacred feminine figure for the Plains Indians, appeared to two youths, who were out away from the tribe, as a beautiful woman coming toward them. One fell into lustful thoughts about her, while the other was respectful, realizing this was a sacred, not an erotic event. A cloud covered the first, and when it departed, his partner saw, to his horror, nothing but a mass of writhing serpents. It was to the survivor that White Buffalo Calf Woman revealed the sacred teachings for the tribe.[17]

The visionary journey is geared somehow to our ethical development, and we may not endure its trials without transformation. "What would you do if you had three wishes?" we are asked, and thus are thrust into a revelatory adventure about motives. In one theme that is very common in Celtic as well as shamanic lore, a horrible old woman guards a well or treasure. The hero merely has to give her a kiss—but few do. In one version, Sir Gawain does indeed give her the kiss and she transforms—but only partially. "Would you rather have me beautiful by night and ugly by day, or the other way around?" the bewitched maiden asks her hero, putting him into an undeniable state of "cognitive dissonance." Tradition has the correct answer as "Whichever way is the least painful for you, lady, since your burden is the greater." This emotionally gracious response usually frees her from the enchantment, so she is always beautiful.[18]

Modern social psychologists have a penchant for thrusting similar existential dilemmas on their subjects. What would you do if you saw something as plain as day and a whole roomful of people disagreed with you? Would you violate your own certainty to avoid social disapproval? What if you encountered someone in trouble on the street? Would you help or succumb to what psychologists have called "bystander apathy"? (This situation is evocative of the myths, where it may be an animal, or even a disguised god, who is in trouble.) Would it matter if he was well dressed? (I think of Odin in his gray travel-stained cloak and slouch hat or Demeter as a beggar woman come unexpectedly to our door.) The gods and goddesses of Norse and classic mythology were always, it seems, wandering the world testing our mortal ancestors in these ways.

Social psychology lies to study ethical development; it tells subjects they are here for this reason and then does that to them. Suppose a psychologist-authority had you strap another subject in a chair and administer powerful electric shocks whenever he made learning errors. Stanley Milgram's "shocking" findings were that a majority of subjects would obey the authority, and overrule their own human sympathies. Later Lawrence Kohlberg used this experiment to delineate cognitive stages of moral development. The few at the top of the ladder were those in the "universal ethical principle stage," whose reasoning relied on personally felt values that transcended for them unjust authority.[19]

But it would be even more interesting to follow up the subsequent attitudes of subjects in that experiment, who revealed themselves (to themselves) as cruel and blind puppets of authority—the authoritarian personalities, or potential Nazis, that Frenkel-Brunswik, Adorno, and others hoped to reveal in their post–World War II studies.[20] What I have observed from years of showing a film based on Milgram's experiment to psychology students is that they swear they themselves would never do what the study itself says a high percentage of the population would indeed do, if placed in a similar situation.

Herein we may see the psychologically instructive side of art, and mythology as well. Seeing the film, hearing a tale, watching a drama, gives one a distance from the dilemma, a chance to make a more objective choice—to consider the whole situation. I think of the biblical story in which the prophet Nathan used a fairy tale to awaken King David to his moral flaw, which was cursing the whole land, archaically always symbolic of the king's self (2 Sam. 11).

Nathan told the king a pitiful tale about a man who had only one sheep, which he loved more than anything. His beloved sheep was seized from him by a richer and more powerful man with many sheep. David judged the greedy man harshly and demanded that he be brought before him, when Nathan said, "You, O King, are that man"; he was referring to David's having lusted after beautiful Bathsheba, whom he had seen bathing, from his rooftop. The Hebrew king already possessed, of course, the best harem in the land. Nonetheless, he wickedly sent Uriah, her husband, and the king's own most loyal general, into the worst part of a battle to be slain, so he could marry her. Only by using a parable could the prophet make a man as powerful as the king see his own moral flaw. "The play's the thing, wherein I'll catch the conscience of the King" (Hamlet).

Psychology acts like myth when it creates its little scenarios based on "as if." And much as humanistic psychology has justifiably criticized the experimentalists for their lies to people, perhaps here is some mythic justification for the experimentalists: by participating in an as-if situation, we mythologize our experience and come to see through ourselves. Thus we may experience the revelation of some of our flaws before we become their victims, a kind of self-knowledge that should be one of psychology's main goals.

The revelation of character and its flaws is one of the guides to inner mythic experience. Is the unconscious mind moral *sui generis,* beyond our social conditioning? This question may yet be answered positively, much to the modern intellectual world's surprise. And the answer may come from observing our instinctive response to fairy tales and from examining sequences of dreams in relation to our conscious attitudes and life experience. In our self-mirroring lies a profound ethical capability.

THE LANDSCAPE AS SELF

Fritz Perls, who readapted Gestalt psychology into a therapeutic form he called Gestalt therapy, devised many techniques to utilize the imagination. Among these is the beautifully simple one of *indwelling,* or imagining-oneself-into, any person, place, or thing in the dream.[21] Most of us may find it easier to do this with persons, or even animals, but Perls was willing to see through any disguise of psyche. He claimed a major insight was triggered for him when he had a person indwell a bridle path in a park (from a dream), which led to the therapeutic issue of allowing anything and everything to "walk on you and crap all over you." In subsequent exploration following this insight, Perls discovered that by indwelling, our entire inner landscape may be found to be alive with feeling-toned issues; the very ground on which the dreamer walks is made of his inner concerns.

One younger male client, in a therapy group I led, dreamed,

> *I am at the college taking a course in field work. S. is the teacher. He takes us into a forest which it seems is an enchanted forest. There are all kinds of strange creatures living in the hillside and the people in our group go running after them. S. is not interested in these, but rather in the roots of the trees. What he is saying seems important. Some kind of petrifaction process going on.*

In keeping with the unitive concept of the imaginal realm, I asked the dreamer to do a guided fantasy with the dream. As he indwelt a hillside prominent in the dream he said, "I'm up here sort of looking down on everything else. I'm a solid structure, hard and permanent." The "creatures" he

FIGURE 11. Giants in the Earth, *view of the living landscape, along the Akra Fjord, Norway. (Pen-and-ink drawing by Robin Larsen, 1983).*

imagined as a transient species living in the holes and grot-toes in him. "They're nice but I don't really need them," he said. Later the dreamer himself would identify the animals as feelings. In the dream, deeper in the unconscious, they seemed to him living things—mysterious and strange. The elaborating fantasy showed them closer to the conscious attitude, as silly, "cute little things," compared with the serious things of life.

But following the lead provided by the dream imagery I asked him to indwell first S., the guide-teacher: "I'm interested in these trees. I've been coming here a long time and I know what's important. There's a petrifying process going on in the roots." Following the process into the roots drew him into a state not unlike deep trance. He became very still and spoke slowly, as if from the depths: "I'm like dead . . . with all this life going around me. There's something going on . . . I guess I'm being petrified."

This could seem to provide a frightening insight for this dreamer, but he emerged from the guided imagery feeling calm and very "centered." The contact with what we might call longer-term structural processes going on in his own root systems sobered but grounded him. He saw his own difficulty with feelings, but also felt more connected with his own deeper maturational process.

Through following inner leads such as these, I learned some interesting things about trance and mental imagery. The "deeper" the imagery, as in that from a night dream, the more the consciousness–altering potential of the image. One could also say that the image is like a code relating to an underlying psychological situation. As the person concentrates on it, it takes him or her (in a way similar to dialing a phone number) to the trance or ASC (altered state of consciousness) level appropriate to encounter the problem area.

Is the unconscious itself aware in some way of its symbolic landscapes? Notice in the following two dreams the almost "conscious" play of the "unconscious":

1. *I run away from a party, which had become loud, with my friend. There is a fairy-tale quality to the landscape. We come*

to a cottage. There are sheep grazing on green hills as we look out through the small window.

2. This is like a movie. There is a strange land covered with something like ice or snow, but it isn't. We have to climb a mountain with switchbacks. At the top is an arbor like you find in Greece. There is a feeling it's all not real.

These were dreamed about three weeks apart by the same dreamer. There is little doubt of the psyche's making use of the device of make-believe, or as-if.

In the following example are three dreams by different dreamers with no knowledge of one another. They provide one of the most interesting illustrations in my dream collection. In each of these dreams, the dreamer is overshadowed by a giant wave, the legendary tidal wave, hanging above, while he or she must complete an ordinary act. A woman college professor in her forties wrote,

I am in Hawaii. My friend A. is doing something; hanging over him is an enormous wave. I am wondering if I should shout and warn him, and wondering if I remember how to body-surf.

Another woman in her fifties wrote,

I am in a stark, empty landscape. A giant wave is hanging over me. The water is a tropical beautiful clear blue. The water will engulf my home. I am sitting at a woman's writing desk in a beautiful yellow light.

The dreamer said of the scene represented in this dream, "There is no place on earth like that. It was like *Fantasia*." Perhaps the most succinct of the dreams was by a highly creative man in his forties, who dreamed,

I am on a rock building a fire. Towering over me are huge waves like in a Japanese watercolor. I must do this ritual (the fire building) correctly, for it is holding off the waves.

The last dream reminded me of a hexagram from the *I Ching,* the Chinese *Book of Changes,* and of the enormous respect for ritual in Chinese and Japanese culture:

Shock comes—oh, oh!
Laughing words—ha, ha!
The shock terrifies for a hundred miles,
And he does not let fall the sacrificial spoon and chalice.[22]

The commentary mentions that "When a man has learned within his heart what fear and trembling mean, he is safeguarded against terrors produced by outside influences." While working on these tidal wave dreams, I was told by my wife, Robin, of a similar one she had had several years before.

People of all kinds, men, women, and children, were doing the things that meant the most to them, while overhead hung The Wave.

The striking thing in all the examples is the frozen quality of time in the face of the wave, which represents an overwhelming event. Are we asked to look at a modern mythologem here, a symbol of our psychological predicament in these times? Even though a giant catastrophic event (of a nuclear or environmental sort) seems to hang over our heads, are we asked to perform the rituals of everyday life correctly, nonetheless?

A woman who seemed frozen in her ability to resolve certain problems of life dreamed about a snow-covered volcano. I asked her to indwell the volcano. Having just come back from the Pacific Northwest, where I visited and studied Mt. Shasta and Mt. St. Helens, I was interested to see how well the fantasy image mirrored the real volcanoes. What emerged was an impression of enormous heat and power, slumbering under an icy exterior. The image from nature showed exactly the state of the psyche. She needed to contact and release the heat within her in order to overcome her icy impasse.

A man in his early forties dreamed he was taken to a well by his grandfather. He was told by that personless voice in the dream that tells us important things: *"This well produces one-hundred thousand gallons per minute."* With his grandfather, the dreamer associated a wisdom figure in touch with the spiritual dimension. The exaggerated yield of the well seemed to refer to a spiritual reservoir that is inexhaustible, and to the existence of which the dreamer was being awakened. This dreamer's business was real estate, and he knew that wells ordinarily encountered would yield only a few gallons per minute. Exaggeration provided us the key to the transpersonal interpretation, and for the dreamer, it awakened his awareness of more inner resources than he had previously imagined.

Water, the circulatory system of the living landscape, shows itself in a variety of symbolic states: the universal surging ocean, to which all returns; waterfalls, cataracts, streambeds now dried-up; flash floods, lakes, or wells; both shallow and deep pools and fishbowls; swamps and quicksands; even a drink of water in a dry place.

A male dreamer in his early sixties, who was afraid of losing the powers of his maturity, dreamed several times of dried-up streambeds. As therapy helped him release some dammed-up feelings, they began to flow again, in one cleansing dream, like the cataracts and wild torrents of spring. In a later guided imagery experience, stimulated by a dream, he relived a real incident in which he had ridden out a dangerous storm at the helm of a sailboat. He had, in a mystical all-night ordeal, come to a mysterious inner communion with the storm. The water imagery also enabled this man to make a strong reconnection with his source of life and power.

Meteorology, too, shows the qualities of the living landscape. Dream days, like real ones, are sunny and bright or gray and overcast, or rainy or snowy. One dreamer's inner weather perfectly described his depression: *"We were down South, under these ominous black and brown clouds. Severe rain was threatening."*

The same man had dreamed of the approach of a great whirlwind from which everybody fled. He stood and watched it come, fascinated by the overpowering quality of it *"till bricks flew all around and I realized I might be dying."* This dreamer was consciously preoccupied with fear of the judgment of God. Like Job he was experiencing the overwhelmingness of the divine, he who speaks from the whirlwind.

Another dreamer, a woman in her fifties, recorded several dreams similar to the following:

I am in a small light yellow car. The atmosphere is very dark and dreary and this large tornado keeps chasing me. I am going around corners, hoping it will pass me, but it does not. It turns every corner I make, and seems to follow me.

The same dream was repeated for three nights, with no essential details changed. This unwelcome attention from the world of nature then was spookily echoed in the real world, in which, as she reported in the "daily log" portion of her psychology journal, a fierce storm came to her indeed, lightning struck a tree next to her house, and it fell through the roof. As in the dreams, no one was hurt, but she seemed to be having "a close encounter of (some) kind," with a ferocious primal power. Perhaps she was learning "what fear and trembling mean," as the *I Ching* said, to strengthen her spirit. In any case, after the real experience, the dreams abated.

Some land under the dreamer's feet may be *"slippery and treacherous, you can't make your way."* Or, *"I see a strip of bright green lawn, but it is really a bog with the grass just emerging."* What appears normal and solid may be treacherous, undermined, unsafe to support our progress. A male dreamer in his late twenties experienced the earth opening up and swallowing his hometown, which had always seemed safe and secure. The imagery reflected his feelings about his childhood world, in the face of drastic changes in life-style and modern culture. Another younger male dreamer with a very unorthodox life-style dreamed:

> I am standing on the shore of the sea, which is frozen. I am looking out toward an island, just over the horizon, where there are people like me, that I can relate to. I start to skate out over the ice. Soon I can't see the shore—or the island that I know must be out there. What if the ocean should melt? I awaken frightened.

This dream captures the motif of "the perilous crossing," the all-too-common disorientation of our times, in which we "lose our bearings"; and illustrates the way in which the whole landscape may symbolize an existential predicament.

Mountains in the living landscape may imply not only phalluses or breasts, as per Freud, but effort and goals to be attained, as well as transcendence of the ordinary. Their vertical dimension breaks through the horizontal landscape of our common daily concerns. For many of us there is something spiritual about a mountain. On the level of psyche are they not like René Daumal's *Mount Analogue;* symbols of the soul's great ascent, their base "accessible to human beings as nature made us, their summit in some yonder realm, attainable only by great effort"?[23]

W. Y. Evans-Wentz, the great folklorist and Tibetologist, also made a special study of sacred mountains, from Mt. Meru, the Himalayan world mountain, to Mt. Cuchama in southern California, sacred to several Indian groups. Anthropologist Phillip Staniford in a 1978 paper on the sacred mountain, commemorating Evans-Wentz's hundredth birthday, described the underlying concept of "the magic mountain" beautifully: "The mountain is the bond between the

FIGURE 12. *The magic mountain, a Tibetan* chor-ten *(Sanskrit, "stupa") at Thame monastery in Himalayan Nepal. The symbolism is complex, but the elemental references of the five stages of the* chor-ten, *in ascending order, are to earth, water, fire, air, and ether.* (PHOTO BY ROBIN LARSEN.)

earth and the sky, man as ego consciousness and man as divine spark. Its solitary summit reaches the sphere of eternity, and its base spreads out in manifold foothills into the world of mortals. It is the way by which the divine can reveal itself to man."[24] And, it should be mentioned, by which humans can aspire to the divine. On a worldwide basis, many cultures have a tradition of pilgrimage to the tops of sacred mountains. An example is the Japanese tradition of *shugendo,* the "way" of mountains, which began in the seventh century and involved climbing as many as possible of Japan's 134 sacred mountains. The pilgrim was believed to enter another world for the world of the mountain, finally attaining spiritual rebirth on the summit.

During a time in which I was preoccupied with climbing mountains, I dreamed of them constantly. After a while, it became apparent that different mountain settings represented different feeling states for me. Frequently, for example, I dreamed of the Black Hills of South Dakota, where I had rock-climbed and hiked. For the Sioux, the Black Hills's central mountain, Harney Peak, was the world mountain. The great Sioux visionary Black Elk called its summit "the center of the world." When I dreamed of these mountains there would often be a spiritual issue involved. Sometimes the mountains were full of "nature spirits," and pre-European scenarios. I also dreamed of Wyoming's Grand Tetons (I had climbed there, too) but they symbolized a different feeling state: more carefree and adventurous.

When I dream-climbed Mt. Washington in New Hampshire, several times, I found the theme to be "much effort with little culminating reward." In real life, after hours of hiking you find a tourist cafeteria at the summit, which is serviced by road and cog railway. The Himalayas, in contrast, represented almost inaccessible spiritual heights on my soul journey. My Austrian analyst, who had climbed himself and had a good symbolic imagination, was able to help me catalog these mountain contexts and understand the mood of the soul they represented.

Mountains are beautiful and beckoning, but may be dangerous; Jung wrote in several places of a Swiss mountaineer acquaintance of his who dreamed about "climbing on," in a kind of ecstasy, even after he had reached the summit of the mountain. Jung warned him of the psychic danger implied by this image and urged him to discontinue soloing and leading. The friend ignored the advice, and a few months later was observed literally to step off a ledge into space during a climb and fall to his death.[25]

Dreamers may experience mountains with slippery holds or good ones. Some of them seem impossibly high and unattainable; others yield unexpectedly to effort. Sometimes the attainment of the summit will yield a "peak experience," sometimes, despite the intensity of effort, a disappointment— something more easily obtained in other ways.

One dreamer revisited his hometown, all spread out on "Pop Wilson's Hill," as it was in real life, except the dream, in an almost caricatural way, showed the mount as a symbol for everyone's economic and social level. The successful people were at the top, the others arranged in descending layers, as on Dante's Mount Paradiso. The dreamer was able to realize Pop Wilson's Hill was a kind of Mount Analogue for him, imitating a certain value hierarchy in his own psychology with which he had long been preoccupied. Where would he be on the hill, at each stage of life? The image not only initiated a kind of an awakening to his unconscious hierarchical assumptions, but allowed him to see it in perspective—spread out on the landscape in an amusingly symbolic way.

THE SACRED MINDSCAPE

When I used to ask therapy clients to engage in guided fantasy, I would first do a hypnotic induction to get them well "inside"; and I still find this procedure appropriate at times. However, I have since noticed that focusing on an inner image, especially one from a powerful dream (as in the hillside guided imagery discussed earlier), pulls the experiencer within anyway, even sometimes into a deep trance. Symbolic images may be thought of as having a "valence," the ability to attract consciousness and pull it further into engagement.

Several modern investigators of mental imagery have observed that as the subject moves in a direction defined as "inward," the tone of the imagery deepens and begins to take on a decidedly mythological or religious character. Masters and Houston, originally psychedelic researchers, wrote that the most profound personality changes they observed in their subjects occurred with those who reached the inner levels they described as *symbolic* (mythological) and *integral* (religious).[26] Bernard Aaronson, a consciousness researcher who has specialized in "altered states," as well as mental imagery and fantasy, agreed:

> The occurrence of religious symbols in daydream is not an isolated occurrence. Patients of the most diverse kinds of personality and with the most diverse kinds of problems, report experiences involving profound religious confrontations. . . . As the dreamer moves within himself away from the world . . . he seems to be caught up in a world of myth and then in a world of eternal confrontation, a world of religious experience.[27]

With the attainment of these deeper levels of the living landscape comes a noticeable change in consciousness. This may be observed behaviorally by guide or therapist. One researcher described the narrative of a psychedelic subject caught up in a deep inner drama as taking place in "a hushed monotone, as if he were describing the forbidden liturgy of a mystery rite." And as another subject, in a guided imagery, approached a child in a manger, "a Christmas Eve hush seemed to fall upon her voice."[28]

One dreamer found in the woods *"a pool that has a special feeling about it. I go to bathe in it, and emerge feeling very refreshed.''* In a guided imagery I had her repeat the experience. She had been feeling rather battered from some recent life experience, but this dream seemed to provide access to a refreshing and renewing quality for her.

When the dreamer enters the Grail Castle, sacred grove, bathes in the healing pool or fountain, or goes up on the church altar, the psyche wishes to show us a different condition of itself, Eliade's sacred as opposed to profane consciousness. We are asked to look at a qualitative change in the very sense of being, ontology. It is my observation that dreams routinely show this boundary (Greek: *temenos,* literally "a frame of reverence"), the threshold between the sacred and the profane.

As Aaronson asserted, the spiritual level is often reached by ordinary people from all walks of life. Human beings need not join a religion to be religious. We may assume awareness of the spiritual to be one perennial modality of psyche. Soul, as Hillman and other archetypal psychologists keep reminding us, is much to be discerned from spirit. They may overlap, but are far from the same thing.

Spirit soars always toward light and toward the heights. Like the moth to the flame, it ever seeks for the One and immolation in eternal things. Soul is a more pagan, creaturely thing, not of the peaks but of the vales.[29] Soul is the rainbow, we remember, and although it seems to be made of supernal fire, it touches the earth and is made of terrestrial air and water refracting nature's light. But we could also say it this way: "Spiritual" is a condition of soul when its eyes are turned toward eternity.

The soul, as it shows itself to us through dreams, is capable of conceiving of itself at worship as one of its activities. Sacred space or events as themes appear with equal regularity in both religious and not-so-religious people. Religious figures such as Christ appeared several times in my sample. The following is one example that shows vividly the living-landscape quality.

I am riding in a car with others over a hilly, surrealistic landscape. Two black-robed nuns appear in front of us and walk across the land and over a hill. An older woman comes out to greet us. As I walk toward the building I notice something: a statue of Christ. His head is alive. He smiles and nods in affirmation. I turn and go in.

In this case, the dreamer, a middle-aged woman who was thinking of entering the religious life as a conscious choice by joining a convent was surprised by this inner confirmation. The appearance of such figures in dreams often seems astonishing to dreamers. Sometimes they look unexpectedly dissimilar to traditional ideas. One man in his forties encountered Jesus in a basement. Unlike some popular representations, *"he was not a handsome man. It was evident he was overworked and tired."* But the dreamer asked if he could do anything for the Lord, who said simply, *"Yes, fry an egg for me."* The dreamer was astonished, but complied. Subsequent insights to this dream confirmed that the dreamer's idealized religious images were being compensated by a need to relate them to ordinary life. His religious attitude needed a daily type of nourishment.

One interesting kind of dream from my sample suggests a revisioning of religious attitudes in our time. My attention was drawn to this genre by Jungian analyst Whitmont, who has studied contemporary personal dreams that seem to prefigure our collective concerns: the myths of our time. Among the many dreams he presented in lectures, the ones that stuck with me were of "colorful athletes being crucified on Golgotha," and another simple one which Jung had also encountered, of "ivy growing upon a church altar." Whitmont (and Jung) interpreted these, especially the second dream (and a whole genre of similar ones), as reevoking an ancient affinity between Christ and Dionysus, whose symbol is the ivy. Both are lords of the sacrifice—personal dismemberment—but heretofore diligently kept separated by Christian orthodoxy. Modern life and culture would certainly seem to make the reemergence of Dionysus mythology (lord of ecstasy, intoxication, and dismemberment) a plausible hypothesis.

My own attention was drawn to the first dream, maybe a different aspect of the same fundamental change being hinted at. One of the early dreams in my sample was:

> *It is Easter Sunday. People are coming down from their apartments to the street. On the way to church they begin to play leap-frog. Everyone is playing joyously, like children.*

Here, in the context of a traditional religious holiday associated with rebirth, we seem to be pointed toward an affiliation between play and the sacred. Several dreams shared the following skeletal structure:

> *I am at church or mass. The service is about to begin. Suddenly clowns and acrobats appear. (Or the priests are these.) They celebrate, even swinging across the altar on trapezes, or roller-skating. One is unsure whether it is now church or a festival or fair.*

These dreams could be giving us a hint to where the missing vitality of our religious traditions may be found: in the sense of sacred play and life understood as a celebration. We are reminded of the *Festum Asinorum,* or Fools Mass, of the medieval Church. On this day, rowdies dressed as priests and made a mess of mass. Animals—especially donkeys—were brought into the church and even onto the altar. Fools preached sermons. Rome publicly denounced the practice and constantly tried to outlaw it, but the populace loved it. The clown societies of native Americans were held to be sacred, and their doings, including mocking the most serious ceremonies, were acceptable (see Chapter 10).

Perhaps my favorite of all these dreams is the following one from my wife, Robin:

I am in church in New England. The service is under way when suddenly the music becomes raucous. In comes a parade of black women with red dresses. They are loud and funny. They are carrying banners on which animals of various kinds are depicted. It seems irreverent but is infectiously funny and everyone joins in the spirit.

We seem not to be told here that religion is merely a sham, as Freud proposed in *The Future of an Illusion,* but rather that it requires some missing ingredients to bring it back to life. Notice too the emphasis is not on despair as in existentialism or Black Mass-like inversions of traditional religious forms, as if to horrify totally the religious sensibility. The context is still the church, or the religious event, but the psyche brings in new life. As if to echo our most liberal ecclesiastical tribunals, its focus is on the neglected dimensions: the feminine and the minority group. This last dream also shows its specifically feminine shadow to proper New England Protestantism and even an unexpected iconographic return of the animal (the instinctive realm asking for re-sacralization?).

These dreams are heartening to me as a believer in the renewing and vitalizing capacities of psyche. It may be that we shall find ourselves spiritually at home again in this great universe shown to us by science. But the mythology will have to expand with the scope of our vision. We cannot return literally to the myths of childhood, but we can recover the sacred innocence and the sheer vitality of children in our worship, and in our play. We may yet find new content to fill our "frame of reverence." We are the most recent inheritors of the eternal quest to find images of the universe that bring meaning into the soul.

Chapter 5

DEPTH MAPS OF THE PSYCHE

If we want to understand the psyche we have to include the whole world.

—Jung

The sense of boredom which . . . appears in analysis is simply an expression of the monotony and poverty of ideas, not of the unconscious . . . but of the analyst.

—Jung

When entering any new territory it is not a bad idea to have a map of the terrain. As we who hike or orienteer know, when one is down in among the rocks and trees, perspective vanishes, and all we see is the immediate surroundings. Maps provide orientation and tell us of the topography and larger features. We know where we are with respect to the whole place. We are then free to experience the details ourselves, as the journey unfolds them in all their spontaneity and variety.

I have used the term *depth* for the maps in this chapter because I believe it is indispensable to consider the "root metaphors" for any way of knowing.[1] The term *depth psychology (tiefenpsychologie)* seems to have originated with Jung and then was used by Freud, at least in their correspondence. Both were highly concerned about depth, and each came to think his mapping was "deeper."[2]

Here, however, I have chosen to go back far beyond modern psychology for my maps. The value of comparative mythology is that its maps have been accumulated over centuries, by different folk from differing ethnicities. The common elements in their journeys should provide us with some general guidelines for the human adventure, whatever its time or place—thus coming around to psychology, after all. The two principal cartographies I have chosen for this chapter—the heroic and the shamanic—are alike in being distillates of an enormous spectrum of recorded human experience, which spans millennia. The value they provide for modern people setting out on, or already in the midst of, what may seem like a terribly solitary journey is a sense of belonging to a timeless community. "We have not even to risk the adventure alone," as Campbell has so eloquently said, "for the heroes of all time have gone before us."

THE HERO'S UNDERWORLD JOURNEY

The hero quest is a concept to which we all may relate intuitively. But the question I introduce in this chapter—and I believe it is a crucial one—is, at what depth? On the naive, popular culture level, he (usually male) has a special endowment by nature: strength, superiority, and integrity (it is hoped). He seems to be here on earth for the sole purpose of easily vanquishing those obstacles on which all the rest of us founder. Although enemies and overwhelming malefic forces may arise, they are put there just to elicit and test his strength and prowess (he is always equal to the task). But the stories tell us Achilles had to watch his heels, and Siegfried had to watch his (both heroes had this vulnerable place). Each hero sooner or later seems to encounter his nemesis, his vulnerable place or wound. In the terms of our modern myth, it seems as if every Superman has his own form of kryptonite. It is only through an exploration of the hero's potential weakness and mortality that we are led away from the impregnable surface layer of this formidable archetype toward its depth interpretation.

Between the latter part of the nineteenth and beginning of the twentieth centuries, Sir James Frazer, Leo Frobenius, Lord Raglan, and Otto Rank, using the growing record of mythologies collected by ethnographers, began to assemble lore pointing to a deeper interpretation of the hero. As the archaic king must die, so must the solar hero, following the sun on its night journey to the underworld. Vulnerable as the naive hero is scatheless, the sacrificial hero, they discovered, must suffer great grief and humiliation, even death and dismemberment. Only after this *nekyia,* underworld journey, or "dark night of the soul," comes the rebirth and return, the boon, or saving of mankind.

In his classic *The Origins and History of Consciousness* Jungian scholar Erich Neumann portrayed the heroic attitude as the metaphor for the early development of individual consciousness. As the child ego seeks to find independence from the all-nurturing, yet all-embracing, realm of the mother, a great inner struggle must be mobilized. The dragon to be slain by each hero is the instinctive bondage to smothering mothering, especially after the child needs less nurturing and more freedom to encounter its own destiny. The aggressive attitude necessary to acquire autonomy is appropriate to the first part of the hero journey, but this is the point beyond which—unfortunately—the naive interpretation fails to go.

Campbell's *The Hero with a Thousand Faces* not only went further than earlier accounts in assembling hero lore from multitudinous cultures and epochs, but after establishing the universality of the pattern beyond doubt, he went deeper into its coherent psychological sense. The human personality, as he portrayed it, is always on a journey of soul making. The adventures may be told as "outer," but they are really inner, into psyche's depth realm. The ego, emissary of the daylight world of consciousness, must encounter the unknown zone of its own origins and secret destiny. The archetypal pattern of the hero quest may well be one of the fundamental ways in which consciousness can encounter that larger, older aspect of itself without seizure or engulfment. It is a timeless adventure, ever, yet never the same.

The psychological task of the hero, as Campbell described it, is "to retreat from the world scene of secondary effects to those causal zones of the psyche where the difficulties really reside." Campbell describes the monomyth as follows: "A hero ventures forth from the world of common day into a region of supernatural wonder: fabulous forces are there encountered and a decisive victory is won: the hero comes back from this mysterious adventure with the power to bestow boons on his fellow man."[3]

Departure, crossing the threshold, initiation, adventure, and return are the ever-familiar stages of the hero quest, whatever the culture, time, or place. And each stage is fraught with its perils and pitfalls, the return no less than the setting out.

As the hero departs the world of everyday, his own locally conditioned variety of reality, he moves into the zone of the changeless archetypes, the wardens of the mythological adventure the world over. Odysseus (too much the warrior still, says Campbell) is blown by the winds of Aeolus (the *pneuma,* the divine wind) from wonder to terror and back again. He encounters enchantment, irresistible attraction to magical women, monstrous inner beings, and always, somehow, moral tests and learning. On this journey the distinct outlines of what previously seemed so certain—a problem or goal, even one's idea of self—shimmer and disappear, to be replaced by what now is seen to be unmistakably more real: the world of myth and dream. A symbolic adventure is enacted, a discovery of something important, the rescue and release of someone who was imprisoned, the seeking and bestowal of a blessing, or a dying and being reborn.

When the hero returns to the world of everyday, his

experiencing has been renewed. As Campbell said, "The objective world remains what it was, but, because of a shift in emphasis within the subject, is beheld as though transformed."[4] The hero's quest brings rebirth not only of himself, but of reality as he experiences it. Odysseus is finally fit to come home.

One of the oldest great heroes of whom we have any record is the Babylonian, Gilgamesh. He was described as "two-thirds god, one-third man." He carried out typical early heroic tasks: clearing a great cedar forest and defeating the giant Humbaba. The legends say, though, that he was too powerful to be gainsaid—in terms of moral development this is good for no one—and became a tyrant of unbridled arrogance. The people turned in despair to the mother goddess, who conceived in her heart, at the suggestion of the other gods, his counterpart, embodying him by casting a piece of clay on the ground.

This marvelous counterpart, whose name was Enkidu, is worth describing:

> The whole of his body was hairy and his locks were like a woman's, or like the hair of the goddess of grain. Moreover, he knew nothing of settled fields or of human beings, and was clothed like a deity of flocks. He ate grass with the gazelles, jostled the wild beasts at the watering hole, and was content with the animals there.[5]

Enkidu resembles the shamanic "lord of the animals," the biblical Esau, or the figure of "the hairy anchorite" from medieval legend. A hunter sees this amazing hairy man out on the plains, realizes it is he who has been tearing up the traps he lays for the animals, but the hunter recognizes Enkidu's godlike strength and is afraid to approach. In dismay he goes to his king, Gilgamesh, who shows himself to be crafty as well as powerful:

"Go my hunter," he said; "take along with you a temple prostitute, and when he comes to the watering hole with the beasts, let her throw off her clothes, disclose her nakedness, and when he sees, he will approach her; and the beasts thereafter will desert him, which grew up with him on his plain."[6]

The hunter does as he is bidden, the enterprising temple maiden discloses her abundant charms, and for seven nights and six days they mate in wild abandon. Thus, in the snares of love, the taming of this strange being of the wilds has begun. After this encounter the animals flee from him as he approaches.

The hunter takes him to Uruk, the city of Gilgamesh, and there in his great strength and pride, he challenges godlike Gilgamesh. They grapple together—"locked like bulls," the texts say, so violently that the temple walls shake and the doorpost shatters. Gilgamesh finally relents. Following this (an almost archetypal pattern for boys who fight), they become fast friends, like brothers.

In this archaic parable there is interesting psychological lore on the taming of the naive hero. Gilgamesh possesses the hero's classic requirements of godlike strength and power. What he lacks, however, is humility and the internal controls to match his power. He needs to experience defeat and limitation. This is provided by the divine powers in the form of this curious double, who manifests Gilgamesh's own untamed nature in symbolic form. His divine arrogance is to be neutralized by being brought into contact with its animal counterpart. Two kinds of "taming" occur: first that of Enkidu and then, through him, that of Gilgamesh.

However, Gilgamesh does not need to be reconciled with the realm of the divine or the animal to complete his hero quest, but the condition that lies precisely between, that of the human. Campbell said of this, "Time, mortality, and the anguish of humanity in a world of personal destiny basically related to our own, give to this piece the quality of an epic."[7]

The meeting with mortality initiates—as it does for all—the master quest of Gilgamesh, the one for which he is best known. Time passes and then, to his immense sorrow, his beloved Enkidu dies. After terrible mourning, he must face his own fear. "Grief has entered my body; of death I am afraid," he says. In the model of Jung, this is the initiation of the second half of life, the encounter with mortality. He recognizes he cannot face death and sets out on the quest for the "herb of immortality."

In brief, after setting forth, Gilgamesh encounters devouring lions, succumbs to fear but prays to the moon god for aid, receives a guiding dream, fights his way past the lions, and arrives at the Mountains of Sunset, "where the scorpion men guard the gate, whom it is death to behold." Again he gives in to fear, but one of them opens the gate, and he passes into a thick darkness. After a sojourn in this shadowland he proceeds to a fair plain. There in a park he sees a wonderful tree, whose branches are exceedingly beautiful and whose fruit consists of living jewels.

Gilgamesh passes then along the shore of the world sea and comes to the residence of a mysterious woman, Siduri, who utters the following incantation on the lot of man:

> O Gilgamesh, whither do you fare?
> The life you seek, you will not find.
> When the gods created man,
> They apportioned death to mankind;
> And retained life to themselves.
>
> O Gilgamesh, fill your belly,
> Make merry, day and night;
> . . . .
> Let your raiment be kept clean,
> Your head washed, body bathed.

> Pay heed to the little one, holding on to your hand,
> Let your wife delight your heart,
> For this is the portion of man.[8]

Despite this instructive counsel on how properly to embrace one's humanity, Gilgamesh insists on his quest. The woman sends him to the ferryman of death, who carries him across the cosmic sea to the Isle of the Blessed, where dwells Ut-napishtim, the immortal Sumero-Babylonian hero of the flood (prototype of Noah), with his wife. They feed Gilgamesh magic food, wash him with healing waters, and tell him of the Plant of Immortality that lies at the bottom of the sea. Gilgamesh once again sets out with the ferryman of death. Arriving at the place in the sea of which the couple has told him, he ties heavy stones to his feet, and plummets into the depths. There he finds the plant, which, as he has been warned, tears his hands as he plucks it. He cuts himself loose from the stones and rises, victorious, to the surface.

But the great strength and vigilance of even this hero has been exhausted. While he bathes in a stream for renewal, the serpent, who more than once has served as nemesis to heroes, creeps out of the water, attracted by the herb's fragrance, and eats it, thereby learning immortality's secret: death and rebirth, the sloughing of the skin, the art of perpetual self-transformation. It is said that Gilgamesh sat and wept bitterly.[9] Thus humanity is still mortal, whereas the serpent transforms.

The tale offers us profound psychological instruction, especially on the conversion of the naive hero into what we might call the "real" hero. Although still human and vulnerable, Gilgamesh has learned wisdom. It is worth noting the role of the feminine initiatrix, both the temple prostitute, who "tames" Enkidu, and the mysterious Siduri, who instructs so eloquently in the simple wisdom of being human. Does encounter with the feminine indeed tame men, moderating both their divine inflation and their animal proclivities? We move now to a parallel story.

In a feminine version of the hero myth, the goddess Inanna—like Gilgamesh for Enkidu—mourns bitterly for her lover, Damuzi, who has died and gone to the underworld. She decides to go and rescue him, whatever the cost. The nether realm is ruled by her dark and awful sister Ereshkigal, Queen of the Underworld, who holds his soul. On the way, she has to pass through seven terrible gates. At each one she sacrifices something symbolic of her high estate in the daylight world: her crown, her necklaces, her breastplate, her gold ring, her rod of lapis lazuli, even her garment. Naked, the goddess stands before her awful sister, then:

> Ereshkigal fastened on Inanna the eye of death.
> She spoke against her the word of wrath.
> She uttered against her the cry of guilt.
> She struck her.
> Inanna was turned into a corpse,
> A piece of rotting meat,
> And was hung from a hook on the wall.[10]

Samuel Noah Kramer and Diane Wolkstein in their excellent recent retelling of Inanna's story, from which the above passage was quoted, mention that she was the most celebrated and beloved of all Sumerian heroes or deities. Damuzi, later Tammuz, the male hero, was expected to die, as in the many goddess traditions where Her consort is the sacrificial victim. But it must have been Inanna's voluntary sacrifice of and to herself, as it were (she being also, as Great Goddess, identical to Ereshkigal), that made her special and endeared her to the people. Like Christ (or Odin), she experienced and triumphed over death, and she was "hung up" as a symbol of her redemptive role—for love conquers death. After those terrible personal sacrifices she brings back Damuzi, who in the same way as Adonis Osiris, and, later, Jesus, becomes known chiefly as a dying and reviving god.

As mentioned earlier, the sacrificial hero, who voluntarily

FIGURE 13. *Night sea journey of the hero.* Heracles in the Vessel of the Sun *(Attic vase, fifth century; Etruscan Museum, Vatican).* (PHOTO ART RESOURCE.)

undertakes the meeting with death pertains to the second half of life, whereas the naive, forceful hero is the symbol of the first half. Only with the full recognition of mortality does the attention turn to the search for spiritual meaning.

In the current time, more than ever, when our grand mythological projections have been so withdrawn—from the theater of outer events to the inner life—do we need to become aware of this psychological dimension of the hero quest. The self is to be entered as the fairy realm of myth and folklore: the dragons and ogres encountered there are primitive aspects of ourselves; the princesses that are released represent our own long-hidden impulse toward beauty; and the kingdom, lying under its wicked enchantment, is the world as we have come to see it in our regressive, outmoded myth and our self-induced trance. Everyone is to take the hero adventure within and there seek the Grail, the hard-to-obtain treasure, the wish-fulfilling gem, and the herb of immortality.

Recently, Whitmont and Woolger have speculated that it is the cult of the naive hero that is threatening to destroy our world. The childish ego is still struggling with the mother, instead of returning to her in reconciliation and for initiation, as does the mature hero. (In "Men's Mysteries" in Chapter 2, I cited the dream of a middle-aged man who must rescue a young hero, like Galahad, who is wounded. The dream shows that resolution will only come from the older man's resources—and divine help.) Woolger said in a paper on death and the hero,

> For at the heart of the very structure of the hero archetype and hence any ego psychology there lies fear and ambivalence: to conquer or submit? to rule or to serve? Or epitomized in the words of the Sophoclean protagonist: "Who is the slayer, who the victim? Speak." The hero in all of us imagines it is his strength, her wits, his resourcefulness that makes possible the vanquishing of one's foes and will bring about the defeat of "the last enemy," failing to see that the real enemy is oneself, the ego-centered reliance on one's "own" gifts, which are in fact divine in origin.[11]

Woolger argued that it is the lunar journey, not the solar, that constitutes the hero's deeper transformation through death. The excessively solar masculine hero is compensated by a self-sacrificing anima who is secretly the bride or apprentice of death. Ariadne, for example, in the classic Greek tale, could not really be permanently "rescued" by the hero Theseus, because she was actually the priestess-bride of the Minotaur, who dwelt in the center of the labyrinth as symbolic lord of the underworld. After her "rescue," she ran away, or some say was abandoned, on the isle of Naxos, and became the bride of Dionysus. In effect she returned to where she began.

All of this may seem quite depressing with its sacrifices and encounters with death. Modern culture understands the solar hero well, but not the lunar. Are there any positive outcomes to this process of transformation outside of a weary resignation? "There is a shift of emphasis within the observer," Campbell has said of the outcome of the successful in-depth hero quest. The goal is not to change the world, but ourselves, and then the world is renewed.

Jesse Watkins was a modern hero who made a journey to his inner depths—designated by his psychiatrists as "schizophrenia," but by himself as a "journey to the dawn of time," and the origins of creation. Like the Celtic bard Taliesin, Watkins experienced his soul entering all the forms of life and growing through the evolutionary ages of the planet. He died and was reborn many times. The complete story is told in R. D. Laing's *Politics of Experience,* but here is how Watkins (a lunar hero) experienced his return:

> I remember when I came out of the hospital . . . I suddenly felt that everything was so much more real than it . . . had been before. The grass was greener, the sun was shining brighter, and people were alive, I could see them clearer. I could see the bad things and the good things and all that. I was much more aware.[12]

LSD researcher Grof reported a similar enlargement of consciousness in those who have passed through their personal hero journey in guided psychedelic sessions. Those subjects who encountered the full gamut of inner experiences experienced "rebirth." "Beyond the barrier of personal hell through which they have just passed," he wrote,

> there seems to be an area of inherent sense for beauty, justice, love, and genuine religious feelings (in the sense of Einstein's "cosmic religion" rather than specific church affiliation). Persons transformed in this way seem to have a higher frustration tolerance, are more oriented toward now and here than toward the past and future and are able to draw satisfaction from ordinary things, rather than focussing on remote, heroic and often irrational and unattainable goals.[13]

Note here the negative use of "heroic." The failure to undertake the personal hero quest may lead to acting out the archetype in the naive way. We strike heroic postures in unnecessary places. The transformed hero does not need to manifest heroism perpetually. He or she has become content within the living mystery of universe, without having urgently to remake it. Especially important to note is the wholesomeness of the transformed hero's outlook and the sacralization of everyday life. Grof wrote, "The subjects feel part of creation, see new dimensions in the universe and tend to sacramentalize ordinary things of everyday life (meals, playing with children, sexual activities, walking in nature, etc.)."[14]

These transformed heroes seem to be seeing the world in a new way. In Blake's now-famous words, "If the doors of perception were cleansed, man would behold everything as it is, infinite."[15] Experience can recover innocence; the hero can find, not his lost childhood, but its open sense of participating in a sacred universe.

THE SHAMANIC MAP

Surely the most ancient maps of the mythic imagination have been provided by shamans. Modern history has not paid much attention to the shamanic journey because its roots are prehistoric and its field of significance has been the loosely organized community of the primitive hunting and gathering tribe. The remnants of shamanism in the contemporary world seem archaic and quaint, peripheral, and third worldish. The venerable role of the medicine man has often been rendered as that hysterical—if not psychotic—fraud: the witch doctor.

The archaic figure of the shaman has only recently become significant again, principally for those interested in altered states of consciousness, esoteric spirituality, and visionary activity. The orthodoxies of the priestly role have provided relatively stabilized mythologies that celebrate a traditional human encounter with the sacred in the long ago. But in times of radical change such as ours, the conditions of life that mythologies address require new encounters, in which the individual soul plunges into the depths of his or her own psyche in the search for renewed meaning and a sense of belonging.[16]

Although individual and personal, the shamanic journey has yielded transpersonal, and very reliable, maps of the psyche. These recurring features are transcultural and transhistoric as well, yielding a kind of perennial psychology of the visionary journey. It seems that whether we look to the upper paleolithic of 30,000 years ago, into the arctic or tropical cultural hinterlands of still-practicing shamans, or even into the psyches of modern people in personal crisis, the imaginal journey of the shaman bears the same features.

First is the call—an animal or bird may announce it. Sometimes it starts with a depression—things just don't feel right. The incipient shaman, with a certain amount of terror, realizes the fragility of the personal ego integrity usually taken for granted. (As in schizophrenia, there is a felt fragmentation of the underlying self.) At this stage, the shaman has no choice but to withdraw from ordinary life into the causal zone of the psyche—we find echoes of the hero journey here, but starting from the wound.

Next is the soul journey, in which the initiate is pulled within, to a world of wonders and terrors. The shaman has fallen into the living landscape. The adventures, as we have seen in regard to the fairy tale, are somehow appropriate to his or her development and potential for growth. Along the way spiritual beings are encountered. Some are traditionally in the form of animals with a special personal significance for the shaman. The initial contact with the animal may be frightening, even violent, but the shaman candidate must not be daunted, for it will later become his ally or "familiar" (see Chapter 7). Other kinds of spiritual beings emerge as well: "little people," as known all over the world; sprites; devas of holy places, lakes, springs, or mountains; elementals of the weather; mythical beings, such as the thunderbirds from native American mythology; or in the creation of "greater" shamans, primordial and universal powers. For example, the Sioux Black Elk had a marvelous vision in which he was taken into the sky to a rainbow lodge with six old men sitting in it, "old like hills, like stars." As he said, "I shook all over with fear . . . for I knew that these were not old men, but the Powers of the World."[17]

The shaman must encounter death, because this is the pivot of the entire transformative process. Sometimes the animal in its ferocious aspect devours or dismembers the shaman. Sometimes he or she may be thrown in a fire; cooked in a giant cauldron; a giantess or a great whale devours him or her. Some shamans go through the process only once, others many times. The only rule of thumb seems to be "submit," which obviously requires a great deal of faith in the integrity of the process. Ethical ordeals are often presented to the shaman, as in the fairy tale; the novice shaman is shown how important personal integrity is because he or she seems to have lost it in the process of "coming apart." Yet the possibility of finding a deeper integrity is invited. This is only obtained, however, by passing through the entire ordeal of inner confrontation.

The shaman is reborn, reconstituted in a new form, with something added. This "something" is later revealed to be a new spiritual integrity, accompanied by a sense of spiritual indestructibility or immortality. The shaman is now fit to return to the three-dimensional ordinary world, but may no longer live in an ordinary way. He or she is now a special intermediary or emissary to the spirit realm. In mythologically inspired communities this relationship between the spiritual and physical dimensions is the single most important reality there is. The aperture between the worlds is to be kept open. (Is it that same "tunnel" that shows up in near-death experiences?) Thus the shaman embodies a covenant between separate realities and exhibits in the shamanic rituals the ability to move between them.

Because in the visionary journey the shaman is "in" the imaginal, mythic realm, the beings of the imagination are real. The magic that transpires is efficacious, indeed, because the mythic figures and events are the precise keys that turn the locks of personal transformation. (Deep within, we all seem to be mythological creatures.) The arrangement of worlds and universes in this realm is vertical (in the mythic imagination vertical movement is sacred movement and horizontal is secular).[18] Some shamanic journeys, then, are to the underworld and some, to a celestial realm. Movement in this vertical way seems to give access to spiritual power and has a causal relationship to events in the ordinary world.

Fierce polarities prevail in the living landscape. There are encounters with the demonic as well as the divine. The roots of a disease or psychological illness are often found in the workings of malevolent spirits who "steal" the soul or have ensorcelled the person's vital energies in a magical snare. The shaman must encounter these forces and, therefore, needs resiliency and strength, as well as spiritual allies. Because the shaman enters one world to effect causes in an-

FIGURE 14. *Nepali shaman with symbolic paraphernalia.* (PHOTO COURTESY OF ROD DORNAN.)

other, he or she is often known as "the master of two worlds." In the initiatory ordeal the shaman begins to learn the terrain of the nonordinary reality, to which he or she will often return in out-of-body journeys of healing or rescue.

The shaman's staff—the magician's wand—is symbolic of the axis of the universe and the vertical arrangement of worlds within it. The pointed hat, still evoked in the magician's cap with its moon and stars, is a kind of cosmic antenna, as were the antlers worn by shamans in paleolithic times. The costume—the wizard's cloak—is a kind of inner-space suit with the symbols and tokens of his or her mythological encounter displayed on it. The cloak or robe is an androgynous costume that shows the shaman to be an ambiguous creature, between the sexes as between the worlds, neither here nor there, this nor that. There is also a symbolic marriage implied in the male shaman's often overt femininity; in relation to the spirit, all humans are female.[19]

Early in my professional practice I was leading training workshops for therapists in an outreach program for the New York State Department of Mental Hygiene. One of these trainees presented a dream that was very mysterious for him.

My therapist appears as a primitive medicine man, dancing and jumping around a fire in a strange squatting position. He drums and utters peculiar cries. I am puzzled but the performance is spooky and powerful.

The trainee had no knowledge of shamanism and did not know about my interest in it. To me it seemed a classic illustration of something I had read in Jung, years before. Jung believed the so-called transference—the intense psychological bond between the client and therapist—involved more than feelings based on just parental figures, as Freud thought. All the archaic, mythological contents of the unconscious were present in the therapeutic relationship as well. The therapist attracted the projection of the medicine man, or wonder worker, especially to the extent that he seemed to have magical powers of healing or intuition. (Is every therapist a shaman, for the mythic imagination?) Does the almost automatic efficacy of the therapeutic encounter—regardless of the therapist's approach or level of skill—reside in such a magical projection of the figure of the wonder worker?[20]

One modern psychotherapist who has incorporated specifically shamanic processes into his therapeutic work is Stephen Gallegos. Following a visionary experience of his own, in which he saw the human mind-body system as a totem pole, with animals arranged on a vertical axis, he developed his own way of engaging in therapeutic dialogue with the animals. Gallegos, whose early education was in psychology, found these inner visionary encounters more helpful for his clients than were his usual therapeutic procedures.

He identified the animals as living sources of power within the psyche, much as native Americans identified their personal animal totems. But from the East Indians, he drew lore about the specific location of the animals on their vertical axis. From therapist Ma Prem Mala, he learned about the *chakra* system, part of the esoteric lore of yogic Tantrism. According to this venerable map, the human spine is the axis of the self, an analogue of the axis of the universe we have been discussing from shamanism. The fundamental energies of the personality are arranged along this axis from the Muladhara, or root *chakra* at the base of the spine, to the Sahasrara or Brahma *chakra* at the crown of the head.

What I found especially intriguing about Gallegos's system was its creative and personal versatility. Although the Sanskrit texts do feature representative animals at each of the *chakras,* these are fixed by tradition. Gallegos's system is open to a more personal mythology. Individuals have their own unique constellations of animals arranged along the *chakras.* The therapeutic encounter is to enter dialogue with the animals and find what they need (some may be sick or neglected, for example). Gallegos said, "In my thinking about the chakra system in relation to the animals . . . I had come to the understanding that the equivalent of a closed or limited chakra was represented by an animal that was injured, caged, or in some way not functioning optimally."[21]

FIGURE 15. On the Rainbow-Path to the Visionary Rock-Crystal, *Huichol shaman journey, by Ramon Medina Silva (yarn painting, 1950)*. (PHOTO COURTESY OF PETER T. FURST.)

Further exploration showed him that the animals had complex interrelationships with each other, a kind of personal ecology within the self.

By failing to recognize our inner as well as outer ecology, we modern folk have cut ourselves off from our sources of life. Our maps of the psyche, like the charts of medieval navigators, need to be mythologized: Here there are dragons, here there are helping animals, here is the realm of the little people, here is my "slough of despond," and here are my inner mountains and my medicine lodge from which I work the shaman's magic. We are in quest of a world of symbolic texture, like the French postmodernists. To have a richness of outer experience requires an inner wealth of symbolic forms; this is both the legacy and the invitation of the mythic imagination.

THE RELATIVITY OF THERAPEUTIC MAPS

Each therapeutic approach presents a valid myth, but it must be appropriately placed on a personal map that describes the stages of the journey for a particular person. There are, as Daniel Levinson has assured us, "seasons in a man's life," the psychological developmental stages of the mature personality.[22]

The therapeutic confrontation represents a powerful moment when the client (with all his myths) meets the therapist (with all his myths). It is a time for demythologizing and remythologizing. It is hoped that the therapist's myths are larger and healthier than the client's, but this is not necessarily the case. The client doesn't have only "neurotic" myths, but probably has a mixture of life-enhancing and life-inhibiting ones. And the therapist should not assume that his or her myths are superior on all levels of the psyche. Is it fair, because a client shows one area of dysfunctional personal mythology, to devaluate his or her whole orientation?

A therapeutic system presents, ultimately, a mythology—a way of conceiving of things—that may bend the whole interpretation of human experiencing to a certain form. By now it is a cliché that Freudian analysts have Freudian patients (with Freudian dreams); Jungian analysts have Jungian patients who, of course, obediently produce archetypal dreams. Therapists of whatever persuasion, it seems, would generate such a potent mythology around themselves and their (sacred) system that it would influence the unconscious itself to produce certain symbolic materials and not others.

Dreams do draw images from waking life (Freud's day residues), but these are never simply recapitulations of outer experience, past or anticipated. Something is always unexpected, added, or changed; a new twist appears, often something quite alien to consciousness. As an experiment, give yourself the suggestion to dream about something, and if you are sincere (and your unconscious cooperates) you prob-

ably will, but never in the exact way anticipated. The unconscious seems to be involved with our concerns, but it is
no mere physical mirror, rather, as we have seen, it is a
magical one.

Some people have experienced details seemingly from other
lives they have lived, in different times and places.[23] In India
this notion is commonplace and unexceptional, in Western
society it seems outrageous and impossible. Some of this
"other-life material" (of varying levels of credibility) originally appeared in the West in the protocols of hypnotized
people who were asked to regress in age. Suddenly they
would seem to pop into another lifetime. The writings of
the theosophists and of Edgar Cayce abound in comparable
accounts. Roger Woolger has developed nondrug techniques
using guided imagery to produce these experiences routinely
in the therapeutic situation. These are often tied in with
actual conditions in the body, connected to a lifetime, or its
"story." He has said, of the bodywork he uses to help elicit
the story,

> Yet it must be stated clearly that any bodywork of this
> sort is only a means to eliciting a story; a story which
> belongs to the imaginal body. Altering body tissues
> cannot be an end in itself from the perspective of past-
> life therapy and moreover is doomed to only limited
> success if the psyche is ignored. So that when a person
> complains of persistent back pain the aim of massage
> would be to allow a clear image of that pain to emerge
> as a key to an imaginal drama involving that location of
> the body in another lifetime. The therapist's task is to
> pursue the story in the understanding, confirmed by
> more and more reports, that it is the re-living of the
> story in all its physical details, psychological drama and
> human pathos that really heals.[24]

Myths are to be found in the body, as Stanley Keleman said,
and this paragraph of Woolger's paper is close to my central

theme. Every detail of the physical body has its counterpart in the imaginal body, which is woven of stories and myths. Does it help us to see through this lifetime if we can imagine another? Herman Hesse shows us the literary power of this visionary technique in *Magister Ludi, The Glass Bead Game,* in which the character of hero Joseph Knecht is deepened, reflected, and elaborated through other "incarnations." These stories imply the existence of a being beyond time and space that "plays" at life in different ways, yet "works" at actualizing an underlying pattern or myth into life (incarnation) and which is always transforming into and out of its several contexts.

Grof observed scores of other-life experiences in the transpersonal zone in the course of his LSD work, several of which he has published. He wrote,

> On occasion past-incarnation memories emerge spontaneously in everyday life; they can have the same beneficial consequences (as they do in psychedelic therapy) if they are allowed to reach completion. This raises a question as to how many opportunities for effective therapeutic intervention have been missed by Cartesian–Newtonian psychiatrists whose patients reported access to karmic levels.[25]

Whether we prefer to take past-life stories literally, or see through them in some way, we must accept their phenomenological reality for many people. Therapists must listen to these stories when they arise in psychotherapy. Ultimately, I expect a recognition to emerge (broadly aligned with humanistic psychology) of a democracy of personal myths, which are respected merely because they are held to be meaningful by individual human beings.[26]

At a given time and place in personal history, the psyche may gravitate strongly to one or another metaphor or system of soul transformation. It is as if modern man in search of a soul stands on a barren plain, in darkness, while all around are the dim presences of great megaliths, the myths of bygone, present, and future times. A single one of these is not enough to help us find our way; we must reference from more than one, like points for navigation. And over-head, now deeper, yet more seen into than ever before, is the night sky, with its bright, clear points for a celestial kind of navigation; our science not in disharmony with but ex-tending, deepening, and rendering precise our vision.

Part Two

DISMEMBERING, DREAMING, REMEMBERING

Chapter 6

INTO THE SHADOWLANDS

Our complexes are not only wounds that hurt and mouths that tell our myths, but also eyes that see what the normal and healthy parts cannot envision. . . .

Our falling apart is an imaginal process, like the collapse of cities and the fall of heroes in mythical tales—like the dismemberment of Dionysian loosening which releases from overtight constraint, like the dissolution and decay of alchemy. . . .

Afflictions point to Gods, Gods reach us through afflictions.

—JAMES HILLMAN

THE LORD OF THE ABYSS

During a time when I was working on initial versions of this chapter, a professional man told me a dream that had come to him a few years previously, at about the age of forty. Like Dante, he was lost in a dark woods in the middle of his life:

I am crossing a city park with a friend when a group of tough-looking youths approaches. My friend flees; but it seems all they want to do is to bring me to their "Master," who is underground, in a basement or subway. But the Master presents an aura of great knowledge and power, and shows me all kinds of allegories about life. Then we go to a movie kiosk where all kinds of perverted and horrible and unnatural things are depicted. He says, "I am this, too." In the last part we are walking together in the mountains and talking. We seem to be looking out upon the whole world.

The dreamer told me that the dream had affected him profoundly at an important time of personal change. Although he was of a somewhat scientific turn of mind, he was unable to dismiss the dream's penetrating commentary on life and his own situation. This dream also introduces two overall themes of this section: understanding pathological imagery in soul growth and the presence of that mysteriously so-well-oriented inner figure we call "the guide."

Do dreams really speak in a language of psychic transformation? We have to start from just where they are to learn where they are capable of going. The core patterns of soul sickness, dismemberment, and the pivotal role of death that show up in shamanism also rise up and come to us at night in our homes. Difficult as these themes are, they are really the genetic material of the transformative process. People seldom expect to be inwardly initiated, confronted by some unbidden interior rite of passage. But at such times the only productive attitude seems to be one of attention and receptivity to an unfolding flood of inner experiences: mental imagery and emotional states, attraction and repulsion to psyche's seeming polymorphous perversity.

The unfolding symbolism of self-transformation is often more complex and philosophically profound than the ego's viewpoint—as in the above dream—and challenges one's very self-concept: to include "this too" among one's inner contents. Where the images are grotesque, shocking, even "sick" in quality, the psyche is provoked to profound self-confrontation. These have ethical implications and, yes, aesthetic sensibilities are challenged. People confronting this zone of their own psyches often stumble through shifting sands of horror, self-rejection, and doubt.

These experiences are often so at variance with our conscious side we find ourselves asking, Is this me? With trepidation people have dared to imagine or personify their source because when we invite the fathomless void to take shape, we invoke a spirit of ancient power. Remember first that formless yet infinitely formidable character that psychiatrist H. S. Sullivan called the "Not-I," and Buddhist philosophy calls *anatman,* the mysterious vacancy of the void: no-self. Carlos Castaneda summons him in truly spooky form in *Tales of Power*—imbuing him with Aztec mythology in naming him the *Nagual,* the unknown one. He is the one who blows the terror-ridden wind of unexpected change to the safe island of the *Tonal,* the ego. It is he who raises the hackles on our necks when we summon him in the telling of ghost stories. He is "the secret cause," that uncanny Dionysian power the Greeks—and Joyce—held as the informing and patron spirit of tragedy. Is not the dreamer's "subwaymaster" an inflection of this ancient daimon: the lord of the abyss?

"Hades is not an absence, but a hidden presence—even an invisible fullness," said Hillman.[1] The lord of the abyss (basement or subway), says the dream, may also lead us into the heights. Some traditions place the lord of the underworld as an equivalent principle, even the brother, of the empyrean lord of the air and the heavens. For the Greeks the deep unconscious was the chthonic realm. Its lord was Hades–Dionysus–Pluto. ("Hades and Dionysus are the same," said Heraclitus, Frag. 15.) The gateway to the underworld is sexuality, intoxication, and self-abandonment. Yet the chthonic realm is that creative deep from which dreams (*oneiros*) arise; Pluto, the euphemistic name for Hades, means "wealth," which the underworld lord was said both to possess and to bestow. The modern dreamer above is invited to the ancient *nekyia,* the underworld journey, as a mode of self-discovery—and thus personal enrichment—invoked by heroes (Aeneas, Odysseus, and Dante) throughout the ages.

The subway-master is to the dreamer as Virgil is to Dante, and he keeps the dreamer moving. As they walk, wonders—and horrors—are revealed. What is going on is soul education. "The psyche," Hillman wrote,

> is using a particular metaphorical language system which is very detailed and concrete and seems to accomplish a specific end. Sick figures—crippled, with venereal disease, hurtling toward an accident, locked up in a closed ward—have an *exceptionally moving power.* We start up, afflicted, haunted through the day, psychologically on edge. The pathologized images have moved the soul in several ways: we feel vulnerable and in danger; our very physical substance and sanity appear to be menaced; we want to prevent or rectify.[2]

In the confrontation we are awakened. Our perspective is enlarged because our boundaries no longer stop short. We are reminded that "the big picture" includes "this too."

THE PATHOLOGICAL IMAGE

It seems curious to me, if, as Freud said, ordinary dream symbolism emerges mainly to disguise the unthinkable, that sometimes the unconscious exaggerates and highlights the pathological symbol, as some of the examples in the following pages show. If the unconscious may pun and play jokes, as Freud well knew, may it not also use hyperbole, or irony? Jung captured these personlike qualities of the darker zone of the unconscious in his concept of *the shadow,* a figure we explore later in this chapter.[3]

Pathologizing may include all of the shadow symbolism of the macabre; of death, disease, unwholesomeness, and the living dead; of curses, black magic, evil, and sinister magicians; or mana personalities, dictators, sadists, and the paraphernalia of torture chambers. Related to these topics we find a strange and perpetual human fascination. Most recently it is found in the symbolic mystique of the punk movement: the celebration of the capricious and grotesque, violence, razor blades, wounds, and mental pathology. These topics are most offensive, though, when we fail to see through them. Children have always (in my memory) told "sick" jokes involving the handicapped and chanted playground favorites like "the worms crawl in, the worms crawl out." They love to read horror comics that make their parents blanch, and in other ways they let the elders know they have few rosy illusions about these concomitants of mortal existence. If death turns a smile toward life (the *risus sardonicus* of the corpse), so too does life, toward death—laughing and joking in the face of the horrific spectacle of physical dismemberment, universal injustice, human ugliness, and monstrosity.

In this zone the iconography often used by filmmakers Federico Fellini, Ingmar Bergman, and others becomes relevant: dwarves, hunchbacks, the mentally retarded, and physical androgynes. In the tradition of the *bouffon* from French improvisational theater, we see the clown actor as a pathetic, disillusioned, even evil, dwarfish version of the ordinary self. This is often a role that carries an extraordinary power for both clown and audience (see Chapter 11).

One middle-aged man in my sample dreamed,

> *I wasn't a good-looking guy. I was ugly and physically twisted like a monster. They showed me a photo and I couldn't believe how ugly I looked.*

The dream here exaggerates, as if to call attention to, a particular self-image of the dreamer (actually above average in appearance). The deliberate exaggeration is both shocking and, a little later, funny and liberating, as one sees the message in the hyperbole. "Don't think of yourself so badly," it says. Another male client saw the following:

A half-man, half-laundry basket on wheels with long hanging arms appears wheeling down the hall. He seems to be one of those sad medical cases who must live his life out in this horrible condition. Another freak appears with a lurching walk. He has canes with bombs attached near the hands.

It is a matter of clinical experience that if in a group open to psychodrama or therapeutic theater one can get the dreamer to indwell such a figure, the thwarted dwarf or hunchback will emerge as a strong protagonist and stage presence. Almost always he or she will have an overdue message for the dreamer.[4]

However, we should not imagine that one may wave away the impact of pathological material by mere play or a magical gesture. By its very nature the pathological image may compel the deep attention we give to events and people who open wounds in us. One man dreamed:

I have a wound in my side that I was supposed to wash out regularly with vinegar. I've been reluctant to do it.

Here an astringent conscious attitude to his wounded condition seemed to be required of the dreamer. This wound, which was psychic, not physical, required a regular and acerbic self-attention for healing. When the patient is also a therapist, sometimes the wound occurs right in the healing context. A woman who does hands-on body therapy with patients dreamed:

I am doing this bodywork with a woman. Working down her spine I feel the skin is split apart. As I get down to the coccyx I see the whole body has been eviscerated from the waist down. I awaken with horror, weeping uncontrollably.

Such a dream bodes to open powerful affective issues for a person, and in this case challenged the healer to "heal herself" in no uncertain terms. She was somewhat exhausted—as happens to many therapists—with her own therapeutic work with others. Fortunately she entered therapy again herself and found the (symbolic) Canopic jar that contained her psychic viscera. Later, through therapeutic "remembering" she would be able to restore them to her imaginal body.

The imagery of this dream evoked a similar one presented to me ten years ago by a highly creative elderly artist who dreamed of a figure—himself? he wondered—with entrails removed (see Figure 17). Neither dreamer had any conscious knowledge of the shamanistic pattern in which the shamanic candidate experiences himself or herself dismembered and eviscerated by psychic forces. The mortal parts are replaced by immortal substance, as the long-term (spiritual) concerns of the patient are addressed. The viscera represent fragile, emotional parts that are to be transubstantiated into the imperishable wisdom body, the *vajra* body of the Yoga tradition.[5]

All life feeds on life, all constituted forms dissolve, as we are eternally reminded by Buddhism. If our dreams show us horrors they do not necessarily predict events in the real world. (However, neither can we rule out that such prefigurements occur among soul's forms of knowing.) What seems to be called for again is the as-if metaphorical attitude that takes the dream and its implications symbolically and yet seriously.

To experience the implications of a pathological dream to the psyche is to be wounded. In French *blesser* is "to wound," and as Jacob said to the angel who wounded him in the joint of his race progenitor's thigh, "I will not let you go unless you bless me" (Gen. 32:26). Is the angel who must be held on to like Proteus, the divinity of the soul image, who both wounds and blesses? Is wounding equivalent in some way to "being blessed"? The relevance of this material to our lives is that to develop the full range of symbolic thinking possible we must overcome symbolic squeamishness. While our culture teaches us to look away from the underside of what

FIGURE 16. *Eskimo shaman drum with spirit figure; man with entrails removed. Collected by Sheldon Jackson between 1888 and 1898. (Courtesy of Sheldon Jackson Museum, Division of Alaska State Museums.)*

FIGURE 17. The Man with Entrails Gone, *by Harry Helfman (drawing, 1970s).* (PHOTO BY ROBIN LARSEN.)

it means to be alive, to see through sickness and suffering, we must first learn how not to look away.

One male dreamer in search of a new purpose in mid-life dreamed,

I was in a stream of beautiful clear water searching for something. Someone who was ahead of me said, "You're not going to find it here." I said, "Yeah, it's too pure, too clear."

The dreamer here is told that he will not find what he is looking for in the clear water. He may be like the man in the Sufi parable who searches for his lost key only in the patch of light, because there at least he can see. This also reminds me of an alchemical saying attributed to the philosopher's stone itself—that precious inner thing that one seeks—often quoted with malicious delight by Jung: "In dung shall ye find me."

A week later, "up ahead," in the words of the dream, the same man (above) dreamed of *"a crude sexual act being taught me by a woman teacher."* In the very revulsion and embarrassment occasioned by this dream, some valuable therapeutic insights were obtained. We could say that only by looking into the "difficult and the dirty" could the next therapeutic step be taken. And it might be added, Freud is fully vindicated by this level of depth mapping the psyche. Although the roots of such a problem may lie in the events of childhood (with its polymorphous perversity), it is now best understood as part of an adult initiation. Perhaps the largeness of soul to include "this too" among psyche's contents is only attained with maturity and enough inner wholesomeness to give it a larger context.

Don't be too offended if your dreams occasionally flush you down a toilet, or have the toilets in your house overflowing, and you must cope with them. *Inter faeces et urinam,* we must go sometimes for psychological as well as physical birth. These are among the most common dreams encountered in psychotherapy. One woman dreamed,

The toilets are overflowing, mess is everywhere. All around are pails full of dirty dishes in stale dishwater. It's too much.

This dream reflected her feeling, not only about household tasks, as any feminist therapist would note, but the "messiness" of some issues in life. Excrement often appears in dreams where the neglected or the despised is at issue or something needs to be eliminated. Sometimes it may be used to characterize, in what seems like a vulgar style on the part of the dream, someone whose humanity or down-to-earth dimension has been ignored. This may be a compensation for idealization or etherealization of people or issues. Consciousness may be dream taught to overcome some kinds of fastidiousness, or squeamishness, and to contemplate the fertilizer of new growth.

But the soul that remains hypnotized in the pathological spell is in arrest by only one of psyche's archetypes. It's not even a nice place to visit, but most certainly you wouldn't want to live there. Psychology must be willing to help assign these elements their legitimate and appropriate place among psyche's many moods.

One of the most profound dreams I ever experienced was quite simple: *"A bucket of disgusting slops was made crystal clear."* Soul was speaking to me about the property of spirit, its ability to make things wholesome. ("Behold, I make all things new," Rev. 21:5.) Spirituality promises ultimately to free soul from its accumulated personal garbage.

One cultured woman dreamer experienced *"a bestial face, ruddy and screwed up, like the face of the Gorgon."* I think here of Nicholas of Flüe, who saw a divine countenance so terrifying, his own countenance was changed by it. People used to travel many miles just to see his face and experience at second hand the power of his vision.[6] The Gorgon, or Medusa, the sight of whose mask could turn men to stone, paradoxically also yielded up the healing medicines of Asclepius (see Chapter 10). Do these curious symbolic talismans remind us we must "face up" to the pathological element in life? The grotesque masks worn by Sri Lankan priests during healing ceremonies seem to show forth the *risus* (the horribly grinning face) of a particular disease. Similarly, the masks of Iroquois healers are twisted assymetrical grimaces with bug-eyed stares that laugh and leer all at once. In both societies, clowning is intermixed with the pathological element so that we come to laugh at the unspeakable and unthinkable, a healing discharge.

One man dreamed he was being tested by a woman psychologist. As the test unfolded she showed him *"the image of a toothless face which he knew to be that of Hitler."* The mask image initiated a profound catharsis in the dream. The dreamer found himself grieving for the innocent people whose lives were swept into nightmare by this evil man. He awoke weeping. Here the grotesque mask seemed to function as the labeling and evocative emblem for a whole zone of profound feelings. It served to announce an area that was asking to break through into personal therapy (even though it is indeed a collective issue). What did his personally ethnic Jewish background mean against the symbol of the Holocaust? Such issues may not be gainsaid when they arise. And it may be that if we neglect our personal pathology too much, the psychopathic dictator may emerge for us all to face collectively.

THE SHADOW, MAGIC, AND THE FEMININE

The "shadow" is, of course, that which is excluded from the light of consciousness, but like all psychic stuff, it is alive and creates a quasi personality, a golem-like shambling creation made up of our faults and fears. In the dreams of Northern Europeans, said Jung, the shadow frequently personifies as a darker or more equatorial person, a black, or a Middle Easterner. However, not just racial characteristics, but psychological ones pervade the image: sinister people, gangsters, and violent thugs. The shadow is also associated with "the primitive," tricksterlike mistakes, and Freudian slips.[7] Whoever accepts the misconception that Jungian psychology is mystical and "airy-fairy" should look at the immense amount of importance Jung attached to this figure, putting "the integration of the shadow" as the prerequisite and inevitable first stage of the soul journey (the "individuation process" as he called it).

Both men and women have shadows, but if women are thought of as inferior in certain cultural milieus, then the feminine "anima" and the shadow get all tangled up, as Jung noted.[8] Women might, for example, be associated with natural sinfulness—veritable handmaids of the devil—as they were for medieval Christianity. The centuries-long witch-hunts have been seen by feminist scholars as deliberate suppression of the natural magic of women (the magic having to do with herbal lore and gynecological mysteries including contraception, abortion, and childbirth) by a specifically male priesthood.[9] Feminists believe the shadow of "female inferiority" extends into contemporary times in many forms, but especially their being expected to perform demeaning tasks and their economic disadvantages.

When women dream of their own shadows, the personification is often fraught with magic (as if this is a disowned but still-present part of their nature), for example, Gypsy fortune-tellers with a malicious quality; witches; the "Wicked Queen," as in *Snow White;* knowing prostitutes; primitive "juju" women; and horrible "trundles" with too many shopping bags, who shout and know one's personal secrets. My wife dreamed years ago of an "unraveler," a primitive but numinous woman figure who "undid" the constructive things she was trying to weave together in her life.

Several years ago two men, one a therapeutic client and one a friend, shared with me dreams involving the same figure: *"An old scrubwoman, often in tatters, or in sordid circumstances; yet with a goddess-like quality of concealed power."* Because I had dreamed of an almost identical figure, and within a few months, I sat up and took notice. My own dream was of

an old crazy scrubwoman who lives in the basement of the Empire State Building. She runs the elevators, and we ride from level to level, just barely in control. She seems full of

*power and secret mystery. There are winds, and sometimes it
feels like we are in the* Sushumna *of the world.*[10]

The three of us wondered, after talking if we lived in a
culture that shared and reverenced collective images, would
this be the birth of (return of) a goddess? I thought of the
"Sedna complex" throughout the maritime shamanic world:
the mother of the sea creatures.[11] My wife remembered the
old nursery rhyme about a similarly numinous old woman
who seems to manifest some of the same archetypal qualities:

> There was an old woman tossed up in a basket,
> Ninety times as high as the moon;
> And where she was going, I couldn't but ask it,
> for in her hand she carried a broom.
>
> "Old woman, old woman, old woman," quoth I,
> "O whither, O whither, O whither so high?
> "To sweep the cobwebs off the sky!"
> "Shall I go with you?" "Ay, by and by."[12]

The old woman flies, like the being in my dream, on a
vertical axis (movement between the worlds). She also bears
that mysterious talisman, the cleaning instrument of the
scrubwoman—the witch's broom. In the last line of the
verse, it is implied that she is almost a goddess, who not
only clears away obstacles (the cobwebs of the sky) but
also conducts souls to the other world.

A woman client who was a college professor dreamed
repeatedly of

> *an old woman who lives at the bottom of a well/deep in the
> sea; she has immense energy, and is flailing her arms, creat-
> ing a maelstrom.*

The image became so strong for her, she began to image the
dream scene while awake—as if her external life were simultaneous with this underworld tableau—frozen in mythic time.

If we interpret this dream personally, it seems the client has a lot of anger. But if we interpret transpersonally, then an angry feminine spirit, or even Mother Nature, neglected and unworshipped, is abroad—and angry—in our time.[13]

The numinous old woman—or goddess—as was mentioned, resembles the primitive mother of animals. This figure is found from paleolithic times far into the neolithic in the worship of the great goddess. At the core of prehistory, wrote Buffie Johnson,

> loom the animal archetypes, symbols of fertility and death, that stand beside the Great Mother in what can only be described as an epiphany. Her animals are neither totems nor the independent divinities of polytheistic beliefs. They embody the deity herself, defining her personality and exemplifying her power. Her sacred animals act in the myths as guides and soul carriers, much as they do in fairy tales and dreams.[14]

Dream animals, then, with wicked, sly, threatening, or violent characteristics also may manifest the shadow of the neglected goddess. These can include domestic animals who have gone mad or seem possessed. The favorite horse balks or throws the rider (see Chapter 7), or *the cat stands up on its hind legs with knowing eyes, and does an evil dance.* In one woman's dream her pet cat did this: *and cracks opened in the ground, with vapor coming out.* In this case the animal—like the one whose image accompanies the Halloween witch—has an evident affinity for, and summons the mood of, the underworld.

These days there is a massive movement for animal rights. I have wondered if this is not a manifestation of the same goddess epiphany hinted in the above dreams. It is evident that our last few centuries have culminated one or two millennia of historical conspiracy: against animals as well as the feminine element. To many it seems as if some funda-

FIGURE 18. *Sedna, Mother of the Animals; "an old woman who lives at the bottom . . . of the sea . . . she has immense energy." (Detail from* Trickster and the Mother of the Animals; *silkscreen by Robin Larsen, 1974.)*

mental change is needed in our attitude toward our very life force, but more on this in Chapter 7.

THE WELL-DRESSED UNDERTAKER

If Hades–Pluto is the lord of initiation who shows us the depths so that we may also come to know the heights, then we may also see that he puts his stamp on virtually every rite of transformation. One man in my sample dreamed that as he sat in his living room, *"little fires broke out."* When he ran to the door he saw *"the man who was responsible disappearing into an aperture in the earth in a horse-drawn chariot."* The ominous quality of the dream seemed to refer to the (actual) abduction of a girlfriend (Jungian anima) by a strange under-world figure (Hades to Persephone), which depressed him deeply. The dream was startling and awoke him to the reality of his unconscious preoccupations with the underworld.

We know, superstition to the contrary, that we may dream our own deaths and those of others many times, without this in any way boding that reality follows suit (the "omenous" approach to dream interpretation). On the other hand, all psychic rebirths seem to require a prior symbolic "death." So while it is true that dreams of death may prefig-ure events in the "real" world (the files of J. B. Rhine are full of precognitive dreams involving death), obviously peo-ple dream of death, their own and others', far more often than they go through it for real. Therefore, I urge a seeing-through attitude to dreams of death, in which psychic trans-formation rather than literal prophecy may be seen as the dream's secret cause. (There is a subtle feeling-toned differ-ence between the actual precognitive dreams and the sym-bolic ones that is not easily described, but may be conveyed through a dream in Chapter 9, p. 223, "the two grandfathers.")

Sometimes the specific life reference of a loved one or relative's dying in a dream seems to be to highlight that person's mortality and give the dreamer an opportunity to recontext a relationship problem against this ultimate fact. If the person is elderly or ill, the dream may help the dreamer prepare emotionally against the inevitable loss, or cue him or her to make use of the time still remaining to resolve difficulties and strengthen love.

The importance of this latter type of guiding dream is underscored by the many times I have seen in therapy the awful personal pain of having a loved one die while the emotional bond is impaired, say, after an estrangement or argument or even after having had a fleeting death wish toward them. These provide some of the most painfully deep wounds I have encountered. Always it is facing mor-tality and the issues around it that proves to be our most difficult task, not the fact of death itself.

Several women in my sample dreamed of death in connection with marriage. The wedding ceremony, with its flowers, turns into a funeral. Read as a symbol of the woman's real feelings about her marriage, this would be an ill portent indeed, but it also may be symbolic of a kind of an inner death of one's total autonomy and the ritual beginning of a new stage of life (death seeming to precede rebirth in the symbolic sequence). Again, the only clue to the dream's meaning is her own personal associations and feelings. These dreams also touch on a theme to which I will return several times, the mutual affinity and divinity of love and death.

One woman dreamer saw Death several different ways in her dreams. In an initial dream he appeared as *"an undertaker, waiting for me in a car by the curb."* Then she saw the same man in another dream as *"a loser, dressed in grey-black, slumped in a chair, seedy, down-and-out. I felt scorn for him."* Later in that dream she returned to the same room to find him transformed. *"He was an impeccably dressed man. He said, "Today is the day we are all going to die."* In a third part of the (second) dream he was revealed as the famous actor Rex Harrison (the king who must die?), who had *"fooled [her] into having a vision of death."*

Like Ghede, the Haitian Lord of the Dead, this dreamer's personal Hades has a sense of humor and a flair for fancy dress. (We think of well-dressed undertakers, the master cosmeticians who make up death's face.) Does death's lively sense of humor push us into paradox? Does what must seem brutally final to us seem less so to the lord of the underworld, so that he puns and plays jokes?

The previous dreamer said, speaking of her feelings within the dream, *"I felt totally 'had.' But now I admired him, and envied his power to convince."* We are here put in touch with death as a trickster, a master of disguise, and ultimately a teacher. Hades–Pluto is attributed with great wealth, and I like the way the dream figure puts on elegant airs and how he first shows up for the dreamer: at the curb in a funeral limousine.

There is an old tradition that holds that death and life are equivalent realms and that, as Heraclitus said it, "When we are alive our souls are dead and buried in us, but when we die, our souls come to life again and live."[15] We only come to understand the full reach of the soul with the recognition of death. And death is really understandable only to the fully initiated soul.

FIGURE 19. *Māhākala, the Great Black One. Time as devouring Death, virtually a skeleton without entrails. Bas-relief over a doorway in Katmandhu, Nepal.* (PHOTO BY AUTHOR.)

MYTHS AND PERSONIFICATIONS OF DEATH

Two modern researchers in psychological thanatology, Robert Kastenbaum and Ruth Aisenberg, have examined the ways in which people's personifications of death interact with other variables in their personalities, including, of course, what we call their "philosophy of life." They asked, "Do personifications of death tell us something about the individual's conception of his place in the universe and the meaning of his life?"[16]

These authors assigned major categories to personifications they elicited from their subjects, such as "the macabre personification," a malign figure inimical to life. There was also "a machinelike impersonal force." The holders of such views, who could be described as modern demythologized persons, usually saw death accompanied by all the paraphernalia of physical extinction, skeletons, decomposing flesh, and the like, as well as images of a more ambivalent figure, a gay deceiver with seductive as well as horrific attributes. We think of the medieval Harlequin, the darker side of the trickster, or the more playful "well-dressed undertaker" above.

In contrast to these were positive images of a gentle comforter: the Christ, who died himself so that men might have "eternal life"; or Mother Nature in a gentle mood, who takes all living things back to her bosom. This kind of image, incidentally, was far more prevalent among personnel who work with geriatric patients than, say, college students, who were usually much closer to the demythologized approach.

Campbell often pointed out the redemptive power of such messages as the boon-bestowing gesture of horrific figures in Oriental mythology (see Figure 19). These figures portray the horrific aspect frontally, but with the embedded wisdom message, "so the Universe appears, but do not be afraid." Such a figure provides psychological as well as mythological support to the idea that the devouring powers of the universe must be seen through in their literally malign aspect. The personification shows forth this idea in image form. Kastenbaum and Aisenberg suggested, "As an alternative to balance the biological approach, personification enables one to express something of his own emotional and symbolic orientation to death."[17]

There can be no doubt that the recent work in thanatology is in the process of changing death's visage. In the work of Elisabeth Kübler-Ross, Raymond Moody, Kenneth Ring, and other near-death researchers, we find people who enter the outskirts of death's land to bring back reports—not of a deceiver fair outside and foul beneath—but of just the reverse.

As a person enters into the death experience, there are psychological encounters with ever-deeper parts of the self, resembling the early stages reported in *The Tibetan Book of the Dead*. A common initial experience in these accounts, and general folklore as well, is the life review. The general themes—and the overall meaning—of the person's life passes, as it were, before the eyes of the soul. "My life flashed before my eyes," says the drowning victim, and we realize we have been psychically "videotaped" all along by an inner faculty with eidetic clarity of recall. Having read Sartre we may be afraid that at death our being is going to escape into nothingness. But if so, the soul's last curious act is this condensation of a life story. Often the review is experienced in a state of consciousness that makes one profoundly aware of all the moral and creative implications of the lifetime: the centrality of some crucial themes, a personal mythology.

The glimpse of a transcendent purpose to life usually attends the near-death experience. The person's personal myth becomes not an existential farce, but a tale told with meaning. In some of the near-death accounts cited by Ring, it was the conscious experiencing of death that seemed to be the positively transformative factor in subsequent improvements in outlook and behavior. (People in a stupor from a drug-overdose suicide attempt did not consciously experience their life stories.)[18]

Many people thought they themselves were "presenting" the life review to an inner being. This being is depicted in the accounts as "made of light," all-seeing of every detail of the life, yet usually gentle, rather than the judgmental figure some aspects of our religious tradition may have prepared us for; even with a sense of humor. One person in Moody's book said, "The first thing he said to me was, that he kind of asked me if I was ready to die, or what I had done with my life that I wanted to show him."[19]

While this kind of experience might to many readers seem like a traditional religious one, often nonreligious people had them. A popular saw has it that there are fewer "atheists in foxholes" than elsewhere, as if the mere encounter with death makes someone instantly religious. But analysis of the kinds of conscious experiences people have in the near-death state shows more precisely the mechanism whereby the transformation may be wrought. Some people have believed a fire-and-brimstone mythology is necessary and desirable for humanity because a wrathful and judgmental God is more likely to keep us in line. They ought to consider, however, the opposite, gentler, approach: the psychological self-correcting that might emerge from seeing the total truth about one's life in the presence of a person who was caring and of whose love you wanted very much to be worthy.

Among the imagery exercises in this book (Chapter 12) is a simple yet powerful one, which often changes and opens life perspective. This is to imagine yourself at your own death, leaving this life, and looking back. You may also imagine having a loved one or caring person at your funeral deliver your eulogy, but with total fairness. (This would be easy for Jewish people who have attended a *shivah*, a helpful ritual of remembrance and storytelling about the deceased, done during the funeral time.)

Psychoanalysis has shown us that the springs of psychic healing may be touched by recovering knowledge of your early childhood. The divergent theories of Otto Rank, an initial follower of Freud, and Arthur Janov, founder of primal therapy, say the same about recovering the memory of birth itself. There, at the beginning, are to be found the keys to healing and freedom from neurosis. We see now that the contemplation of death—and the end of life—may do the same. If Grof is correct, and I think he is, life and death each contain an inner symbolic representation of the other. These great "portal mysteries" call into question the whole meaning of a lifetime. They give more substance to this sometimes ethereal-seeming quest, for one's personal myth. Telling

one's story—to someone—seems to be necessary for each of us (and is an important ingredient in psychotherapy).

Even "making up" a whole alternative lifetime can be a powerful experience (see Chapter 12). Important symbolic themes may be found in these experiences that also connect to meaningful themes in one's ordinary life. Special attention is usually given to the zones of birth and death in this fantasy exercise. Inevitably we learn through changing our perspectives. Consideration of life against the background of death brings its wonder and mystery to the surface. Consideration of death "in another life" does the same. In this zone especially we are forced to recognize that not only do we live our myths, but we die them as well.

PLAYING DEAD

Thanatomimesis is the imitation of death by something that is living: "Playing dead." As if to disprove John Locke and the baseline social-learning theory, this pattern of ritualized behavior is, by definition, not acquired. (You don't have to die to know how to do it.) Furthermore, thanatomimesis is practiced by insects, animals of all sorts, and humans.

We wonder sometimes when we see children "play dying" with such innocent enjoyment 'where this intuitive rapport comes from. Kastenbaum and Aisenberg said, "We might increase our respect for children's death impersonations if we keep in mind the strong likelihood that this play is a significant part of a developmental process that will have implications for their total life view and adjustment."[20]

Spiders, possums, and human children can all give Academy Award–winning performances of dying. It seems that this imagery—and its dramatic enactment—is carried in our RNA and DNA, our genetic material. The medieval *ars moriendi,* the art of dying well, was thought to be acquired in the hospices and monasteries, and doubtless these contemplative places were able to provide a spiritual orientation

to the yonder-bound soul. But is the art and imagery of dying not at basis an instinct? It may well be out of an instinctual reservoir of knowledge about death that the soul generates its perennial imagery of transformation.

Kübler-Ross has told how during her youthful visit to the concentration camps of post–World War II Germany she found, endlessly repeated, a primary symbol of the soul's transition drawn on the barrack walls by the countless children who faced death there: the image of a butterfly or night moth breaking free of its chrysalis. The moving insight precipitated by this iconography may have been one of the more important determinants that set her on her adult path of insight and compassion related to death and dying.[21]

Altruism is based on a principle very hard to understand in a fully Darwinian universe. We know that humans are capable of it, although some researchers say only through the socialization process. Ethologists have been eager to see if animals possess it, and sometimes they do; for example, "higher" animals such as nonhuman primates and canids have been known, under certain circumstances, to sacrifice themselves for each other (usually "family" or friends). "Greater love hath no man," said Jesus (and we might add, no beast), "than that he lay down his life for his friend" (John 15:13). Among many species of animals, there are signals of submission that stop and defuse even the most serious battles—for supremacy, territories, and mates. The animal who is losing offers his throat or belly to the aggressor—as if saying, "Go ahead kill me"—and the aggressor, instinctively it would seem, quits. (Would that all human beings were in touch with an analogous mechanism!)

It may be a long time before our learned academies agree on whether human altruism, when and where it is manifested, has an instinctive aspect, as I am suggesting, or whether it is only the result of a "socialization process." What is more important to point out at this time is that individual souls carry about, and may act on, a vital inner ethic: the life of another is held to be as important or more important than our own. This means also an image in the soul of man (or beast) that knows something of the nature of death and mortality.

The "little deaths," Kübler-Ross and others pointed out, that attend many of life's transitions and disappointments also follow the classic stages of coming to acceptance of actual death: with the phases of denial, anger, then catharsis, and (it is hoped) coming to acceptance.[22] These, too, illustrate the principle of thanatomimesis. Masters and Houston noted that the opportunity to experience a symbolic little death in the psychedelic session seems to short-circuit a suicidal urge or self-directed death wish.[23]

Obtaining vivid inner recapitulations of the death experience in LSD sessions is proof of a nonconscious than atomimetic knowledge. People are never conscious of inventing the death experience, it "happens" to them. The hardest things to imagine—personal destruction and dissolution, overwhelming annihilation of the ego—are faced in these encounters. The inner iconography in the earlier stages is usually filled with negative personifications of death, the evil tricksters, machinelike impersonal forces, or sadistic monsters. Not until these stages have been undergone in a mood of surrender are the transpersonal images glimpsed beyond. Through the charnel scene of the battlefield great Shiva is seen dancing his terrible, beautiful dance; above the Hill of the Skull rises the Crucifixion and a God-man in voluntary death for the world.

SEEING THROUGH DEATH

Our imaging and personifying of death affects life values. Each of us mythologizes death differently, based on personal variables and developmental stages. We also know that the depth encounter with death is almost always positively transforming. (Whereas the shallow or unconscious brushes, or the fearful running away from, produce pathologies.) There are profound psychological as well as social and ethical implications to this knowledge.[24]

Freud, sobered in the second half of life and exhausted by "beyond the pleasure principle," came to portray Thanatos as an instinct of equivalent power to that of great Eros.[25] Freud's book was written in 1933. This mid-life metanoia in Freud seemed an unexpected and puzzling shift to many of his followers, who thought they were following a priest whose god was Eros.

Was it just that Freud had moved into the "second half of life" (Jung's notion) and that his new theory reflected his life-stage myth—a preparation for death? Or does the power of love always contain a secret seed of death, as the French term for orgasm, *le petit mort,* "the little death," seems to imply? Unchecked, Eros turns to Dionysus, as the imperious pleasure principle divides and dismembers itself and the world into hedonic centers. The only way in which the god of desire will desist is expenditure, cessation, and death.

Hence death's mysticism for the German romantic tradition; death is the hero's great apotheosis, his mystical reunion with the feminine source, Faust's realm of the mothers. This is ultimately his only chance for revitalization. Germanic mythology resonates with the theme of the *Liebestodt,* or love-death. And the Hindus long ago knew what Freud found only in the second half of his life: that the lord of desire and death, Kama-Mara, is one deity with two aspects.

When we love, we lose ourselves, and conversely when we have become lost to ourselves, the spiritual traditions tell us, we become capable of inexhaustible love. We see through carnal love to find death, as in the Buddha's Graveyard Vision (the experience that started the young prince, whose parents tried in every way to keep him from it, on the spiritual path). He beheld the beautiful houris and dancers sent to distract him, unconscious—some say from drinking, some say a spell of the gods—with mouths agape and arms akimbo, resembling corpses.

And we see through death to find only love, as in Christ

on the cross. "Perfect love casteth out fear," said the gentle master (I John 4:18). The early Christian *agape,* or love feast, was an attempt at a sacramental transmutation of *eros* into *agapé,* selfish personal love to unselfish transpersonal love; martyrs were rent apart, blessing and loving those who laughed and set the beasts on them. Perhaps Christianity's greatest contribution to the world has been to sacralize the principle of self-sacrifice, the consecration of the idea of "perfect love."

People who consciously enter death's realm are enriched thereby (Pluto's wealth). Mother Theresa and Kübler-Ross are examples of modern people transformed, almost transfigured, by a conscious facing of death. Kübler-Ross tells that when she began her work in thanatology, people shunned her as if her interest was somehow morbid. These people obviously read her deep interest from their relatively shallow level. Now she is venerated by thoughtful people all over the world.

Death, then, is the wisest counselor of life. To be aware of him looking over your left shoulder as you live makes a warrior of you, Don Juan tells Carlos Castaneda. The message of the roughest initiations is to learn the proximity and reality of death. The transformation of the soul through death is the central message not only of Christianity but also of the oldest religion in the world—shamanism. For the greatest percentage of our two or three million years of existence, the major evidence, not only of religious awareness but even of culture at all, are the ceremonial burials of people and animals. These latter were usually, as Campbell and others have shown, involved with rites of propitiation to the spirits of the slain animals to be reborn again, to complete nature's great cycle (of which the human food chain was known as just a part), and to ask the master or mistress of the animals to pardon the violence of the hunting and killing.[26]

"Do you wish to be food for the moon?" the brilliant and unconventional consciousness-teacher Gurdjieff would ask his pupils. Gurdjieff taught that lives lived like machines, without conscious awareness (a higher vibratory frequency than "mere nature" in his system), passed in a natural ray of transmission to the moon, portrayed in some mythologies as the abode of dead souls. Gurdjieff believed, like many teachers before him, that an alchemical or gnostic transubstantiation of our lower selves was necessary to become immortal. And to do this, we must first become conscious of it, even, as we have seen, the parts we would rather avoid. The "unexamined life" always needs to die, it is "food for the moon." It is only through encountering both life and death consciously, the wisdom traditions tell us, that we build the adamantine, the diamond, the *vajra* or thunderbolt body of immortality.[27]

> To seek God too soon is not less sinful than to seek God too late; we must love, man, woman or child, we must exhaust ambition, intellect, desire, dedicating all things as they pass, or we come to God with empty hands.
>
> —YEATS

Chapter 7

BEASTS AND
BIRDS OF
THE MIND

*Understand that thou hast within thyself flocks of cattle . . .
flocks of sheep and flocks of goats . . . understand that the
birds of the sky are also within thee.*

—ORIGEN, *Leviticum Homiliae*

ANIMISM AND THE ARK OF THE MIND

Anyone who listens to lots of dreams will be struck by the numbers of animals that appear. They are far more numerous and exotic than any theory of "day residues" could explain. (Freud's "residues" theory says that the major contents of a dream come from the material of the previous day.) The animals are sometimes, although by no means always, found in the dreamer's habitat, but sometimes they are not even from this world.

It is rather as if all the animals of the biosphere, and even some (we call them mythological) of the psychesphere, were available to the unconscious of the dreamer. Do we still carry within us, in Paul Shepard's words, an ark of the mind?[1] Several dreams presented to me in therapy contained the image of great parks or forests filled with many animals, as if glimpsing Eden itself. These would be understandable if the dreamer had just completed a visit to a zoo or game farm, but the dreams often appeared with no such external context. Sometimes the animals would appear peaceful, or neutral, but sometimes threatening; several times they appeared like a "gauntlet" of beasts through which the dreamer had to pass. The following is an example of this type of dream, by a woman in her fifties:

> I am living in a house in a triangular area between two roads, the roads are dusty country roads. I have to go on foot to an old general store in town. The woods are full of animals, all around, one coming toward me as I enter the house. A second time I have to go, this time carrying a child. I almost meet a brownish animal like a deer, face to face, as I make it back. An older woman berates me for taking chances with the child's life. To take chances with my own was okay.

While the animals do not menace the dreamer, the older woman figure brings up the danger element. In this case the instinctual powers might pose a threat to new life.

This genre of dream seems to harken back to a time in human history (or rather prehistory) when human beings were surrounded by animals and recognized a kinship with them. It speaks of a theriogenic—an animating, animal-creating—zone of the psyche, where the animal powers still reside and are created anew always from the raw stuff of mind. Perhaps this is the timeless place to which the Sioux Black Elk went on a visionary journey. He told Joseph Epes Brown, "I was taken away from this world into a vast tipi which seemed to be as large as the world itself, and painted on the inside were every kind of four-legged being, winged being, and all the crawling peoples. The peoples that were there in that lodge, they talked to me, just as I am talking to you."[2]

Black Elk was a spokesman for the view, prevalent among native Americans, that animals are spiritual powers as well as earthly beings. To this ancient view, found everywhere throughout the paleolithic world, Campbell addressed the first volume of his *Historical Atlas of World Mythology,* which he called *The Way of the Animal Powers.* Men and women living in close proximity to the natural world felt not only its permeation by the same life force they felt in themselves, but the whole to be an intelligible revelation of divine power. The roots of human mythology are to be found in the beast realm and the endless now-forgotten ages of the paleolithic hunt. If the human psyche has been shaped by our few millions of years of terrestrial existence, then animals are our oldest teachers, as well as "relatives." (How many modern hunters—who may kill for pleasure or trophy rather than survival—apologize, as did the ancient ones, to the beasts they slay? "I'm sorry, Uncle, but I need your fur coat." "Grandfather, this is painful for me too." "Please come back and be with us again.")

Animism is not the worship of animals, but the tendency to see the entire world of nature as spiritually alive. Archaic people had "relatives" and allies in the plant and mineral worlds (the shaman's herbs, stones, and crystals) as well as the animal world (shamanic tokens of skin, bones, feathers, and animal masks). But the special role of animals seems to have been to embody specific aspects of psyche, literally and symbolically (some would say through a correspondence in the world of nature to the soul, others merely through receiving mind's projection).

The informing sentiment of this world view, as Campbell wrote, "Nor is only man made in the image of God: so, too, are the jaguar, buffalo, bear, eagle and serpent, butterflies, trees, rivers and mountains. For 'All things speak of Tirawa' [the Pawnee creator god]."[3]

ANIMALS AND RELIGIOUS TRADITION

When we look to a spectrum of religious traditions, modern forms contrasted with the ancient, we find a division of opinion on this subject, represented in the following two views.

1. **Animals are closer to the divine source than we are.** Each animal species has a prototype, a "master animal" that is also a spiritual power and to which one must relate all doings with his "people." Animals are to be treated with respect.

2. **Animals are lower than our human condition.** We may dominate and enslave them for our purposes, because of our mental or spiritual advantage. One certainly should never consider an animal comparable in any way to a human being.

In the Judeo-Christian religious tradition, as opposed to Black Elk's, there is little doubt that the second view has been the favorite. In the Bible: "Thou hast put all things under his feet: All sheep and oxen, yea, and beasts of the field; The fowl of the air, and the fish of the sea, and whatever passeth through the paths of the sea" (Ps. 8:6–8). This is reflective of the condition of our "fallen" state, replacing the wonderful early symbol of the garden (Eden) where the animals and people lived in paradisal harmony, like the beings in Black Elk's tepee, or the aboriginal Australians in the *alcheringa* time, the dream time of the ancestors. But it is this second view that has motivated our post–Iron Age ancestors, who have rendered extinct untold hundreds of species. Others we have merely subjugated or "trampled on" in literal ways. By comparison to our clumsy domination, Black Elk's native American kin lived in what might be termed a *biospiritual symbiosis,* an exquisitely self-governing ecosystem. As author and naturalist Barry Lopez said, in a *Parabola*[4] article, "We once thought of animals not only as sentient, but as congruent with ourselves in a world beyond the world we can see, one structured by myth and moral obligation, and activated by spiritual power."[5]

The eighteenth-century scientist-visionary Swedenborg interpreted the entire Bible as a great allegory of the growth of the mind, or development of the psyche. Following his intriguing lead we can see a historical transformation of the psyche's relation to animals through the Hebrew Scriptures, or Old Testament. In the garden, Adam and Eve speak the language of the beasts and are in harmony with their instincts. The exile is a fall from the integrity of this instinctual life of *participation mystique* with nature.[6]

Later Noah became a prototype of the savior figure, by saving the animate ecosystem from a destruction sent by God, but provoked by human wickedness. But the biblical patriarchs increasingly alienated themselves from animals, particularly wild ones, by a system of taboos that hints at suppression of the first view: "Ye shall not make your souls abominable by beast or by fowl or any manner of thing that creepeth on the ground, which I have separated from you as unclean" (Lev. 20:25). It was said by Josephus Flavius in the first century A.D. that "the curtains of the Hebrew temple were composed of purple and scarlet and blue and fine linen, and embroidered with diverse kinds of figures, excepting the form of animals."[7]

The Hebrews were an aniconic people who were very serious about having no images of the deity, and especially no animal deities in their temple; this was to be their one great distinction from the multitudinous goddess-worshipping cults of Asia Minor. The creation of the Golden Calf by the Israelites (while Moses waited high on Mount Sinai for a revelation *in words* of the Hebrew laws) was doubly troubling, according to Raphael Patai in *The Hebrew Goddess,* because the calf was an animal god-image and because the usual response to the public exhibition of the god in this form was sexual rioting.[8]

The only statuary or "beasts" of any sort allowed in the temple were the mysterious and wonderful cherubim, which had quasi-human bodies and faces and the wings of great birds, with which they covered the Ark of the Covenant.

The priests were eager for outsiders, especially Hellenic or Roman intellectuals, to know that these were not "graven images" of any living thing, but were "divine beings stationed near the throne of God." What they most resemble are the animal and human "guardian figures" at the entrances to temples from the Middle East to the Orient. These are the "watchers" and portal guardians of sacred space: often mythological or semidivine animals such as the Sphinx in Egypt or the Garuda in India. Patai, however, thinks they are the remnant of the archaic Androgynous One, a deity whose representation is made from a pair of opposites in tension—the two snakes or spirals intertwined, the Hindu Yab-Yum, or the Chinese yin and yang.[9]

In the first three centuries of Buddhism (600–300 B.C.), contemporary with the Hebrew Temple, the Buddha, like Yahweh, was not to be represented, save by footprints or a throne or parasol. The Buddha also is much associated with animals, in legend and iconography, especially through the *Jataka* tales, which are wonderful stories of how the Enlightened One in his "great awakening" remembered all his previous incarnations—lived in various animal forms. Animals are thus brought forward in religious tradition and resacralized, since Buddha entered "their condition" (in an analogous way to Christ's incarnating, or entering "our condition").

Christianity kept some of Judaism's animal taboos, as well as adding a few of its own. But it is interesting to see how the positive animal connection keeps emerging. Jesus first appeared in a manger among animals. So that in the crèche scene, one of the most publicly exhibited pieces of Christian iconography, the world savior appears in the midst of beasts. And for his adult vision quest, Jesus was "there in the wilderness forty days, tempted of Satan; and was with the wild beasts" (Mark 1:13).

Like Buddha, who "lived as" an animal, or the later Celtic Merlin (sometimes called the "Hairy Anchorite," a figure with ancient roots), who himself ran with the beasts of the forest, Jesus illustrates the curious symbolic paradox of having the figure representing the highest spiritual principle be also a secret initiate of wildness. He warned the disciples, who must also have been initiates, in the beast language: "Behold I send you forth as sheep in the midst of wolves. Be ye wise as serpents and harmless as doves" (Matt. 10:16).[10]

The master of the animals, or the beastmaster, as in the title of a recent film, is he who knows and uses the ancient connection. He is Tarzan of the Apes and Mowgli, heroes of our youth. He is Whistling Dan Barry, whose friend is a wild wolf and who, like Orpheus, is master both of music and, through music, animals.[11] Remember also fairy-tale specialist Von Franz's assertion that meeting and rendering assistance to the animal is the one stage of the hero journey that may not be omitted. The guide of souls must be a friend to the animal realm because the soul is, in part, made up of animals.

We remember that Medieval neoplatonists compared the human soul to the sea deity Proteus, he who takes the shape of all things. The mind is polymorphously perverse; the imagination ever outstrips the poor limited body in possibility. The human imagination is the source of the worldwide tradition of *theriomorphism,* the capability attributed to some humans of turning into an animal (i.e., the werewolf).

Now if we can consider briefly the implications of two modern scientists' theories to this discussion of "renegotiating contracts," we may come to see our responsibilities to the animals of both psyche and world.

Cleve Backster is an ex-FBI interrogation expert who hooked up geranium plants to a skin conductance meter, and found they responded at the precise moment when live brine shrimp were dropped into boiling water in the next room; the plants even responded to (human) feeling-toned thoughts of anger or hostility. His message: All life is in communion at a very deep—probably unconscious—level with all other life. Animals may not know our thoughts, but they do sense our feelings. Hence through our emotions we live in a psychological as well as biological ecosystem.[12] Rupert Sheldrake's controversial theory of morphic resonance holds a similar idea to be true: that there is an invisible communion between all members of one species, so that all feel in some way what happens to one. The extreme example of this is found in insects, but Sheldrake proposes that it is true of all species. His theory is not really much different from the ancient shamanic notion that there is a "group mind" and an archetypal or "master" animal for each species. In the light of his speculations, this ancient shamanic idea becomes eerily plausible.[13]

These researches may stimulate us to ask, Are we "lords of creation" in more than an archaically metaphorical sense? Are we by nature, and "polymorphogenetically" (if the reader can stand such a ponderous term), in resonance with all life forms? The myth of the paradisal garden or even the ark of the great rescue shows us a kind of spiritual ecology, an unavoidable connection and responsibility to the world of animals. And shouldn't we rephrase *Nihil humanum mihi alienum est* ("Nothing human is alien to me") to *Nihil animale mihi alienum est?*

"The two claims," wrote Campbell,

> on one hand, of an individual existence, and on the other of transpersonal identity, alternate and compete in the lifetimes both of beasts and of men; and whenever the larger force takes over, the individual forgetting itself in a seizure, acts in manners stereotyped to the species, often with little or no regard for self-preservation. The courtship dances and displays of birds and fish are examples of such performances.[14]

Both myth and instinct are concerned with ritual, and people as well as animals come to know each other through rituals. (If you are a disbeliever, see what your dog knows of ritual or observe carefully the body language or social behavior of any animal). Is it possible there is an exact mirroring between our mythologies (and treatment) of animals in the outer world, and our approach to the inner world of instinct, the birds and beasts of the mind?

Animals tell us of our compulsions, instincts, and the human equivalent of innate releasing mechanisms (IRMs) such as imprinting behavior among young fowl to follow a mother figure (usually within a time "window," during which, if no mother is present, the chicks or ducklings may follow the family cat or even a mobile toy). Some behaviorists will try to tell us we don't have instincts, but see what happens when a child misses a developmental stage, or try to get a teenager to skip puberty, or your own heart not to beat faster in the presence of certain living and breathing "incentive objects" in your immediate environment. To find replicas of nonhuman dominance hierarchies you can go to any sports club or workplace.

Some visionaries have tried to bring animals back into our religious consciousness, such as twelfth-century Saint Francis of Assisi, who was almost canonized by the animals themselves who befriended him, apparently recognizing his spiritual state. In the sixteenth century, Francisco de Osuna, Francis of Assisi's namesake, wrote *A Meditation on the Creatures* (Osuna is better known for his *Spiritual Alphabet*); the mind of the spiritual meditator was systematically to contemplate this living branch of God's creation as a metaphor for the conditions of the soul.

In the eighteenth century, Swedenborg developed his theory of "correspondences," which says "there is nothing in nature that does not symbolize something in the world of spirit." What is without, in the natural world, is only a counterpart and later transformation of that which is within, the living images of the spiritual influx into the soul: "by beasts and animals were anciently signified affections and like things in man." Swedenborg also boldly asserted that he who does not know "what each beast specifically signifies, cannot understand what the Word contains in the internal sense."[15] For Swedenborg's symbolic purview of the Bible, then, not only the natural features of geography—the mountains, seas, gardens, and wells—but very specific qualities of the sacrificial animals—the ram, ewe, bullock, or the one forbidden by Talmudic law, the pig—are full of spiritual significance. One who fails to read the "book of nature" within the historical book, Swedenborg thought, misses the "internal sense" of the West's primary religious document. A later interpreter of Swedenborg's view says, "Is there in the mind a class of objects which is sensitive to pleasure or pain? Can I hurt you without touching your body? What do I hurt? . . . Are these same feelings capable of enjoyment? Are they warm? Are they active? The feelings or affections are the animals of the mind."[16]

Children's comic books have talking animals, which, we are told, make more sense to them than talking adults. Psychologist Henry A. Murray recognized that the version of the Thematic Apperception Test developed for children (the C.A.T.) should use animals instead of people, in typical situations. The children empathize with the animals and feel them to be peers. Adults are inscrutable and distant from the child's world by comparison. And adults mostly get their opportunities to visit zoos in the company of children.

The sheep is agreeable, the goat contrary, the tiger ferocious, the rabbit frightened, the elephant ponderous of person and memory. Animals invite our stereotypes, receiving them far more unequivocally than people, who are always too complicated. Each animal shows a characteristic quality or state of the mind, an instinct, an affect. Animals are to be studied, as well as revered, because they are manifestations of the hidden archetypal powers that lie behind the transformations of the human soul.

In the next section I suggest that the animals of our dreams not only speak of our personalities, but often show their connection with the spiritual source realm. Is our unconscious mind really "archaic," as the depth psychologists have told us, and are its images a few thousand years out of

date in catching up with "progress"? Or is it rather that
archaic people were in touch with realities of the spirit, still
applicable today, and although we have consciously forgotten them, our unconscious has not? (What consciousness
forgets, the unconscious remembers.)

In the soul's remembrance of things past there are animal
forms from all evolutionary levels; psyche knows well how to
wear the scales, feathers, and fur. It puts on skins and antlers,
like the *sorcière* of *Les Trois Frères,* and wears a tail, like a million
children galloping about their backyards. Proteus remembers
the experience of changing into all beings. The Celtic wizard
Amergin says, "I was in many shapes before I was released."

> I am a stag of seven tines . . .
> I am a shining tear of the sun,
> I am a hawk on a cliff,
> I am fair among flowers . . .
> I am a salmon in the pool,
> I am a hill of poetry,
> I am a ruthless boar,
> I am a threatening noise of the sea . . .
> Who but I knows the secrets of the unhewn dolmen?[17]

In a tradition closely related to that of Amergin, Celtic
Taliesin (who in some traditions is identical with Merlin),
like the Buddha, has visited the earth in many incarnations,
not only as men and beasts, but even "the bubbles on beer,
and the drops in a shower."[18]

"I was in the ark," says the poet, "with Noah and Alpha
. . . / And I was with my lord in the manger of oxen and
asses . . . / I was revealed in the land of the Trinity."

> And I was moved through the entire universe
> And I shall remain till doomsday,
>   upon the face of the earth.
> And no one knows what my flesh is—
>   whether meat or fish.[19]

The worldwide belief that humans can change into animals, theriomorphism, includes not only our familiar fuzzy werewolves from Europe, but the berserkers of Scandinavia, who hallucinated changing into bears to go more ferociously into battle. Also on the savagely feral side are the leopard men of Africa, the werejaguars of South America, and the shark shamans of the Pacific atolls.

Although biologists would certify them physically unchanged for all their magical identification, humans have played this metamorphic game for a long time. Theriomorphism tells of a condition of soul: psyche, not flesh, changes easily to beast form. We are pointed ever inward toward a source realm close to our psychogenic as well as genetic roots.

DREAM ANIMALS

My sample of about 3,000 dreams contains the following animals: alligators, apes, bats, birds, cats, cows, crocodiles, deer, dogs, dinosaurs, dragons, eagles, elephants (and baby elephants), fish, fox, hawks, horses, goats, insects, lions, kangaroos, mares, mice, monkeys, monstrous unrecognizable animals, panthers, rats and rodents of different kinds, reptiles, serpents of many sorts, squirrels, tarantulas, tigers, turtles (including giant ones), werewolves, whales, and wolves. This list contains the major categories and animals that appeared several times, but is not exhaustive. My dream list also includes several theriomorphic dreams, where people experienced "being" animals or actually transforming into them. Although some dream animals are clearly of the domestic variety or to be found in local zoos, many are not and seem selected by the dream playwright for an exemplary or symbolic quality that they represent.

Snakes are among the most primary and powerful of symbolic animals; they lend themselves to multiple representations. Freud's favorite was of the phallus, but why not also the spinal cord—our more "instinctual" part of the central nervous system—or the digestive tract, which expands to swallow? Snakes live in hidden places in the earth or in water. They carry poisons, also potentially usable as medicines. Their legendary serpentine movement we now know as an elementary form of energy, the sine wave. Most important for the archaic world—as in the tale of Gilgamesh—was their ability to shed the skin, which became a primary and perennial symbol of transformation.

One woman dreamer had a long-term phobia of snakes and would panic on the rare occasions she encountered one in nature. Her dream was a very simple one: *"I meet a snake on a path in the woods. He looks at me with intelligent eyes, that say he means me no harm."* Earlier in therapy this client herself had proffered the explanation that snakes reminded her of phalluses; we explored the implications of this, for a while. But it was not the work on this insight, but the dream of the I-thou encounter with the snake that enabled her to deal with the irrational intensity of her fear.

Another woman dreamer saw a snake crawling across her bed. She was going into panic, when suddenly the snake looked at her *"with brown human eyes in a flat face. I felt he looked at me like he knew me."* She felt the shock turn into wonder, as she woke up. The next day she was surprised to find an actual live snake in the desk drawer of her study. Panic was avoided, and, with help, the snake carefully removed and let loose in the woods, rather than destroyed on the spot. (Panic at the sight or proximity of certain animals would seem an atavistic leftover in our psyches. Archetypally this emotion is connected to Pan, the Arcadian lord of the animals, who could fill both animals and humans with "panic.")

One of the most fearful types of dream is that in which there are lots of snakes, as in the memorable scene in the film *Raiders of the Lost Ark,* where there is a whole tomb full of snakes, or as in the theme of the snake pit, a herpatological horror some medieval folk liked to keep around to properly entertain their enemies, if they caught them. In the nineteenth century, being lowered into such a pit was even used to frighten mental patients out of their delusions, because it was thought to be worse than anything their imaginations could conjure. The following dream by a woman in her fifties has something of this flavor:

I am walking along a path, freshly dug earth to the left, trees. I look down . . . it is not grass, some fluffy material covered with tiny writhing snakes, all over everywhere. I look up ahead and there is a tree in mid-path with a huge fat snake coiled around a branch overhanging the path.

The paradisal garden atmosphere in this dream was so strong, that I checked back through the dreamer's journal to find another reference. It came to the same dreamer, and just two days before, the dream quoted on page 149. The dreamer was clearly experiencing the theriogenic zone I have been describing; its presence is signaled by "lots of animals" of one kind or of different kinds.

Sometimes the dreamer is bitten by a snake and has strange consciousness alterations in the dream from the "poison." Two asps appeared specifically in dreams. One was carried in hand by the male dreamer's stepmother (no comment) and the creative woman dreamer above was warned by a dream voice as she began an underworld journey, or *nekyia,* *"Watch out for buzzards and aspy stinging creatures."* Both of these animals would seem to belong to the darker side of the Great Mother archetype.

It may be important to note here that snake venoms are also used as medicines (for example, the homeopathic remedy, *Lachesis*). The sinister side of the snake has gotten such bad press that its positive dimensions are overlooked. The understory of the Tholos temple of the Asclepia at Epidaurus was probably filled with sacred serpents, like the legendary snake pit. These would be allowed to frequent the sleeping quarters, or *abaton,* where the patients slept, awaiting a healing dream. It was an especially auspicious omen if the snakes crawled on one while sleeping, or licked the dreamer's wounds. Having snakes in your bed is a very unpleasant thought for most modern folk, but it was a blessing for these ancients. The animals were sacred to Asclepius, the healing god, and still appear on his symbol, much like the caduceus, intertwined around a central staff and surmounted by wings, a winged globe, or a helmet.

One dreamer in my sample had a snake lick his wound and the Asclepian interpretation astounded the dreamer, but the dream actually seemed to initiate a phase of healing for him.

Other dreamers felt they had snakes crawling up and down their spines, as if to evoke the activity of the mysterious *kundalini* serpent from Yoga tradition. The two subtle channels of *prāna*, the *ida* and *piṅgalā,* look just like the caduceus's serpents coiled around the central channel of the spine, the *sushumnā.* The symbolism points to a profound symbolic connection between the serpent and the vital force of life itself. The yogi's task is to waken the dormant *kunda-lini* serpent (the spirit force asleep while the body lives), which is coiled around a phallus, or lingam, at the base of the spine, and bring it through that central channel. If the yogi's system is "pure," when the serpent reaches his head, or crown *chakra,* he will experience *samādhi* (or cosmic consciousness); if impure, something more like schizophrenia.

Curiously enough, in regard to this latter notion, several modern psychiatrists have reported experiences and dreams by their psychotic patients, of snakes crawling up and down their spines. Needless to say, few of them had any knowledge of the esoteric *kundalini* system.[20]

Flying snakes appeared a number of times in my dream sample, as if to defy their earthbound quality. Sometimes these images went along with instincts that seemed out of control in the person, or detached from ordinary existence.[21]

Mythology usually portrays serpents oppositionally to birds, terrestrial to celestial, as in the *Nagas* and *Garudas* of India.

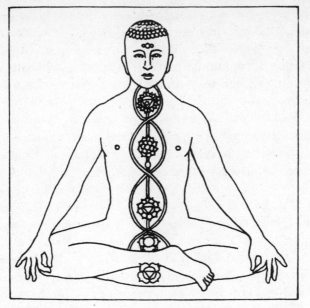

FIGURE 20. The Kundalini System & Serpent, *by Robin Larsen (drawing, 1984).*

Spirit and nature may oppose each other, the elements of the earth and air in contradiction. We think of the image of the eagle with the serpent in its claws. However, figures such as Quetzalcoatl, the Mesoamerican feathered serpent, seem to point toward a union of opposites, a coming together of the hereditary enemies, perhaps a clue to the secret similarities of reptile and bird, even to the union of spirit and matter.

If serpents symbolize some aspects of psychic energy, horses do as well. Horses may be either tame or wild. They are familiar, although not necessarily often encountered in the flesh by most people, but are more numerous in my sample than dogs or cats. For better or worse, it seems they have the connotation of an energy that "carries us" (or refuses to). They appear often in the dreams of those who do not ride actively, as well as those who do.

One woman who had not ridden for many years dreamed

weekly during her therapy of horses, especially ones that balked on the rider. Sometimes this happened while doing ordinary things like going downhill on a trail, but especially on entering an unknown place or a dark barn. There were currently no horses in her outer life, but there was no doubt either that concurrently her instincts were "balking," in opposition to her conscious mind. As time went on the dreams showed the conflict becoming more serious, before hints of resolution were to appear. Following is a very interesting sequence from these dreams:

> I'm in a field, planting. A group of riders enters on horseback. One horse goes berserk with a rider on him, attacks another horse with a woman rider. They go down, and I'm afraid she'll be killed under the weight of the horse. He rushes around the field, having dumped his rider. He comes at me, and I think I'm supposed to stop him but I'm afraid.

This dream shows the male, or masculine, style of control failing, and the horse not only throwing his own, but endangering another, woman rider. I have actually heard more than one woman riding or dressage instructor complain about the masculine style of control, which uses *force majeur* to try to control the beast, rather than winning its cooperation.

The dreams continued:

> There's a horse show. My nieces are longeing horses but they're wild and angry, out of control. My sister (their mother) goes to a stall but one backs up wildly against her. She surprises the horse by shoving it against a wall, which almost splinters. I admire her quick and aggressive action. Then I'm walking near a corral with a paper bag full of popcorn and candy. A black horse smells it and gets excited. He charges me breaking down the fence. The dream fades, but I'm scared.

Here the women have had their own chance, with mixed results. The dreamer associated her sister, however, with a more masculine style, often with a preconceived notion of how things should go; an expert Jungian analyst might call it the animus, an inner masculine personification that sometimes takes over in feminine psychology. The dreamer somewhat admires her sister's style, but the horses remain unruly and menacing, especially the black horse. About ten days later she dreamed the following:

> *An Indian chief is on a white stallion. The horse must be kept behind barriers. Later, though, I bring him into my kitchen. He's my friend, listens to me; but there's always the chance he'll act up.*

Here both the rider and the horse are male, but there is no overt violence. The Indian (animus) is more in touch with the animal, perhaps appropriately, its "chief." Although the white horse theoretically needs control, the dreamer's relation to him now is different. There is a friendship, and the horse is invited into a feminine space, the kitchen.

Following this came a dream of visiting the therapist's (my own) farm, where there are horses, and of being introduced to them (by my wife) in what seemed like a more safe and supportive atmosphere. She also dreamed of another potentially dangerous beast:

> *I've tamed a bear. He loves to be scratched and rubbed all over. People are surprised. He occasionally gets excited and I have to warn him not to stick his claws in me, to pull them in like a cat.*

The dreamer associated the bear with a novel she had just read (one of Robertson Davies's *Deptford Trilogy*), in which the bear, Felix, was a friend or spirit-guide to the hero. Perhaps this influence from literature, as well as her therapeutic work, was helping her to attune to her more instinctual side.

About a month after the Indian dream came one of those wonderful clarifying dreams that addressed the whole sequence:

> *I'm taking care of my sister's horse. It's in a stall, and seems restless, hungry and agitated. I climb up on the side of the stall to put its halter on. But he just walks out the stall door which I've left open. Then he talks and matter-of-factly tells me I've been trying to put on the wrong halter anyway. I've been trying to put a white halter on. He gets the right one (darker), and puts his head down so I can reach it.*

Here the horse belies his own membership in the category of "dumb beast," and shows there to have been an intelligence behind the refractory and stupid-seeming behavior all along. The dreamer had had an impaired relationship to her own instinct and intuition. The dreams were helping her find an improved rapprochement with the unconscious (the dark horse). The unknown one requires a dark halter.

I think of the biblical story of Balaam's ass, who balked three times along the way through the plains of Moab, although his master tried to flog him on. (It was the beast, not the master, who saw the angel with the drawn sword in the road, blocking his path.) When the conflict escalated, the ass, being forced, crushed Balaam's foot against a wall, then fell down. Balaam, enraged, began to beat her with a staff.

And the Lord opened the mouth of the ass, and she said unto Balaam, "What have I done unto thee, that thou hast smitten me these three times?" And Balaam said unto the ass, "Because thou hast mocked me: I would now there were a sword in mine hand, for now I would kill thee." And the ass said unto Balaam, "Am I not thine ass, upon which thou has ridden ever since I was thine unto this day? was I ever wont to do so unto

thee?" And he said, "Nay." Then the Lord opened the
eyes of Balaam and he saw the angel of the Lord
standing in the way, and his sword drawn in his hand:
and he bowed his head and fell flat on his face.[22]

Balaam had to change his direction and also to learn to trust
his animal's perception. In the series of dreams above, the
dreamer also had to learn to value the intelligence of her
beast and to value a more feminine, receptive style of relationship (the dark halter), right for her—not anybody else—to
the wisdom of the unconscious.

In *Memories, Dreams, Reflections* Jung told the story of a
woman who came to see him for an unusual therapeutic
encounter. Years before she had committed a murder for
which she was never caught, poisoning a friend to marry the
man whom they both loved. She felt that conscience was a
type of ephemeral thing that couldn't bother you if you
didn't let it. But things went badly. Her husband died early
in life. Her relationship with their son was poor. Finally she
began having trouble with her dog, and horses, which were
important to her. They became unruly, and her favorite
horse threw her badly. It was the uncanny behavior of the
animals that made her finally seek Jung and confess the
crime, hidden carefully all these years. The confession and
psychological insights that went with it initiated a change of
life for the woman.

A woman with a very different problem, in her early
twenties, and having twice dropped out of school, dreamed:

*I am in a valley encircled by mountains. My girlfriend and I
have a destination to get to. We are on horse-back, but my
horse is too small and weak. My legs are almost touching the
ground.*

This dream captures in a simple little metaphor the dreamer's "depression," as she described it. She had no motivation
to accomplish her elected goals. In a later section of the

dream she was given some therapeutic advice by that mysterious dream voice: *"Let your horse run with the wild horses."* It was understood this would restore her mount's vitality, and move her out of the impasse. She looked up in the dream *"and saw a hawk hovering above."* Her association was to spirit's freedom of flight. Subsequently in therapy, her decision to not return to school right away, although against external expectations and her own superego promptings, turned out to be "right"; and she experienced relief from a painful long-term neurotic symptom, which was one of the principal factors that brought her to therapy.

I have seen dream horses terribly neglected; one has forgotten to feed and care for them. Because in real life they are so often penned up and dependent on human care and concern, they well symbolize "neglected" areas of the instinctual psyche that need our awareness. They also may show the state of the relationship to the physical body. How well does the conscious psyche (rider) treat the body (horse)?

Dream horses resent maltreatment, throw the rider, or run away with the carriage. They have an ancient association to war, both bearing the predatory aggressors into peaceful communities, as in Mongol invasions or the symbolism of the horsemen of the Apocalypse, and also becoming tragic victims of human warfare, which they cannot understand. Sometimes this quality shows up in dream montages of wounded horses and other beasts that resemble Picasso's *Guernica*. In these images we see natural beauty and the nobility of living creation mutilated through human blindness.

THE NUMINOUS ANIMAL

This section carries the symbolism of the horse into an area central to our task of understanding dream animals.

One evening, when the long red sunset of Carolina was blazed out across its huge sky, the uncle took his niece

out into a pasture for some reason or other. There it was that she saw—really saw—the Mare. The Mare was standing on a low hill in all that flat landscape, silhouetted against the fiery backdrop of sunfall. All around the edges of her body she was made of molten bronze, so hot she was at each moment about to dissolve into the sky, which was her true element. Her head was contoured of knife-edged lines so fine it hurt to look at them . . . her eyes black as mirrors. The Mare said what the gods say: See and don't forget. Then, like all gods revealed, she shut down her revelation, so as not to burn up utterly the human eyes which had seen.[23]

The foregoing was a waking revelation, not a dream, but so was young Black Elk's, who saw in his great vision horses "with eyes like the daybreak star and manes of morning light." The numinous animal serves as a window to the transpersonal dimension. Its eyes, when seen through, open into the abyss, the realm of the *Nagual,* the secret cause.

If ordinary eyes are "windows to the soul," the eyes of such an animal may open deeper still to the spirit realm. The following two dreams were presented to me during the same week I had begun work on this chapter. (It should be noted that I alone knew of my inner meditation on beasts.) The first was presented neatly typed in a therapy session and the second, volunteered in a psychology class during a general discussion of dreams.

> *I am driving past a field near our home. Deer are out and I stop to watch them. They seem unafraid of my presence. Suddenly I lock eyes with a big, antlered buck. He holds my gaze, and as I look into his eyes, I feel a wonderful sense of calmness and permission to be there.*

It is important to know that this woman dreamer had anxieties about being "seen," and especially eye contact with

FIGURE 21. *Detail of horses "with eyes like the daybreak star and manes of morning light," by Robin Larsen, from the* Rhiannon Series *(detail of an untitled drawing, mixed media, 1989).*

men. In previous dreams she had experienced the fearfulness of visibility. We know from animal ethologists of the role of direct gaze in dominance hierarchies. Usually, before the "dominant male," all others must avert their gaze. Here the buck seems to serve as a "helping animal" for the dreamer. Clearly the type of the dominant male, but of a different species, the dream buck shows her the way to meet the eyes of males without automatic deference. An animal ordinary to the dreamer's environment (the woods are full of them this fall) acts in an extraordinary way.

The following dream shows a less-ordinary animal in an unusual setting:

I am in the state of Florida with majestic mountains surrounding me. I see an eagle flying in a circling motion way up. I feel the wind blowing oh so gently and powerfully. I say, "What's an eagle doing in Florida?" He circles and lands where I am standing. He stands as high as I do. We exchange glances and travel deep within each other's eyes to a place of peace and calmness. Every shape and color is real and vivid. I notice the feathers of the head so bold and neat, the strong upright chest. I feel I could stay within those eyes forever. Then he ascends above my head. He opens his wings and I feel the wind. I can hardly believe my eyes; I suddenly see ten white doves sitting on the wings, five on each wing.

As the dreamer told me the dream (for which she had almost no personal associations), she was overwhelmed by feelings, and her body began to vibrate uncontrollably. I have seen similar reactions from other people to transpersonal images: they may function as a literal "power source." Like many who experience "big" dreams this woman had told no one else, for fear of being laughed at or misunderstood. Yet the sharing may sometimes be necessary, completing a circuit between the imaginal and the physical worlds.[24]

The references throughout the dream between the eagle

and the wind show us his spiritual connection. We think of Gwaihir, Windlord, from Tolkien's stories, who saves Gandalf from Saruman's tower. And countless folktales celebrate the high flight and keen gaze of the eagle. But it is the incongruous presence of the doves that signals a Christian reference to the lord of the winds in the esoteric sense: He is the Holy Spirit who breathes life into all things (in Hebrew, *Ruach*, in Greek, *Pneuma*). "The wind bloweth where it listeth," said John, in the most pneumatic of the gospels, "and thou hearest the voice thereof, and knowest not whence it cometh or whither it goeth, so is every one born of the Spirit" (John 3:8).[25]

At Jesus's baptism, the spirit of God descends on him in the form of a dove, and it is a dove that is sent forth from Noah's ark of beasts. We remember it returns with an olive branch in its beak, the perennial symbol of peace and, along with the rainbow, of the covenant between God and man.

Can a dream combine totemistic and Christian symbolism, eagles (hawks) and doves, emblems of war and of peace? Apparently so, and with no apologies for the syncretism. In this dream the spirit seems to wish to come to the dreamer urgently, so he has assembled his symbolic clothing from different wardrobes of the psyche. The tradition of birds as spiritual symbols is ancient and far-reaching. Are we asked to discern an ever-deepening symbolic network of comparisons: eagle to dove, high flight to deep gaze, the seeing through eye to the transparent, omnipresent wind? But the impact of a big dream such as this on personal psychology is enormous.

Campbell wrote of the role of the animal eye and its symbolism in the paleolithic caves. It is associated with the sun, or solar eye, and also with the lion and the eagle. It is the sun door, the "shaman's doorway," the passage through the world of matter into spirit. Jung, in a number of places in his writings, also explored this aspect of animal and spiritual symbolism.[26]

Many other animal-spiritual manifestations appear in my dream sample. One woman therapist in her thirties dreamed of

> *a male and female lion. The lioness approaches and begins to tell me about surgery, and I see she has a wound in her hip. The meat is gone and I can see the bone. She is licking the wound and then begins to lick me all over.*

The dreamer awoke with a mixture of awe and amusement, tickled by the memory of the rough tongue. The licking of wounds is associated with healing, as well as nurturing of the young. The dream presents an animal version of the "wounded healer" motif, and suggests a comparison to the mysterious Fisher King of the Grail Castle, who was wounded in the thigh. The healer-therapist felt somewhat wounded in her healing ability, yet here she found a wounded animal who offered to help her (a little different from the fairy-tale version, where the hero initially must help the animal).

Lions appear in my dream sample a number of times, sometimes fierce, but often paradoxically gentle, as is the great lion Aslan in C. S. Lewis's *The Chronicles of Narnia*. Narnia is a land reached through a magical wardrobe (and other interesting apertures between the worlds). All the animals speak, and are major characters in the stories, along with the human children protagonists. The lion Aslan is the king of beasts, naturally, and symbolizes the ruling spiritual principle of the adventure. In Lewis's Christian perspective, the lion is a Christ figure, who becomes a willing victim in a great sacrifice, to save one of the children. Christ's animal personifications include the lion, lamb, unicorn, fish, and, esoterically, the serpent.[27]

In a more archaic association of the lion, another woman healer presented a simple, but powerful dream the week I was finishing this chapter:

> *There is a dishevelled, cat or lion-faced woman, with cat-*
> *whiskers, standing in a doorway. She looks angry.*

We did active imagination work with the figure of the cat-woman as starting image. The dreamer at first did not like her at all, especially because of her angry quality. The imaginal figure dropped to all fours and became a literal lion with terrifying power who tore up the room; whereupon I suggested she might want to get out. In the imaginal forest at night, the anger changed to a kind of mystical energy.

Subsequently, the woman, who had a special talent for holding on to and working with mental images, found this symbol connected her to an energy source, with a power and vitality that she could feel in her daily life. This may be the same experience that in totemistic societies continues to keep a clan or group connected to the living energic fountainhead of their animal sponsor. More than "mere symbol," the totem is a vital force on the imaginal level. But there is more to the story. Just two weeks before, the woman had presented a dream of *"the sun, so huge and bright you could not keep your eyes open."* She thought the dream took place in Egypt, as had some previous ones, with barges on a great river and scenes from life there. I asked her if she knew the figure from Egyptian mythology of Sekhmet, the lion-headed woman goddess; she did not, and she did not have any awareness of the ancient mythological affinity of the great goddess for the sun or for lions. However, she told her grown daughter about the dreams. The daughter was surprised and intrigued because she had experienced, and even drawn, the same imaginal figure a few months before. She had never shown her mother the lion-headed (and whiskered) woman, with the sun arranged as a halo. Actually Egypt abounded with cat goddesses, including Pekhet, also usually shown lion headed, and Bubastis, mistress of house cats[28] (see Figure 22).

If the previous dream figure shows a solar-animal-goddess affinity, the following one shows the lunar equivalent, hint-

FIGURE 22. *Sekhmet, Lady of the Place of the Beginning of Time. Egyptian, ca. 1250 B.C., approximately the time of Rameses II.* (PHOTO COURTESY OF JEAN HOUSTON AND ROBERT MASTERS.)

ing that more than one ancient form of the goddess is abroad in our time. A woman in her forties dreamed:

> It's very early in the morning, barely light enough to see. I'm by an old road in the country, near woods and a meadow (hilly). I'm with an older "father" man and feel protective towards him. We stop by a tree and I see some beautiful bucks, lying majestically in the field, barely visible in the dim light. I try to point them out to him. Suddenly a dark van pulls up and I realize it holds hunters, who want to kill the deer. With a sense of horror I warn the older man to get ready for the bang of the guns, but nothing happens. There's confusion, then coming away from the deer, emerging from the shadows, is a mysterious girl. Apparently she's been there all along and the hunters didn't dare shoot. She has white makeup on her face, an enigmatic smile, a strange primitive grass skirt, and black hair. I'm intrigued by this wood nymph creature. I ask her, "You saved the animals, didn't you?" She's so shy and wild and mysterious, and just keeps coming past us, but she smiles warmly and I know I'm right.

This figure is perhaps less specifically emblemed than the lion goddess, but her white face, surreal serenity, and association with the antlered deer suggest Artemis (Diana for the Roman world). The dreamer herself wrote, "She's some kind of pagan goddess looking out for animals and other wild creatures. A very beautiful and mystical dream." Her identity as a transpersonal figure is underlined by the fact that this dream came after literally hundreds of animal dreams, over the space of about a year and a half, by the same woman dreamer. I have never seen anything quite as symbolically dramatic and continuous as this creative woman artist's dream journal. The animal dreams included many horses (related earlier in this chapter) as well as bats, bears, deer, elephants, fish, lions, hawks, mice, and snakes—a rather complete symbolic menagerie.

"Have you hugged an animal today?" a New Age bumper

sticker might say, or better yet, "Have you indwelt an animal today?" Our generation must find a "meditation of the creatures" for this century. In his experiential workshops shaman-teacher Michael Harner often begins with reconnecting modern people with their totemic animal, or animal spirit helper. Likewise, Gallegos, whose shamanic system was introduced in Chapter 5, helps people locate animals on their internal totem pole and guides them in developing a healing relationship with and among the creatures within.[29]

It is no surprise how readily we reconnect with an animal in this archaic, yet spiritual way. Our mythological roots are deep and yet alive.

In personal mythology workshops my wife, Robin, and I have helped people explore their animal roots with similar results. We have found people have plant and even mineral "allies," too. It is only through specific and personal connections such as these that we truly are in a position to find ourselves at home, rather than in exile, in the world of nature. Then collectively, we may come into a better position to "renegotiate our contracts" with the vast sentient kingdom, the ecology that surrounds and sustains us—within, we now see, no less than without.

Chapter 8

THE INNER CAST OF CHARACTERS

And he asked him, What is thy name? And he answered, saying, My name is Legion: for we are many.[1]

—Mark 5:9

We walk through ourselves, meeting robbers, ghosts, giants, old men, young men, wives, widows, brothers-in-love. But always meeting ourselves.

—Stephen Dedalus, in *Ulysses*

Some significant figures that may appear within the context of the inner mythic journey have already been mentioned: guardian figures, the lord of the abyss, animals that represent spiritual powers within us, and a glimpse of the inner guide who helps us find our way (the subject of the next chapter). This chapter introduces the concept of inner characters. In addition to symbolic analogues of the world of nature—mountains, oceans, springs, beasts and birds of the mind—a magic theater is always at play within us, at once human and divine.

For each person the constellation is different, yet as archetypal psychology assures us, the characters are recognizable: the hero or heroine figures we have already touched on and their counterparts, the villains, who partake of the shadow element. But there are also wise old men and women in our inner theater; tricksters—including deceivers as well as the helpful clown sidekick (more on this in the next section)—contrasexual figures who open our creativity or guide us toward potential soul mates, but also false tempters or temptresses to be learned from but ultimately bypassed; figures who exemplify a realm of activity such as crafts or the warrior domain; healers; our twin or the figure of the double (Doppelgänger); and many others.

At first glance we seem to be in a specifically human realm, whose characters exemplify the personality characteristics we find in the endless parade of our fellow human beings. But mythology shows us this realm is also contaminated with the divine—and the demonic. Zeus, for example, often acts like a human tyrant, as well as a divine power—lord of the thunderbolt and the upper air. Hera, his consort, engages in very recognizable human soap opera in the form of family arguments with her spouse and children yet, at the same time, is the feminine divinity who rules the family and social propriety. Throughout the mythology of the world, in fact, we are introduced to deities who border on the human (including Yahweh of the Old Testament with his demiurgic fits and starts of creation and notable jealousy) and humans who are ever threatening to cross the threshold to the divine. Heroes like Heracles come to embody an archetypal quality such as strength, and ancestral race progenitors like Erechtheus of Athens and Don of the Celts gradually become deified, as history and myth conspire selectively to forget their human flaws and worship their archetypal virtues.

THE PERMEABLE SELF

To understand this intriguing but baffling mix of divine and anthropomorphic metaphors, I began to look again to the most ancient mythology: shamanism. What emerges is a

FIGURE 23. *Other selves: person and persona.* (PHOTO BY ROBIN LARSEN.)

model I call the permeable self. The basic nature of this world view is that a human being dwells simultaneously in two worlds, the familiar natural one and a spiritual one. The natural world encloses or enfolds a spiritual one "within" it. The spiritual world—although seemingly insubstantial—is recognized as more potent than this natural one, enfolding it in turn, for the spiritual world is thought of as identical with the realities existing before birth and after the death of the physical body. In traditional societies, the spiritual almost always has priority. In addition, the bright world subtly guides and interfuses events in the three-dimensional world, especially events that become timeless, luminous, or intensely meaningful—in short, mythic. "I knew the real was yonder, and the darkened dream of it was here," said the great Sioux shaman Black Elk when he saw a vision in the clouds that was evoked by the enactment of his own childhood vision.[2]

The mythic world is "within" in the form of our dreams and visions, but also "without" when the outer world seems full of archetypal coincidences and we enact our myths (not always to our advantage, as was discussed earlier). In addition, part of the power and privilege of a human being, whether we refer to this as magic or religion, is to control (magic) or to propitiate (religion) the powers of the spiritual realm. The shaman is the prototype of the traveler between worlds and also brings the messages of each to the other (his Hermes-like quality). In possession (which I call "mythic identity"), however, the shaman does more than travel, and may assume the role of trance medium, embodying, as it were, a spiritual power, and loaning it his human voice box to broadcast the spirit's message to the human community. Furthermore, in this view, everyone is subject to spiritual invasion, which may result, on the one hand, in physical or mental illness (if the spirits are malevolent, or even rebuking benevolent ones) or, on the other, in the human privilege, as it is conceived, of manifesting a kind of supernatural power, for example, in the possession of oracles by tutelary deities for the sake of prophecy or healing. This is what the Greeks meant by our overused word *enthusiasm,* literally, "filled by spirit."

In the psychology of this ancient model, a human being has no real or fixed identity, but a kind of hollow space or receptivity that may become filled with spiritual or archetypal energy. When a young man going into battle is filled with the numinous power of the bear or the eagle that has come to him in vision, this might be seen as a positive possession. The legendary prowess of the totem animal, which has become his own, enables him to transcend human fear and frailty. However, when someone becomes obsessed or identified with an animal in a psychotic way (such as certain hebephrenic schizophrenics who think they are chickens, for example), the possession is unhealthy, indeed, because in the process he loses his human autonomy, the ability to choose his own behavior. In traditional societies in these latter cases, some variety of exorcism may be employed, visualized as a kind of spiritual eviction procedure, whereby the unwelcome tenant is magically asked to quit the premises. It is curious to see this ancient (and, most moderns feel, superstitious) belief surfacing in modern cinematic myths such as *The Exorcist*. People still seem to be toying—fascinated and horrified—with the ancient myth of possession by an archetypal power.[3]

A PERSONAL EXPERIENCE OF INNER CHARACTERS

When anyone first visits New York (or any other large city), it is not unusual to find an interesting variety of what some call "street crazies," people who wear old costumes, sometimes carry multiple shopping bags, and brandish naked umbrellas—the subway sorcerer's wand of power, I suppose. In 1964, while working as a novice therapist for the New York State Department of Mental Hygiene, I came on what I thought was the ultimate in this line: a man attired in a cloak, strange broad-brimmed sombrero, and wraparound Italian sunglasses. To complete the picture, his lower face was covered by the traditional bandit's kerchief. He moved along Broadway with a peculiar slinking motion, seeming to sneak from one vantage to another, whereupon he would suddenly stand up straight, peer around in the hackneyed scout's posture of hand over eyes, as if beholding some wonder. Occasionally he would blast on a police whistle concealed beneath his kerchief, which made the nearby busy folk, on their urban pilgrimage, almost jump out of their skins. Now and then he would stop someone, peer into his face and ask him, sphinxlike (and to their intense discomfiture) some homemade riddle. Fascinated by this living myth, I followed at a safe distance. He seemed to me a veritable incarnation of a strange being I had first seen in an Al Capp comic strip called "The Fleegle Eyed Floogle."

To my not so great amazement he entered the doorway of the clinic where I worked, and went upstairs. He sat in the waiting room and then obediently went into his appointment with the psychiatric social worker in an adjoining cubicle. From her I was later able to obtain the thick record of this man's clinical history, which provided such fascinating reading that I remained in the office long after hours, caught in rapt attention. I particularly loved one scene I came across, described in clinical language, in which (in full regalia) he climbed into the empty bathtub of a major metropolitan psychiatric hospital and would not come out. Furthermore, this modern Diogenes in Floogle's clothing engaged in philosophical dialogue on the meaning of existence with the supervising psychiatrist, whose repartee was not only pale by comparison, but made him look like the straight man to a figure out of Samuel Beckett.

The case history was a human mixture of mythos and pathos. From a poor socioeconomic background, the man had a series of economic, personal, and marital failures that led up to his rebirth as a mythic character. After a while, with nothing left to lose, he had evidently decided that reality was so ridiculous, he was needed to remind everyone of the absurdity of what we call "normality." Half-willing, and half-coerced by an involuntary possession, he came to incarnate his strange alter ego. I felt I was peering into the very genesis of personality. Do we make it up? Does it make us up? Who are we anyway?

I will admit to an infatuation for the freedom of thought and expression this man enjoyed in the midst of outer circumstances most of us would consider intolerably confining, including mental hospitalization. By living out a myth he had freed himself from our conventional myths of social constraint. He was an artist of life, with a total commitment that makes a chosen, delimited art as a field of endeavor seem like a compromise. But on the other hand, I wondered, was his art communicable, could it be appreciated? Certainly innovative street people liven up the otherwise bleak sidewalks of Manhattan, and I pitied the psychiatrists who tried to swap koans with him—although it is possible they needed someone to shake their role-induced mantle of superiority. Then I came across some copies of poetic letters to his mother about human tragedy, meaning, and love that—though rife with misspellings—were extraordinarily moving. His poetic style reminded me of the works of John Donne.

That night, returning home, I sank into a troubled sleep and experienced what may be called a big dream. In it I was inside "the House of Many Rooms," a theme from dreams since my early childhood.

Around me is an amazing assortment of mythical characters: clowns, dwarves, puppets and masked beings, giant talking birds, and wicked tricksters. With me is my newly wedded wife, shy and somewhat frightened. I am told that she now will have to marry one of the beings that surrounded us. "Me," they all yell in their cacophony of voices, "Me," each one whines, pleads, cajoles, or threatens. There is no escape, and I am powerless to prevent it.

I awoke from this dream in a kind of nightmarish terror. My first thought was of the fearful fragmentation of schizophrenia. "So that's what it feels like," I thought, "maybe

I'm going crazy." Then I remembered my thoughts on retiring to bed, which were a romantic kind of envy for the purity of life evinced by my strange mythic figure and which now gave me a context for understanding my dream. Fortunately I had just entered Jungian analysis. I understood what I had experienced was an inner metaphorical event, perhaps with an instructive aspect. My "wife" in this context was to be interpreted as my anima, or soul, not an actual person. The beings were my "inner cast of characters"; in and of themselves, none were fully human. The reason I awoke with fear was that for my soul to become identical—married—with any part-personality would be a psychological disaster. And that was indeed what had happened to my poor, terrible-wonderful Floogle.

To be human and fully autonomous, we need our many masks. The Greek word *persona* means "mask"; hence a "personality" is a plurality of our inner masks, not a single one. The figures in my dream were inner "masks," or potentially individual aspects of self, but my resolve in the dream, automatically coming from the feelings, was correct. "No, none of you can 'have' her" (the soul). In this aspect— and since then I have seen the same inner iconography in the lives and dreams of schizophrenics—when there is war between the part-personalities for control, they indeed manifest as cruel, dismembering forces. Later, as I studied the shaman journey, I recognized the relationship of my inner characters to the "crowd" of beings that comes to dismember the shaman during his or her inner crisis.

Psychologically, if the central unitive principle of the ego has lost control, a cacaphony of inner voices and subpersons emerges; we are literally self-devoured by our own plurality. Thus the ego either "falls to pieces," or, as we have seen, embarks on an inner hero journey, along the stages of which these powers may be encountered. If the inner rite of transformation is satisfactorily completed, there is a renewal of the unitive principle, and a higher version of internal harmony comes to reign. The shaman is revitalized and renewed after the encounter with his or her inner "demons."

However, in mythology there are many other ways in which the drama of internal conflict may play itself out, hence the endless variety of stories in which we can imagine all the characters as parts of ourselves. For example, the anima, or soul, of a man may have a naive, overly idealized relationship to life; then the dark figure Jung calls the shadow, left out of conscious life, dwells with waxing malevolence in the underworld. We have here the preconditions for a kind of Persephone myth in which the image of the spring maiden, innocently plucking flowers in the beautiful daylight meadow, is surprised by the dark lord of the abyss, who suddenly breaks from the ground in his fiery chariot and carries her into the dark. A depression invades life, and creativity dries up (as Demeter mourns for her daughter and withholds the life principle from the grain).

In a dream that was very frightening to him, a young student dreamed that *"my friends and I were all roller-skating happily down the Thruway to a rock concert. Suddenly great cracks in the earth opened up and began to swallow us one by one."* Eliciting his associations, I was able to find some things about the characters of his friends that appear as the cast of this simple-seeming dream. He and his friends often went to concerts in someone's van or car, all of them very drunk and stoned. The newspapers not too long before had been full of awful tragedies (the dark side of Dionysus) involving youthful intoxication and sudden death, usually via automobiles. His conscious feeling was, "It couldn't happen to me," but the dream scared him and woke him up with the starkness of its underworld imagery. We began to talk about the useful concept of designated drivers and other examples of "square"-world prudence that might be applicable.

When one or another of our internal characters, whether the lover of inebriated pleasure, the prude, the paranoid, the emperor, or the child, "takes over" we have a potential catastrophe. As I meditated on my subject, I began to see that a "personality" is indeed a kaleidoscopic overlay and interpenetration of many subpersonalities or inner characters. These need to be in constant interplay or dialogue, in which there is an ongoing compensation for the one-sidedness any one of these characters may represent. In effect, the actual dynamics within our personality often unfolds as mythic drama or dialogue.

Jung's inner cast of characters is probably the most mythological of all. He sometimes rather whimsically referred to them as "the little people." The persona, or mask, is the first layer of the personality, an ideal version of ourselves turned outward. It is the self we like to show the world and the one that best conforms to our social role. Behind and within, however, is the sinister shadow. (Being solid physical beings, we all cast one, Jung said.) Like Freud's id, or Perls's underdog, the shadow may undermine our ideals and our best intentions. It is the prototype of the beast, the renegade, the undoer. Coming to terms with it, Jung said, is the start of the process of becoming whole (individuation).

Among the most intriguing and useful of Jung's formulations are the contrasexual characters, the inner ghosts, he calls anima and animus. We carry around with us ideals and expectations in the form of images. Almost invariably these images are attracted to people of the opposite sex and externalized, or, in psychological language, "projected" on them. The image I always have of the anima at work, for example, is Tinkerbell, the little airborne sprite in *Peter Pan,* who sprinkles a kind of illusion-producing pixie dust on people, sometimes right in their eyes. For men, the effect of the anima is a glamour or illusion that surrounds actual women, and transforms them from ordinary people into creatures of mystery and inexhaustible wonder. This is sometimes a blessing, but at other times quite the opposite, in that the glamour may conceal someone not adequate to the projected image or perhaps, even more seriously, impair a potentially creative relationship between human individuals. On the psychological—not sociological—level, the role of the anima in masculine psychology is to open the psyche to creativity.

The animus, according to Jung, is less magical and more substantial. He incarnates archetypal attributes of the masculine principle such as status or credibility or an ethical sense. For a woman, the animus is imbued with qualities of her father, or even an idealized Father from religious tradition. At its negative pole the animus can lead to impoverishment of creativity and to fixed ideas. At its positive pole, it is a source of values and interior guidance. Some post-Jungian thinkers such as Irene Claremont de Castillejo have emphasized the animus's role as a guide or bringer of illumination. Again the figure contains potential blessings as well as the curses of limitation. John Sanford wrote an interesting book on this subject called *Invisible Partners,* which explores the subtle aspects of relationship in the influence of these "little people."[4]

The Self is the psychological source of the God-image, said Jung, and exists in all, irrespective of the particular religious tradition of the person. It is as if each person bears within himself or herself a fragment of the divine. The wrong kind of identification with this inner figure can lead to the worst megalomanias and paranoid religious inflation. On the positive side, the Self sponsors our internal growth toward wholeness, embodied in myths such as the quest for the Holy Grail; and generates the transpersonal images at the root of world religions, the Savior, the Saint, and the Bodhisattva. Again, it is not the presence of the archetypal figure, but our relationship to it that seems to determine whether its effect is benevolent or destructive.

As I studied cases of multiple personality, such as *Three Faces of Eve* and *Sybil,* I learned many fascinating things. The subpersonalities acted "as if" they were real people when they were in control. The manifestation was accompanied by all kinds of "personality characteristics," voice, body language, style of posture and movement, and personal idiosyncrasies. Eve White didn't drink, Eve Black could enter hard-drinking "chugalug" contests. Eve Black had an allergy to nylon stockings that Eve White did not share. Every time she "came out," the stockings Eve White had put on and comfortably worn would annoyingly begin to itch (an interesting comment on how allergies may relate to our personalities).

When handwriting samples of the three subpersonalities were submitted to experts for analysis, they were able to read the personality characteristics correctly from the samples, but the experts did not guess that the samples actually came from the same person. Psychiatrists and psychologists have become fascinated by these cases because they speak to us of the very genesis of that walking enigma we call a "personality." What and who are we at root? Can we indeed be pluralities or committees as well as "individuals" (which usually is taken to mean entities not capable of being further divided)?

Our very language takes up the topic when we talk about a "together" or "not very together" personality. The implication is that we all have inner committees, and we are healthy when they (mostly) agree, and unhealthy when they do not, especially when they disagree in serious ways. The other enigma that emerges is that in multiple personality, at least, the fragments of the self actually are recognizable people. They may not be whole or healthy but they are seemingly human, with names, style, preferences, and personal history. Jung must be credited with the first clear formulation of this principle, that the personality breaks up into persons in at least one of its modes of fragmentation; whatever the "stuff" of the psyche, even in pieces, it forms recognizable people.

On a theoretical level it is tempting to see the above "personifying tendency" as consonant with the holographic principle. Like the hologram, fragments of the picture resemble the whole (contain a model of what it means to be a "whole personality"). As in the fragments of a holographic negative, however, the pieces are blurry; they are not as clear as a fully integrated or individuated person would be. (Do the truly striking—clear—people in our lives go more deeply into the nature of what it means to be human?) Somehow the fragmentary or partial people in the teeming human encounter slip away and are more easily forgotten. But there is a paradox here, because people that are incomplete in a powerful way violate the rule and are remembered; herein lies at least one gateway to understanding the relevance of myth to personality. People who devote their lives to enacting a tragic flaw are the cocreators of both great drama and life as we know it.[5]

THE DIVIDED SELF

In about the third year of my psychotherapeutic practice, I encountered a clinical example of the subject to which this chapter is addressed.[6] What I recount here is the aspect of my client's journey that shows—in a vivid way—what it feels like to have one's inner characters activated, and the exciting, sometimes frightening, zone where they touch the mythic. In this case the woman in therapy, whom I shall call Betsy, kept a detailed personal journey of her experiences, which included dreams as well as reflections on her own experience. The story also has a happy ending, in that the dissociation was relatively brief and the therapeutic remedies that were used, efficacious.

Betsy sought therapeutic help for an acute case of claustrophobia, especially when she was in social situations from which there was "no escape" (i.e., a classroom once class began, or public transportation once the bus or train was rolling). The events related here happened after about three months of treatment.

Betsy came to group therapy on this particular day manifesting what almost seemed the signs of a psychotic episode. Although normally she was very self-possessed and composed, her very continuity of consciousness seemed to be fragmented. She made peculiar remarks, was deeply serious one moment and giggling the next (known as "inappropriate affect," this is often associated with schizophrenia). Members of the group were quite surprised by the radical alteration from her usual mode of behavior and expressed this. She would agree that she was "acting funny" one moment, and deny it the next.

We move to her psychological journal entry recorded the next day, to see how this kind of thing feels from the inside. She wrote,

> My head felt strange, maybe fuzzy. . . . Things were changing quickly. . . . I was fluctuating between laughter and depression. I was feeling very self-conscious and hostile because everyone refused to respond in keeping up with my feelings . . . my own deep primitive feelings. . . . I couldn't involve myself, characters were popping up inside me. I wanted to say, "George, you bore me," to George in a southern drawl. I wanted to be the Wicked Witch of the West to Sally. "I'll get you, my pretty, and your little dog Toto, too."

While leading the group I became aware that something rather drastic was happening in this one person's psyche. I verified that she had taken no psychoactive substances—although her state of consciousness was not unlike an LSD trip. I wondered if it were possible for an acute psychotic episode to come on so—drastically—fast. Two considerations affected my next move, which was to rearrange my schedule rapidly so as to see her for a private session of about three hours. The first was that there was no external "precipitating incident," the psychological alterations were coming from within. The second was that in my training with Grof I had learned that, whether pharmaceutically prompted or not, such experiences must be allowed full space to emerge. Also—this I learned from Jungian analyst Whitmont—timing is important. Like the blacksmith in the old saw, working his materials, the wise therapist "strikes while the iron is hot."

As the session started, it seemed difficult for her to speak. As she tells it in her own words,

> I asked Stephen to pull the shade, I felt the characters taking over, wanting to speak. My own voice was out of place . . . weak and strong. If I were to speak at all it would have to be a character. I was very torn between letting the characters out and handling the roles properly. I tried to tell him in sign language that I couldn't speak. He didn't understand. I was physically sitting on the voices. Then I managed to say "character" and partially explained how I was feeling. I told him about Sally and the Wicked Witch of the West.

Sally was a woman who had been in the group, with a somewhat bubbly Pollyanna-like quality. The main thing that had been happening was that Betsy felt witchlike to Sally, whom she wanted to attack, insult, or even literally tear to pieces. Being (usually) a more gentle person with good habitual social controls, Betsy held back—mostly. But what was inside was powerful enough to leak through; Sally was frightened. When inner characterology becomes involved, one can indeed act badly "out of character." (Apologizing later, we might use the old favorite, "I don't know what got into me.") Group therapy is efficacious because it allows us to project inner characters on other members of the group. If the group is a successful one it will provide the context for "working through"—related to "seeing through"—those dynamics.

As I began to get a sense of what was happening, I encouraged Betsy to act out the witch. This she did without further prompting, in a truly fear-invoking performance, frightening herself, sole protagonist, and me, sole member of the audience and a somewhat green therapist, with the power of what seemed to be speaking through her. I remember particularly the lines "I'll get you, my pretty!" and "Do you want to be torn in pieces?"

You may recall this terrible figure from *The Wizard of Oz*. Dorothy and her companions, the Scarecrow, the Tin Woodman, and the Cowardly Lion, are given a perilous assignment by the Wizard, before he will grant their requests. It is to find and slay the Wicked Witch. The original story version describes the witch as follows:

> Now the Wicked Witch of the West had but one eye, yet that was as powerful as a telescope, and could see everywhere. So, as she sat in the door of her castle she happened to look around and saw Dorothy lying asleep, with her friends all about her. They were a long distance off, but the Wicked Witch was angry to find them in her country; so she blew upon a silver whistle that hung around her neck.
>
> At once there came running to her from all directions a pack of great wolves. They had long legs and fierce eyes and sharp teeth.
>
> "Go to those people," said the Witch, "and tear them to pieces."[7]

The wolves came, but the Tin Woodman managed to kill them with his ax. But the witch blew her whistle again, summoning wild crows with instructions to "tear out their eyes and tear them to pieces." Again the menace was beaten back, this time, appropriately enough, by the Scarecrow. The Witch flew into a rage and summoned a swarm of bees to "sting them to death," but again the companions survived. Finally, using a powerful magic spell, she sent winged monkeys, who managed to capture them, imprisoning Dorothy and the Lion, and (temporarily) destroying the Tin Woodman and the Scarecrow—dropping the one onto sharp rocks from a great height and "unstuffing" the other (the threatened dismemberment). But Dorothy herself was unhurt because of the mark the Good Witch had put on her forehead.[8]

A few years ago I took my young daughter to see the original version of *The Wizard of Oz,* the same film the client had seen in her childhood. Whenever the Wicked Witch appeared— so potent is this figure for children—little sobs and whimperings could be heard throughout the theater. Betsy remembered being a child and begging to leave the theater, because she was so frightened by the witch.

The symbolism of the terrible or devouring mother is familiar from myths the world over: Kali, divine demoness of the Hindu pantheon with her necklace of skulls and cup filled to the brim with blood; the weapon-wielding and bloodthirsty Morrigan from Celtic mythology; and Baba Yaga, the Russian ogress whose house is surrounded by the bones of her victims. (We are dealing here with one of those personifications of death introduced in Chapter 6, the universe, mother of all that lives, who, in her aspect of death, devours her own children.) This figure was awake and alive in Betsy during this time.

Jung wrote of this figure, "The so-called Oedipus complex with its famous incest tendency changes at this level into a 'Jonah-and-the-Whale complex,' which has any number of variants, for instance the witch who eats children, the wolf, the ogre, the dragon and so on."[9] Psychologically, we return to the matrix of creation for rebirth, but first we must let her eat us. What allowed this client to "work through" the encounter with this formidable figure was the creation of a safe and sheltered space—the ritual enclosure of the therapeutic situation—to allow room for the feelings and their dramatic enactment (see Chapter 2).

In the dream she brought to the therapy session she had, indeed, just encountered both devouring and death:

I am walking down a street with K. [her husband]. *I know death is there, behind walls or around the corner, just waiting for the right moment. It is going to finish me. I challenge death to come out: "Come on out, come on out, I'll devour you."*

What is peculiar is that her statement in the dream is the inverse of what we expect, death devours us, not we it. But in enacting the witch as powerfully as she did, she became identical with it, annexing some of its dreadful power to herself. Following the enactment she said, "I felt as if something had been yanked out of me. I was dazed and shaking and weak." Thus the healing efficacy of psychodrama—in this case with an archetypal aspect. But there is more to the story.

Already, the experience Betsy had in the beginning of the group, and several days leading up to it, was a kind of dismemberment, the very thing the Wicked Witch was threatening. She came apart—into her part-selves. Betsy had to go through several characters that came out that day, illustrated in Figure 24. They included (1) Louisa, soft-spoken and beautiful, (2) Cora, an angry, complaining bitch (as described), and (3) the archetypal witch. It was obvious as we worked with these personifications that Louisa was close to her ego-ideal, whereas Cora lay squarely in the shadow. Both figures, although opposites, were human. She could, in fact, at that time and more deeply in subsequent sessions, identify them as present in her daily psychology.

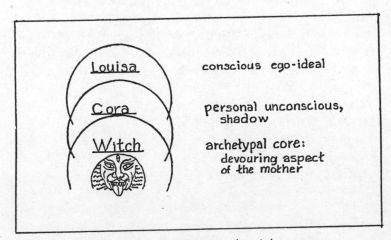

FIGURE 24. *Diagram of feminine archetypes, the witch.*

The witch, however, was a totally different order of being. To meet the dark side of a goddess is not easy (see Chapter 6). The fragmentation Betsy experienced seems to have been brought on simply by proximity to this figure, as if there were a nimbus of destructive power about her. By itself the fear-inspiring enactment was not enough. She herself had to go through "the death experience." Claustrophobia and panic surfaced in an extreme form in the therapeutic situation, worse than ever before. I encouraged her, however, to abreact with it, give in to the trembling, crying, and nausea, which arose in powerful waves. At times she was not sure whether she was dying, giving birth, or being born—as I had seen in Groffian sessions at the Maryland Psychiatric Research Center.

Eventually the waves subsided. She was able to breathe more freely (the claustrophobia had unbearable suffocation feelings with it). Physically she said she felt like "there was no more tension anywhere, inner peacefulness, going with the flow." She also used the word *together,* which implied just that blessed ordinary state we so easily take for granted. She was interested to find two other dreams recorded immediately before this dramatic session, prefiguring the as-yet-unknown outcome. In one she was rescuing a little girl, her sister. In another she was *"in a classroom giving birth. It was a matter-of-fact experience."* But really, her experience of giving birth was a matter of metaphor—not fact. She was giving birth to herself, as well as somehow saving the child within her.

The acute onset of schizophrenia or multiple personality that had seemed so imminent was no longer discernible. Had she only come apart for the sake of the experience—and ultimately to come together again in a new way?[10]

Later, I found this quote in Jung, which summarizes many aspects of Betsy's case:

Now it is a fact amply confirmed by psychiatric experience that all parts of the psyche, inasmuch as they

possess a certain autonomy, exhibit a personal character, like the split-off products of hysteria and schizophrenia, mediumistic "spirits," figures seen in dreams,
etc. Every split-off portion of libido, every complex,
has or is a (fragmentary) personality. At any rate that is
how it looks from a purely observational standpoint.
But when we go into the matter more deeply we find
that they are really archetypal formations.[11]

Meeting the "core" of her complex—the dark aspect of the
goddess—freed Betsy from its spell and ultimately set her on
the next step of her journey to wholeness, without the
claustrophobia. "Here the ego makes contact with the . . .
archetypes which have a compensatory and curative meaning such as has always pertained to the myth," Jung wrote.[12]

LIVING WITH THE DEVAS

There has been much interest recently in the "devas," or
deities, of nature. William Irwin Thompson and David
Spangler portray them as the invisible presences that make
the cabbages grow so beautifully in the Findhorn Garden.
However, the word *deva* is really of broader application than
this and is found in the Indo-European languages, hence
Greek, Latin, and Sanskrit. It is incorporated in the root of
the words *divine, divinity, deity,* and *theology.* In the conclusion of this chapter, I would like to move to a more constructive aspect of inner characterology, one that connects
specifically to its mythological and spiritual aspects. The
devas I wish to invoke, then, are not the ones in our garden,
but in our psyches.

Our contemporary world is no less thirsty for a sense of
spiritual belonging than that of our myth-susceptible ancestors, only we have, thanks to science and the emergence of a
truly planetary culture, a new relationship to the bright
world of myth. We no longer take myths as literal (perhaps

ultimate) descriptions of reality, but we can use them as seeing devices, especially if we learn to "see through" them, as discussed earlier. Furthermore, we can no longer pretend that the myths of a specific tradition or culture are the only ones. Scholars such as Campbell introduced us to the universality of a wisdom tradition embedded within the mythological lore of hundreds of cultures around the planet.

These observations may provide a context for us to consider the curious, and age-old, notion that the gods and goddesses of antiquity reside within us. Within the last decade, a multitude of books have been dedicated to the goddess, both she who is called the Great Goddess and her sister-daughters, or lesser inflections.[13] Moreover, some of the titles, such as Goddesses in Everywoman, by Jean Shinoda Bolen, announce the latest locus of the once-banished deities: they reside within each woman. Other therapists and writers, such as Roger and Jennifer Woolger, in their book The Goddess Within: A Guide to the Eternal Myths That Shape Women's Lives, have worked with the theme of the goddesses as overlapping dimensions to personality, which may appear at different developmental stages of the mature (female) personality (and not only in female psychology—and I like this about their approach—but in aspects of the male anima as well). Hillman, in Revisioning Psychology, and David Miller, in The New Polytheism and Gods and Games, were among the first to argue for a psychological perspective on the self that includes these mythic-divine persons.

What is the lure of this psychological neopaganism, as it must seem, especially to Christians? Isn't it enough to have Christ and The Devil? That makes our choice clear enough! But in this one tradition, the potentially inexhaustible richness of self-concept is restricted to a single inevitable conflict, not too different from Freud's id versus superego—its secular analogue perhaps. Also caught between antithetical supernatural powers, the self-determination of the human soul seems to become negligible, as when Job is torn apart by a secret wager between God and Satan. Such spiritually simplistic psychologies can rip the soul into pieces as well as impoverish its growth.

Devas, however, are more suited to the scale of the human imagination than these almost imponderable cosmic principles.[14] Artemis and Aphrodite probably disagree with each other, and squabble, as they do in Greek mythology, but also each would rather not rule the other's domain. Aphrodite, happy in her love bower, does not envy or seek to destroy Artemis's forest groves and secret pools. Each deity (deva) has its place in the mythic ecology of the universe. On the male side, Zeus, who sometimes seems very close to Yahweh with his wrathful judgments, heavenly abode, and thunderbolts, is happy to delegate the underworld and the ocean of the Hellenic cosmos to his brothers Hades and Poseidon, respectively. In the polytheistic universe every spiritual power has a special place or connection to the world of nature. This is quite different from a deity who is imagined as totally *other* than sinful nature (usually human nature along with biological nature).

But how do the devas of nature relate to what is inside a human being, how do the gods and goddesses get "within" us? The ancients took the concept of "as above, so below" very seriously. For them nature, human nature, and the cosmos were all interconnected, interpenetrating. One way the specific mechanism was rendered was in the colorful mythology of astrology. The gods and goddesses, unquestioned powers in the universe, were projected on cosmic bodies: the sun, moon, and planets. These in turn, through their cyclical movements, against the relatively fixed backdrop of the starry sky, impressed themselves on the human psyche at the moment of birth (or at the moment of conception in the Indian astrological system). Furthermore, the originally imprinted patterns of the psyche continue to be susceptible to the movements of the heavenly bodies through the calendar, so that as a planet moves through a zodiacal sign, or goes retrograde, for example (apparent movement backward through the signs, caused by the motion of the earth relative to the other planet), the corresponding faculty in the human psyche is affected.

While astrology enjoys very little approval from the world of contemporary science (it simply doesn't fit the dominant assumptions about how the universe hangs together), it is remarkable how insistently it knocks at the doors of both pop psychology and intellectual culture; and it is conceived of as very scandalous when national leaders are known to have personal horoscopes done or even (heaven forbid!) make political or national decisions on the basis of astrological predictions.[15] (That this is a cultural issue may be seen from the fact that in the Middle Ages and in certain third world countries of today, it would be unthinkable *to fail* to cast a horoscope at the birth of a successor to the throne, or in a time of national crisis.)

I was once at a dinner during which—unexpectedly—both a Freudian clinical psychologist friend and a very bright astrologer friend were at the same table with me. With some amusement, as well as trepidation, I was able to sit back and watch the dynamics unfold. The psychologist, I must say, was less tolerant of and more indignant about the profession of the astrologer. She couldn't see how an intelligent woman could "believe that crap." But the conversation grew more interesting when the two came to the topic of typologies. They were aware that each one had a typology for the human cast of characters. For the psychologist it was oral, anal, phallic, and so on. For the astrologer it was Capricorn rising, moon in Scorpio, and so on. I was aware of looking at a mythic paradigm clash.

While I am quite conversant with psychodynamic theory and understand the soundness of some of its assumptions, I couldn't help noticing how much richer, and in some ways more complex, the astrological typology seemed. In astrology the personality was portrayed as made up of a multitude of overlapping archetypes. Saturn could afflict one's natal Jupiter in the sixth house, say (but that condition was far from a struggle between God and The Devil or the ego and the id), and at some later time Jupiter, with its expansive alternative to Saturn's constriction, could carry the day; relationships with other people that had previously seemed afflicted (Saturn in sixth house) would open up.

In the Freudian stable of psychosexual characters there are some less-than-likable figures: the overbearing oral aggressive, the stingy anal retentive, or his profligate twin the anal expulsive. Among the derivative bioenergetic and other neo-Reichian therapies there are types that may be recognized by their characteristic body language, including those famous team members sadist and masochist, the schizoid, the psychopath, and the subcategories of the rigid: the compulsive, the phallic narcissistic, and the hysterical. Much as these types may have pedagogical or analytic value, I can't think of a single one I would like to be called.[16]

The problem with names is that in addition to carrying images and myths with them, portraying a person in a more vivid way, they may also stick to us. Because of this problem, I believe that characterizations about people derived from pathology should be used very sparingly, including in the clinical case conference, where they can lead to very demeaning and reductive discussions about human beings. Here then is my pitch: not that we all necessarily start practicing astrology, but that we allow, with a certain playful receptivity, the bright, multifaceted images of the gods and goddesses back into our lives.

In both Jean Bolen's and the Woolgers' books I have found wonderfully useful characterizations of the goddesses that are genuinely helpful to understanding human women: Demeter's endless ability to nurture and grow things and Artemis's almost opposite freedom-loving quality and unwillingness to be tied down (she likes backpacking and rock climbing). But Aphrodite types don't do so well with lots of children and think hiking is a bore, especially when there's no place to put on makeup. Athena rules the upwardly mobile woman of the workplace, especially in the intellectual setting, and Hera, the proprietary rights of the mother and the society. Very different from these is the Persephone woman with her underworld-bound psyche, especially her affinity for dreams and drugs and her potential for destructive relationships (Hades is a hell of a husband).

Just recently men's mysteries have been catching up again. Jung pointed out that many men, living in a society that (heretofore) visualized God as male, engage in an unconscious *imitatio Dei,* an "imitation of God." This is certainly true in the form of that righteous old man von Franz called the *senex.* Righteous, pompous, cut off from feelings and sexuality, he is all too much with us in the persons of our fathers, lawmakers, and political leaders. His eternal opponent is called the *puer,* the eternal child: the hippie, the stereotypical rock musician, the youth who never grows up. Closely allied with the latter archetype are the Dionysus figures of Punk Rock, with their inclination toward intoxication and dismemberment. Their managers, and lawyers as a general category, probably are closer to Hermes; they have tricks up their sleeves and don't always tell the exact truth. There are the Apollonian "golden boys" of Hollywood and the Hephaistos figures of industry. The military and the "martial arts" are full of figures who easily put on Ares (Latin, Mars); they have few doubts that aggression is really what it's all about, when you get right down to it.

But stereotypes, as we have seen, are archetypes unexamined. My special concern in this chapter is more the inner, than the outer cast of characters, and I am more interested in revealing the nature of our inner characters than in labeling people. It is possible that when dealing with a particular situation, any of us may be dealing with a whole constellation of the above archetypal persons. For example, I may find that in a particular situation I am inclined to use authority (Zeus or Yahweh). If that fails, I may actually consider force (Ares), but if I reflect a little further I might find that communication or even guile would be the best approach (Hermes). The richest and most fully human response is not inextricably wedded to any of these figures, but may turn the kaleidoscope of the self to see which pattern fits the situation best.

While the Greek mythology is very rich and complete in its rendition of the divine human archetypes, it is not the only one available. Campbell's scholarship has presented in accessible form a multitude of analogous traditions, so that we may find in any pantheon of figures some new knowledge and interesting psychological revelations. On one level the psyche may be Christian; on another, classic Greek; on yet another, animistic or shamanic in nature; and each and all of these perspectives have something to teach us.

Campbell particularly liked the Hindu-Buddhist tradition, with the grandeur of its scale and representations: Great Vishnu who dreams the lotus of the world while sleeping on the cosmic sea, imponderable Brahma who creates, and terrible-wonderful Lord Shiva who ever threatens to destroy the world and so must be kept meditating. And more rich and complete than the Christian Trinity in this aspect, there are their goddess consorts: Bountiful Lakshmi, Gracious Saraswati, and Shiva's eternal Shakti-Parvati, daughter of the mountain. Like the Greek Eros, there is Kama, god of love, who wounds us with his arrows, and Mara, lord of death and the underworld. In addition, there are the wonderful avatars of Vishnu, who appear as emanations in the field of time and space: Rama, hero of *The Ramayana,* and beautiful blue Krishna, he of the Gopis, who dances and plays irresistible music like Orpheus.[17]

Among these bright and varied devic images from all over the world, we may find not only patrons, but divine doubles, figures who present us to ourselves in eternal form. By remembering that our souls are made up of persons—and, yes, gods and goddesses—who seem the best possible expression for powers and patterns, things for which we have no other symbol, we find ourselves not only with a sense of meaning, but of belonging to a timeless drama. Jung has said, "To serve a mania is detestable, but to serve a god is full of meaning."[18] By learning to recognize and tolerate our inner multiplicity we grow in self-knowledge and are not so surprised when life occasionally has us fall apart, as it does. We gain in wisdom and lose our egocentricity when we recognize how conditional is our very existence and that men and women have always lived in this precarious suchness. But when we recognize the divinities within us, we catch a glimpse of immortality.

To conclude this chapter I return to my own dream that precipitated so many early insights for me. What is truly frightening in madness and possession is the cast of characters that is out of control or has gotten caught in some warped inner drama of ultimate struggle. The dangers seem to lie in imbalance and incoherence. None of our internal parts has the right to seize exclusive control (the dictator), and all do best when they recognize the existence (and the right to exist) of all the others.

In our personal mythology our story ultimately is told, and that story includes characters. The ego, I, or sense of self, whichever we choose to call it, is both immensely powerful and, at the same time, confusingly fragile. Our most important task, though, is the gaining of self-knowledge. More than merely actors, at best we are skilled directors. To put on the "good show" that comprises life we need to keep track of our inner cast.

Chapter 9

THE INNER
GUIDE

The night is dark, and I am far from home, lead thou me on.

—"Lead Kindly Light"

Mythology provides us with abundant examples of the figure of the "inner friend": from the spirit-guides of the shamans, who aid them on their visionary journeys to the supernatural realm; to the *psychopompos* of the Greek mysteries, who takes the initiate through his underworld *nekyia;* to the animal helper in fairy tales, who always shows up at a difficult time to return the favor that was granted him by the hero. In the guide, we find one who not only knows the terrain, the pathways and the obstacles, the wonders and the terrors, but who offers the companionship of a living presence with whom we may confer as the journey unfolds its challenging—and not always predictable—features.

Mythologically the guide is portrayed in such divine figures as the Egyptian soul-conducting deity Anubis, Hermes for the Hellenic mysteries initiate, the Christ "within" for Christians, the indwelling Atman for the Hindus, the Yidam for the Buddhists, and Khidr for Islamic mystics. But the guide may also be found in the human figures of Tiresias for Odysseus, Moses and Aaron for the wilderness-wandering Israelites, Merlin for King Arthur, and Virgil for Dante.

Whether represented as divine or mortal, the function of the guide is the same: spirit comes to conduct the pilgrim soul on its journey.

The oldest representations of this figure we know of are the shamans, cloaked in a robe of skins, with antler headgear or pointed hat—a kind of cosmic antenna—and a staff, symbolizing a connection with the holy center, the axis of the universe. In the classic world, Hermes the divine *psychopomp,* messenger, and conductor of souls, also appeared with staff and cap— and winged heels to show his movement between the worlds. By the Middle Ages the spiritual guide had become associated with the figure of the holy pilgrim, cloaked, with staff and lantern, like the Hermit in the Tarot deck (see Figure 25). He is shod for the journey, knows its perils and pitfalls, but, most important, is in touch with the spiritual principle that gives meaning to the entire adventure. He calls us back when we get lost or sidetracked, and lends meaning and context to experiences that otherwise seem random, chaotic, and fragmentary.

AN OLD FRIEND

When we experience in dream an encounter with "the wise old man," "the wise old woman," or "the animal who knows the way," the psyche is showing us a representation for a principle from which spiritually attuned people have always sought counsel. The Nascapi Indians of the Labrador peninsula call him Mistapeo, their "million-year-old man." Human beings, especially today, enjoy a wonderful freedom and autonomy, but meditation on human history, current events, or even our own lives will show how seriously flawed are both our vision and our wisdom. Every generation of humanity faces its own problems, some left behind for us by our ancestors, some newly created, and we, too, are in the process of bequeathing immense problems for our descendants. Self-determining we may be, but with a tragi-

FIGURE 25. *L'Hermite,
from the Tarot
de Marseilles.*

cally partial vision. How then to gain a larger perspective, "the wisdom of the ages"? Reading history and studying traditional knowledge is worthwhile, but so much lore that was valuable at its own time now seems hopelessly outdated. The Nascapi Indians would tell us to seek a kind of living counsel, the million-year-old man who brings the wisdom of our ancient roots into encounter with the present and who is still very much with us—if we are willing to listen for his voice.

Psychologically, the guide may personify as an actual figure who conducts a dreamer through an inner realm of experience—Virgil to Dante—as the subway-master in Chapter 6 does, or he or she may appear at a crucial moment to point out what is being overlooked, announce something, or warn of impending danger—as in some of the dreams cited later in this chapter. On the other hand, the guide may manifest much more subtly: in the form of a hunch, or intuition, that, when followed, turns out to be just the right thing, a sequence of ideas that leads to a new way of seeing a problem, or a series of dreams that—when examined—opens new vistas of insight. The guide does not need to be literally represented, for his or her presence to be felt. In this chapter, I am interested primarily in the anagogic (from the Greek, "guiding") *principle* and only secondarily in its often fascinating *personifications*.

In modern times, the figure of the guide has become assimilated to the psychotherapist. His or her task is to provide direction for the pilgrim soul lost, like Dante, *nel mezzo del cammin di nostra vita,* on the road or in the dark forest of the midst of our lives. I will consider the role of this outer guide—the psychotherapist—but more important, his or her necessary relationship to the inner counterpart— the anagogue of souls. For those without a therapeutic guide, I believe this inner figure, however, may be found directly by the methods described in Chapter 12, particularly "The Inner Guide" exercise.

This mythic figure's winged heels and magic staff carry him between the divine, which, tradition tells us, "knows the whole story already," and the human, whose lot is to encounter the divine only piecemeal: adventure by adventure, spread out over the measurable realms of time and space. But the human psychotherapist also dwells in the human realm. The doctor does not always "know best" and is often at his or her worst when swollen with such convictions. All too rare these days is the therapist who consciously invokes the healing faculty within the psyche and involves its voice in the therapeutic dialogue.

Mythological images tell us that the inner guide moves through the rooms and stories of the universe, from the inaccessible realm of transcendent omniscience, to the terrestrial world of matter, beasts, and men, surrounded by its "cloud of unknowing." In between, he or she passes through the realm of self-luminous forms—the human imaginal, midway between ignorance and omniscience, where we, too, may contact him or her in dreams and imagination. The guide's task is to help us in one of our major adventures: to encounter the fantasy we call life, deeply and authentically enough to extract its truths from among the delusions. There is no way we can know everything and still be human. That is why we sometimes see this figure represented with his finger to his lips—as the Greek Mystes—for all whereof he knows he may not tell.

In modern times, a fascinating confirmation for the aliveness of the mythological soul journey comes from psychedelic research. While the destructive consequences of unsupervised and casual experimentation with these substances is all too apparent in the contemporary world, the evidence from controlled studies is just the opposite. I have never read of psychosis or any kind of negative effects from "guided journeys" conducted by responsible and appropriately trained therapists; instead, the experiences conduce toward psychological integration rather than disintegration.[1]

Masters and Houston urge the appropriateness of the term *guide,* because the subject so often conceives of his or her experience as a journey, a "trip," in the vernacular. I would only add that the experience need not be psychedelic for the journey metaphor to arise. In guided imagery or Jungian active imagination the most frequently occurring plots are mythical journeys and quests through an unknown realm.[2]

Masters and Houston's favorite metaphor for the psychedelic journey was Dante's *Divine Comedy,* with its tour through infernal and paradisal regions. Grof has described a similar sequence: hell and purgatory are usually encountered before paradise. The journey should be recognized "teleologically," these investigators believe. The brutal initial adventures seem cruel only without knowledge of their anticipatory relationship to the later stages.

Throughout *The Divine Comedy,* Virgil, the guiding principle, explains the logic of the labyrinth, the meanings of the wonders and the horrors, and of their relationship to the moral life. Perhaps most important, Virgil keeps Dante *moving* through the realm, keeps him on a journey rather than transfixed at one of its stations like the many human sufferers they encounter. (Notice that for the mystery tradition hell and heaven are not portrayed as ultimate destinations, their true purpose is not the administration of final and appropriate rewards to souls, but rather stages on the soul journey.) The guide did not necessarily design the labyrinth, but he becomes its revelator and spokesman, implying a secret affinity with the architect.

While the psychedelic journey shows us the guiding principle we have been describing in a microcosmic form, so too does conventional psychotherapy, but in much less clear and distinct form, because it is blurred with details from daily life and must be seen against the conscious *Weltanschauung* (world view) of the time. Also, in the many exchanges between therapist and client, personal myths are mingled, and the therapist interjects his views of where the client is on his or her journey, and how to proceed.

THE WISE OLD MEN

During the time of his friendship with Freud (1906–1913), Jung could be seen as not only "apprenticed" to Freud, nineteen years his elder, but in some sort of filial relationship. Freud in his more expansive moments kept referring to him as the "crown prince" of the psychoanalytic movement (and we know what that made Freud). He speaks of "shaking his wise gray locks" in reproof at the younger man's youthful folly. There is no doubt Freud wished to be in the position of "wise old man" to Jung, and there is no doubt that he thought of the role of father of psychoanalysis as "guide" for a chosen people (their followers). He wrote to Jung, "We are certainly getting ahead; if I am Moses, then you are Joshua and will take possession of the promised land of psychiatry, which I shall only be able to glimpse from afar."[3]

Earlier Jung had written to Freud, "I dreamt that I saw you walking beside me as a very, very frail old man."[4] Jung puzzled over the dream, which took place in Vienna, for some time after coming back to Zurich. Freud was a wise old man to Jung, for a while. But this dream shows the projection to be weakening, into frailness, as early as 1909. The younger man had begun to follow the wisdom principle within, and the inner and outer guides were diverging.

Jung's view of therapy was evolving more and more toward helping his patients make contact with their own inner source of guidance, through dreams. Jung also claimed he knew while writing the chapter on sacrifice in *Symbols of Transformation* that publishing this book (in 1911) would cost him his friendship with Freud (his personal sacrifice). But publish he did, and (probably with other factors affecting it as well) their friendship was certainly doomed. One of the key disagreements was the guiding (anagogic) capacity of the unconscious.[5]

Another, but inextricable issue, had to do with the profound relationship between the worlds of psychology and myth. Freud wrote in a paper, "The Horror of Incest" (later incorporated into the book *Totem and Taboo,* but without the following quote), "Jung shows . . . that the fantasy images of certain mental patients (Dementia Praecox) presented the most striking parallels to the mythological cosmogonies of ancient peoples, concerning which the uneducated among the patients cannot possibly have had scientific knowledge."[6] Here Freud seems close to accepting a theory of "the collective unconscious." However, in a letter to Jung in which he praises the younger man's contribution to the development of psychoanalysis, he also wrote, "but . . . you hide behind your religious-libidinal cloud." Earlier, Freud had complained of his own work:

> My study of totemism and other work are not going well. I have very little time, and to draw on books and reports is not at all the same as drawing on the richness of one's own experience. Besides my interest is diminished by the conviction that I am already in possession of the truths I am trying to prove.[7]

This last remark may be one of the most ingenuously accurate self-criticisms ever uttered by this complex and subtle mind. Jung was still trying to follow in the master's footsteps and come out of his "religious-libidinal cloud," but it wasn't working. Previously, Jung had written to Freud,

> I am having grisly fights with the hydra of mythological fantasy, and not all its heads are cut off yet. Sometimes I feel like calling for help when I am too hard pressed by the welter of material. So far I have managed to suppress the urge. I hope to reach dry land in the not too distant future.[8]

Jung reached "dry land," but it was a different terrain than where his mentor dwelt. He never could cut off all those heads. His mythological scholarship was not only broader, but began to deepen in different ways than Freud's. The myths kept coming to life, talking to him, instructing him. He failed as a psychoanalyst[9] because he couldn't sustain the conviction that he "was already in possession of the truths he was trying to prove."

Jung not only stayed with his belief in the anagogic, he was eventually to document the appearance of specific guiding figures such as the wise old man in patients' dreams. Later he wrote,

> The figure of the wise old man can appear so plastically, not only in dreams but also in visionary meditation (or what we call "active imagination"), that, as is sometimes apparently the case in India, it takes over the role of a guru. The wise old man appears in dreams in the guise of a magician, doctor, priest, teacher, professor, grandfather, or any other person possessing authority. The archetype of spirit in the shape of a man, hobgoblin, or animal always appears in a situation where insight, understanding, good advice, determination, planning, etc., are needed but cannot be mustered on one's own resources. The archetype compensates this state of spiritual deficiency by contents designed to fill in the gap.[10]

This "plasticity" idea can be considered to favor wisdom figures of more than one gender. Jean Houston, an influential contemporary American psychologist, has underscored the epiphany in our time of the "wise old woman" as a guiding figure more appropriate to administer specifically feminine forms of wisdom, and I return to this theme again at the end of this chapter.

Jung was to personify the character Philemon, an ancient Gnostic figure, for his personal spirit-guide. He painted the image of Philemon on the second-story bedroom wall of his tower, because he so intimately felt the influence of this imaginal guide in his daily life. Over the gateway to his first, and then his second, tower he carved: *Philemonis sacrum Fausti Poenitentia*, "Philemon's shrine, Faust's penitence." Philemon here had a second meaning. In a Greek legend, as the gods Zeus and Hermes walked the earth in disguise seeking hospitality, only two old people opened their hearth and their hearts to the gods: Philemon and Baucis.

In *Faust*, Goethe has the old couple murdered in the furthering of Faust's ambitious plans for progress (the desacralizing demon of modern consciousness). Jung, who believed himself to be both biological and spiritual descendant of Goethe, read *Faust* as a youth, was strongly affected by it, and considered himself to be the avenger of Philemon and Baucis, who, as he wrote in a letter (not to Freud), "unlike Faust the superman, are the hosts of the gods in a ruthless and godforsaken age."[11] This may help us to understand Jung's resistance to Freud's godless unconscious: an important theme in Jung's personal mythology was to recognize the ancient gods and offer them "hospitality" in modern life.[12]

In a 1983 keynote address, religious philosopher Jacob Needleman asserted that the human quest for meaning and a spiritual place in the universe must be accorded no lesser place in the hierarchy of instincts than any other. In fact, he portrayed it as the crown of our true humanity. Only when we add this last ingredient are we fully and truly human. Abraham Maslow, especially at the end of his life, would have agreed. Beyond self-actualization, in his hierarchy of motives, he believed there to be self-transcendence. The guide, whether portrayed as spirit being or human being in touch with spirit, is the personification of that meaning principle known only to those who have followed it a while, in themselves or someone else. The Ariadne thread of inner guidance only leads somewhere when you pick up the end and follow.[13]

GUIDED IMAGERY AND ACTIVE IMAGINATION

The foregoing discussion paves the way for our look at Jung's technique of "active imagination." To make sense of a comparison between this and other methods of working with mental imagery, we need ever to clarify the values embedded in each. Consider, for example, the process involved in behavior therapy's "systematic desensitization."

The imagizer is to summon mental imagery for the purpose of manipulating it, for example, imagining oneself in the very situation that brings out a phobia—a bridge or elevator—observing the physical and emotional state that follows, and then extinguishing or reducing the fearful response according to a prearranged program of stages. The role of the mental imagery is to simulate life and eliminate a dysfunctional response to it. The mental imagery is not invited to be spontaneous or autonomous, nor do we follow it to see where it leads or what meanings it bestows.

I feel strongly that we must be cautious about seizing the initiative in the imaginal realm. It is not that I believe we must never do so, but especially not until we fully understand the larger context in which images are embedded.

The clearest example of this value split I observed occurred at a national conference in front of several hundred humanistic psychologists, at a presentation on the Neo-Senoi method.[14] A man from the audience told of a recurring dream that he prefaced by saying it came to him in times of outer catastrophe and inner loss of meaning and always had a positive effect. The gist of the dream was this: *"a man in a loincloth, who ordinarily sits in a box in meditation,"* would arise and, as the dreamer watched, *"perform a completely captivating dance."* At the end of the dream dance, the dreamer said he would awaken—feeling somehow better, "and with a renewed appreciation of life." It was evident the dreamer was really more interested in sharing the dream, and its mysterious quality, than in any kind of analytic interpretation. The workshop leader's advice was so oblique to the anagogic approach and so Freudian-Senoi that I found myself publicly challenging his interpretation: "That is your infant self," he said, "it is wearing diapers. I advise you to put him back in the box and make it smaller and smaller until it goes away forever and you can be a grown-up."

The transpersonal approach, to which the leader seemed oblivious, would notice first the figure's resemblance to

Shiva, the terrible wonderful aspect of the Hindu trinity who in ordinary life is to be kept meditating, because when he dances, although it is beautiful, it represents the destructive forces of the universe. Here it seemed this guiding figure would instruct the pilgrim soul through this dance, which portrays both the terror and wonder of life. The dreamer himself used the term *loincloth,* which the interpreter read as the symbol of infant diapers. But for a more symbolically open imagination even a literal diaper could point to a rebirth motif. (The renunciate, which is Shiva's special aspect, is called "twice born.")

For me, it was the disrespect for an imaginal wisdom figure that elicited the value-laden response. Remember Hillman's concern: in the realm of the imaginal the persons of the imagination are real. Archetypal psychology, which differs from Jung's classic analytical psychology in some respects, here is firmly aligned with its parent.

Neo-Senoi techniques, which manipulate or destroy threatening dreams or mental images, may have their applications. And there is a growing literature on the amelioration and healing of pathological conditions by such deliberately manipulative methods. For example, in the Simonton method, which personifies a battle between invasive or cancerous forces and the body's defenses. The defenses are made—in the imagery—to win: overwhelming, eating, or driving away, the "bad guys."[15]

To become aware of the conscious ego while it is "in" the imaginal world is to realize immense symbolic power. The Senoi tradition has rightly awakened us to the possibilities of *lucid dreaming,* waking up in the dream and even taking an active role rather than the merely passive one we are used to, in regard to dream dynamics. But to assume this active role does not (automatically) entitle us to exercise its prerogatives ruthlessly, especially without regard to the autonomous source of our imagery and our symbolic life.

Mental images are, in psychoanalytic language, "over-determined," that is, redolent with concealed meanings.

If they must be deciphered—rather than simply felt or experienced—it must be with an inexhaustible sense of openness to the many meanings that may be found. Resistance to particular interpretations should be noted, but not made the sine qua non of the interpretive method as Freud urged: "The more you resist, the more correct I am." People should be trusted to comment on how valid or "right" a particular interpretation feels to them. We must learn to see any level as possessing meaning—Freudian no less but no more than Jungian, and better yet, both at once, as one intuits the real depth and transparency of the psyche. It is also important to refer images to the body, where they frequently are found to resonate.

"By deliberate concentration upon a sequence of images . . . emerge fantasies that 'want to become conscious,' " said Jung.[16] His causal assumption—the fantasies' almost anthropomorphic "wish" to become conscious—is revealed here as closer to the metaphysics of the Iroquois than to that of the Senoi.[17] The Iroquois metaphysics stressed dreams as produced by the desires of the soul, but incited in man by a divine source, Tha-ro-hya-wa-ko, the lord of the sky. Thus to ignore the advice given by dreams was for the Iroquois to court illness, madness, or disaster.

There is a voice in dreams that comes out of nowhere and tells the dreamer astonishing things. I have quoted that voice a few times in the dreams rendered throughout this book. Sometimes the dream events take an uncanny turn and we realize the workings of an unseen choreographer. Sometimes the dreamer hears a song or sees a work of art, pregnant and scintillating with suggestive meanings. (I have several times read parts of excellent novels and poems and woken with astonishment. Maybe their author is the same invisible genius who dictated "Kubla Khan," all of a piece, to Coleridge.) The figure or faculty I have been calling the guide resembles a hidden or concealed god, the deus absconditus.

Overtly personified figures may be less frequent than the

subtle insinuation of a kind of co-consciousness in our dreams and everyday life. Unlike the fragmentary personalities of which we seem to be constituted in part, the guide does not make us forget the rest of the self; rather he/she awakens us to it. Sometimes a part-self may be hostile to other parts, or even to the whole, as we saw in the last chapter. When we slip into it we are obsessed, or possessed; we act unconsciously; we forget. The guide seems always to awaken consciousness, rather than steal it away for its own purposes. It leaves the ego in freedom, to choose and to know and to grow in personal awareness.

When we do guided imagery there should be two guides: an outer and an inner one. (If you lack an outer guide you can fulfill the role yourself.) The outer one does well to be always respectful of the inner. His or her purpose is to set the stage, and provide an initial or "seeding" image that awakens the unconscious. This may be something such as, "You are in a meadow at the edge of a great forest. It is dark and cool and you wish to enter it. Do that now, with a sense of anticipation, and tell me what you see." Hanscarl Leuner suggested particular quests and adventures, to find a treasure, a journey in a cave, a heroic quest in which you own a sword of power, or the like. In general, Leuner's German school would seem to have the outer guide be more directive in the proceedings. Desoille and the French school allow the inner imagery more initiative and follow its lead.[18]

I once observed a guided fantasy session in which the therapist became very aggressive about his suggestions to a person to manipulate her inner imagery—to the point where the fantasy simply stopped dead, a negative outcome. The therapist was thinking "magically," in the Freudian sense, that an impasse in the imagery could be solved by a wishful elimination. Magical attempts to deal with real problems presented by inner imagery, instead of allowing the fantasy to unfold in its own manner, often abort the imaginal self-healing process.

In guided imagery the conscious perspective does play a

part, and must be taken into account throughout. When something frightening or blocking is encountered, the outer guide may assist with suggestions to "go further," "be confident it will come out all right." But this does not mean the guide or the ego may exercise a unilateral prerogative or treat the fantasy as something unreal and simply to be manipulated to our intended outcome. (The psyche seems particularly sensitive to this type of attitude and withdraws from meaningful contact.) Although the unfoldment of mental or affective imagery often seems to imply a magically plastic dimension, this does not mean that the problems presented may be solved magically, by ruthless intervention of the conscious perspective.

Feed your dream monsters (in lucid dreams or guided imagery), especially ones that are characterized by gaping jaws and big teeth. The Senoi of Malaysia, those astute dream psychologists, knew the prevalence of oral aggression and recommended the same strategy. And we have a sort of imaginal "civil rights" in the dream world as well as in the outer one. We have a right to fight if we are cornered. Or ask dream persecutors or imagery monsters why they are there. At best, this kind of work is a dialogue that enters into what Jung called the transcendent function. Imagination is followed by interpretation (and response, if needed) and more imagining again—Image:Idea:Image, and so on. This basic pattern seems to be the way in which creativity best unfolds: "inspiration" and "perspiration" follow each other in a rhythm, like a sine wave of receptivity and response.

In one therapeutic session a young male doctor was working on his tendency to explode in anger. Rather than offer "helpful suggestions," I invited him to enter a light trance and find his inner guide to see what he advised. He said, "I find him in a cave, sheltered from the world. He is anchored, he can't be harmed here, in his own place. He speaks only when necessary. He is radiant." I asked if the guide would show him something that would help him with the anger. He was shown the image of a mudra, or sacred hand position, that formed a kind of triangle, with its base under the heart. He was to hold his hands in this position and breathe in a certain way, deeply and powerfully. The young man continued, "There's a kind of flame in my heart I'm supposed to make and keep there, burning continuously, it's supposed to warm my heart. The breath intensifies it, and there's something about the blood. It feels revitalizing."

The doctor remembered a dream that had come to him months before:

> There's an evil woman following me, she's going to stab me in the heart. She comes right up to the window of the car with her dagger. She turns into a skeleton. I awake shaken.

"The woman is coldhearted," he said, reflecting on this dream; "I guess I live in my head a lot, instead of my heart." The skeleton had invoked a long-term fear of death, of which the client knew, but had been unable to resolve. (Perhaps some kind of fear related to the theme "to be, or not to be" was the urgent force beneath his explosive anger.) He "lived in his head," to escape feelings connected to this fear. The guide gave him an almost tantric guided imagery to do regularly, to warm his heart. In addition, he felt that even though he himself might continue to pass through stormy times, the guide was in a secure place. And he could call on him whenever he especially needed him.

At the finish of this guided imagery I felt once again vindicated in my willingness to trust allies some people think are ephemera. Some weeks later, writing this chapter, I asked the young man to rate on a scale of value, say one to a hundred, how useful he felt the advice received from within was, whether it had come from a relative, friend, or therapist. He said "a hundred." Given his situation and personality, what came to him felt "right on." He acknowledged that the images were still very real for him, and he had been doing the flame-heart meditation regularly since.

The next few, concluding, dreams in this section are of a rather extraordinary nature. In many of the guiding dreams I have worked with over the years, the anagogic factor is apparent only in the spaces between the events, and the guide's presence must be intuited. But in these dreams, the guide seems to have been willing to assume a personified form, perhaps for our instruction. The first is also a telepathic dream, but that is not the quality I wish to emphasize. Instead, please notice the feeling tone and its effect on the sensibilities of the woman dreamer:

(I was in India and dreamed about my paternal grandfather back in the U.S.) *He was sitting on a porch with my maternal grandfather (dead two years), talking and laughing about a trip they are going to make together. We had lunch and they were both telling me to take care of myself and don't do any heavy work (I was pregnant). Then they got up to leave. I wanted to go, but they said this was not a trip for me. They walked down the porch stairs and down the street into a light that was almost blinding. I noticed they did not have suitcases . . .*

"Two days later I received a telegram from my dad saying Grandpa had died at 4:30 A.M. on the day I had that dream," she wrote.

Here are two "wise old men" setting out on a journey. Both share their warmth, as well as a farewell with the dreamer. She was close to her grandfather and couldn't have found a better way to learn of the news (halfway round the world, pregnant, and helpless to respond or attend the funeral). Rather than an emotional void, she had a mysterious but treasured personal contact.

The second grandfather showed his guidelike qualities on another occasion. Again the dreamer was pregnant, this time in the United States:

Grandfather comes in and it is quite obvious he is upset about something. I can actually feel his distress. I ask him repeatedly what is wrong and what I can do to help him. He tells me I must accept God's will. Then he is gone but I hear someone crying. I awake frightened.

The next afternoon, as the dreamer wrote in her journal, "I miscarried a son. I had no symptoms of a problem pregnancy and the person in my dream who was crying must have been me because I cried for days after the miscarriage."

In the dream of another woman the guide figure was directly identified as a healer. It is important to note this dreamer had had a serious illness, cancer, and an immunological problem:

I was lying in my own room and my friend said, "Here is the doctor." The man was big and tall . . . had a smaller man with him. The big man kneeled down by me and put his hands on my shoulders, the smaller one by my feet. The people turned to black forms. I closed my eyes. I felt waves of healing power moving down my body. I remained lying there but felt myself getting well.

Whoever this mysterious twentieth-century dream healer was, I knew what they would have named him in ancient Greece. And the healing god Asclepius was frequently known to travel with a dwarf or dwarves (the *telesphoros*).

The last dream is eloquent in its simplicity, and speaks of a form who seems to offer herself for our respectful attention in these times.

Lots of small snakes in an area I'm walking through. Then I'm driving; stop at a station for gas and walk into a house nearby. A woman in jeans and a blue shirt says, "There is someone I want you to meet." A door to my left opens and a woman in a dress, head covered, walks towards me as I walk to meet her. As I am walking closer to her I see she is not just old but ancient (I have never seen such a face, such age). And yet her eyes are eternally young and alive and full of love. I am startled and feel a thrill of fear at her face just before we embrace, and I feel such love for her. Then she is gone. Those eyes!

This dreamer had had a number of male guides appear, including several dream visits of a well-known Indian guru. Often they would give her advice that went oblique to her feelings. But this dream figure, the wise old woman, went the deepest for her; through simply "being there" and not actively counseling, the wise old woman helped her to establish an inner sense of validity. It is wonderful and gratifying to see people improve their feelings of self-worth, not through the aggrandizement of the perennially inflated ego, but through realizing that in their own depths lie transpersonal wisdom figures and an inexhaustible and creative life force.

Part Three

CONSCIOUS MYTHMAKING

Chapter 10

CREATIVE MYTHOLOGY

Were it not for the leaping and twinkling of the soul, man would rot away in his greatest passion, idleness.

—C. G. JUNG

I should have mentioned that the supernatural might at any moment create new myths, but I was timid.

—W. B. YEATS

I have borrowed my chapter title from Joseph Campbell's fourth volume of *The Masks of God.* In that work, he suggests that the civilized West is the growing matrix for a new sense of mythology geared to the creative life of "an adequate individual," who seeks his or her own way in the world and, through following this personal path, develops a relationship to the archetypal and mythological powers that inform life. Aligning himself with the creative spirit that began to arise among the Orphic mysteries and the philosophical humanism of classic Greece, Campbell traced this special recognition of the autonomy of the human soul in the Western tradition through the medieval Courts of Love and into the rich mythology of the Arthurian Round Table.

THE ROOTS OF CREATIVE MYTHOLOGY

It was a passage in the twelfth-century *La Queste del San Graal*, Campbell said, that triggered his insight. Each knight went his own way ". . . striking out into the forest, one here, one there, wherever they saw it thickest and wherever path or track was absent," to enact his personal quest-adventure.[1] Only later, returned once more to the unifying symbolic locus of the Round Table, would they reassemble, recount their adventures, and in so doing, create the tapestry of a rich, and complete, larger mythology from their personal stories.

In the twelfth-century Renaissance, particularly in the elite intellectual courts of southern France (with their troubadours) and Germany (with its own *Minnesingers*), the theme is carried into the tradition of courtly love, and the right of each person to follow the dictates of his or her heart in regard to personal relationship, thus the celebrated romances of Lancelot and Guinevere, of Tristan and Isolde. In the *Parzival* of Wolfram von Eschenbach, the individual journey is given a psychological twist through Parzival's naïveté, leading to his initial failure of the Grail Quest (failure to ask the question), his meeting with the wise old man, Trevrizent, and the dark brother with whom he is reunited, Feirefiz; and perhaps most of all, in his constancy to his chosen love Condwiramurs, despite numerous encounters and temptations involving the feminine archetype.

In *Creative Mythology* Professor Campbell moves finally into our present time of fragmented—but still living—myths, rendered in the art of Picasso and abstract expressionism, and the works of Joyce and Mann. In sum, Campbell boldly suggested that it is this individual path to the mysteries, not necessarily the collective participation enjoined on us by all the religions, that may well constitute the ultimate human adventure.[2]

Jung too, in the field of psychology, was not only walking his own individual path, but outlining the lineaments of the personal journey for the West, which he would call not sainthood or heavenly bliss or enlightenment but *individuation*. This mysterious outcome is never fully attained, yet it must always be sought for. The path of individuation constitutes the developmental psychology of the mature human being, the achievement of personal wholeness.

Jung, like Campbell, felt the roots of the Western journey into personal wholeness were to be found among the Greeks, where he encountered the tradition of dream incubation, of the healing god, Asclepius, mentioned earlier. The preserved stelae at Epidaurus, which served the ancient world for more than a thousand years as a healing center, are full of personal testimonials as to the efficacy of this technique to heal and to empower life.

Another source from which Jung drew were the Gnostic traditions. These came in several varieties, both Christian and non-Christian—the latter often connected to the Hellenic mystery traditions. *Gnosis* is the Greek root of our word *knowledge* and has to do with personal knowledge of the divine (that very knowledge our modern *agnostics* say, honestly enough, they do not have). As Elaine Pagels has pointed out, in her influential book on early Christianity, *The Gnostic Gospels,* the difference between the Gnostic and the orthodox traditions that suppressed and tried to eliminate them was the right of the individual to have an experience of divine revelation outside the provenance of the Church. In the translations of the Nag Hammadi manuscripts, around which her scholarship is based, Pagels said, Jesus "speaks in sayings as cryptic and compelling as Zen koans." For example, the words that he addresses to Thomas, but are transparently intended for the reader: "while you accompany me, although you do not understand [it], you already have come to know, and you will be called 'the one who knows himself.' For whoever has not known himself has known nothing, but whoever has known himself has simultaneously achieved knowledge about the depths of all things."[3]

It is easy to see why sayings such as this were perceived

by the early Church fathers as inimical to the establishment
of a religion of the collective. Rather they seem to conduce
the individual to a personal journey into self-knowledge
(Gnosis). Pagels quoted the legendary ire of Bishop Iranaeus:
"every one of them generates something new every day,
according to his ability"—which, as an act of religious devotion, infuriated the bishop. He accused them of creating a
new kind of mythological poetry or imaginary fiction. Pagels
said, "No doubt he is right: first- and second-century gnostic
literature includes some remarkable poems, like the 'Round
Dance of the Cross' and the 'Thunder, Perfect Mind.' "[4]
Many modern people who still feel a spiritual connection to
Jesus, but resist the blandishments of orthodoxy, are finding
a sense of inspiration, reconnection, and creative empowerment for their own personal spiritual search in these texts.

But the orthodox traditions, by a kind of hegemony of
legend, controlling how the great story shall be told—and
how it shall be lived—have created historical Christianity as
we know it. In later centuries, according to Jung, the quest
for direct and personal spiritual experience went underground
in the tradition of the medieval alchemists. At a time when
the church had already succeeded in suppressing any version
of spiritual development that was personal—outside the authorized sacraments—the alchemists found that in solitude,
in their laboratories, and in a mystical dialogue with matter,
they were mostly let alone. Jung's conclusion on investiga-
tion of hundreds of obscure manuscripts from the Middle
Ages was that they were outlining a mythology of the soul's
personal transformation, but in terms seemingly related to
chemical processes and that disguised their true intent.[5]

In contemporary times the psychology of Abraham
Maslow, and the humanistic psychology movement have
stressed "self-actualization." For Maslow, self-actualization
was to be seen as the peak experience of a hierarchy of
human motives related to—at the lower levels—safety, secu-
rity, and belonging. On the highest level Maslow placed the
individually creative—and yet socially contributive—life. Hu-

manistic psychology and its stepchild transpersonal psychology have opened us to all kinds of learning experiences related to growth and personal transformation. The offerings at growth centers—in some ways not so very different from those Asclepian centers of healing—include dream workshops; instruction in meditation; yoga; healing techniques; and new inner-directed approaches to art, athletics, and even politics. Dimensions neglected in the mainstream society such as conscious dying, the use of guided imagery in healing, and all kinds of techniques for personal growth are celebrated and offered at these centers.

In my own search for the roots of creative mythology, I first encountered shamanism (see Chapter 5), which is personal, indeed, because it antedates the historical beginnings of organized communities and systematic belief systems; then I was led by its universal underlying premises to contemplate a kind of perennial search for personal Gnosis that always has flourished where people of intelligence and integrity live their lives. I have referred to this elsewhere as "the visionary tradition."[6] While the historical church has withheld recognition from such activities, one has merely to examine the lives of the saints (hagiography) to find many examples of great souls, such as the Renaissance mystic Meister Eckhart, who have recognized the importance of personal experience. My growing perspective, then, has been that "creative mythology" is not something that we must learn how to do, but something that flows naturally from the human spirit in the absence of social constraints toward mythological conformity.

Heretofore, (mythic) orthodoxy has dictated much to consciousness of what forms it shall revere as holy, which mental imagery shall constitute an epiphany, and which a trip to the stake; even the words of our inmost prayers have been prescribed. Remembering that mythological ideas are eyes for the soul, it seems in some ways our spiritual vision has been obscured, living in a world in which only the mythically predetermined was to be visible for us. The post-Enlightenment movement of science has taken it on itself to clear the mind of these persistently enforced illusions (Blake's "mind-forged manacles"). Remember that the cardinals who were trying Galileo wouldn't even look in his telescope. Modern science and the Eastern disciplines of meditation each in their way seem determined to hold the mind back from mythologizing—especially when it limits our vision.[7]

Conscious mythmaking, the title of this last section of the book, enables the reader to enter the realm of the inner explorer, the creative artist, the contemporary shaman. The modern mind still thirsts to drink at the well of mythic meaning—and hungers for stories and folklore. But even more, it yearns toward an experience of the world sacralized— luminous with its own "suchness," the world itself becomes a forest of symbols, as in Baudelaire's poetic metaphor.[8] Yet we are rightly cautious about losing our way in that forest. Like it or not, the modern mind has in no way established its immunity from charismatic madmen, strange belief systems, and compulsive forms of worship (including the cult of the mythologized personality; see Chapters 3, 5, and 8). Contemporary life has also seen an epiphany of neoorthodoxy, in which people seem to prefer to regress a few centuries in their belief systems, rather than integrate the honest revelations of biology, paleontology, and archaeology. (Does the vision of the universe seen by science induce a kind of metaphysical vertigo, so that the human gaze must be withdrawn from the abyss?)[9]

As I see it, the purpose of conscious mythmaking is twofold. The first aspect seems to offer that needful kind of immunity to destructive (shallow or hysterically appealing) myth forms. By willingly entering into dialogue with myth we forestall being taken unaware by it—in the vulnerability and neediness of our mythic deprivation. And if we are fortunate and search with integrity, we will see into the deeps of the myth world and subsequently avoid—to reverse the popular image—"the perils of the shallows." The second aspect involves the "living" nature of myths and the necessity for them to address the circumstances of our lives. We need to explain both the universe and ourselves, to ourselves; and to do this, the myths must arise from within us in moments of genuine need—"crying out for a vision," as the Plains Indians would say, or seeking the Asclepian sanctuary of the ancient Greeks.

Everywhere, nowadays, the rights of the individual are being tested, human rights constituting one of the principal issues of our time. Any enterprise such as creative or personal exploration can only take place in a free society. For the most part, in our pluralistic social environment, once we have entered adulthood, we may leave behind the often cumbersome shells of traditional meaning to seek our own—personal—one, a project not without its terrors as well as rewards. In addition, unlike our myth-bound ancestors, all of culture and history lies at our fingertips; therefore, our ability to see myth from all sides—and thus see through it—is unparalleled. But, Campbell has written,

> one cannot predict the next mythology any more than one can predict tonight's dream; for a mythology is not an ideology. It is not something projected from the brain, but something experienced from the heart, from recognitions of identities behind or within the appearances of nature, perceiving with love a "thou" where there would have been otherwise only an "it."[10]

Thus our emerging myth forms may not be created, but only invited. The responsibility of the conscious mythmaker is merely to construct an appropriate "frame of reverence" into which the power is invited to flow. The ritual forms I introduce in this part of the book could in a sense be called "spirit traps." The "play" modality introduced herein, however, is just as important as the seriousness and respect. In Dora Kalff's "sandplay," for example (see Chapter 11), a childish-seeming adventure in a sandbox may be converted into a revelatory adventure of personal transformation. The same is true of mask making, an especially powerful agent of self-recognition and healing, which is the next subject of this chapter. You can know that you are in the presence of living mythology simply by how you feel when you are there. "That in which the lightning flashes forth, makes one blink, and say Ah!—that 'Ah!' refers to divinity," Campbell wrote, quoting the *Kena Upanishad*.[11]

THE HEALING MASK

> *Jesus said, "If you bring forth what is within you, what you bring forth will save you. If you do not bring forth what is within you, what you do not bring forth will destroy you."*

—THE GOSPEL ACCORDING TO THOMAS

Since ancient times masks have been worn in trance rites, initiation ceremonies, festivals, and theatrical events. Less well known is their specific healing function, but aspects of "healing" in its widest sense, including education, psychotherapy, and spiritual instruction are also to be found in these familiar masked rituals.[12]

But there are also cultures in which masks are used specifically for healing: the sickness demon exorcisms of Sri Lanka and the False Face Societies of the Iroquois. Taking our starting point from these ancient traditions, about fifteen years ago Robin and I began to study the use of masks in therapeutic groups. From this work, abundant comparisons emerged that confirmed the healing role of the mask, when used respectfully, in a ritual manner. This section moves from a consideration of mask in traditional myths, to mask work as an example of creative mythmaking.

The mystery interpretation of the mask involves the recognition of the mask as a gateway into and out of life. With its rigid form, the mask speaks of death and yet of a quality that endures through time. It may be worn by different generations, and as each living person animates the shell, breathing his or her spirit into it, the mask is brought alive, reborn. Thus the mask may evoke images of life in death and death in life.

In ancient Greece the mask appeared in the rites of Dionysus and the mysteries. Masks were hung on poles or on trees in the woods, to be filled by the spirits of nature, the wind, and the light of the sun, moon, and stars. The passerby would be surprised and held by the sight of the mask inhabited by emptiness itself. Does this type of image evoke the idea of the masks of God referred to by Campbell in the title of his four-volume series?[13]

There is a Zen koan in which the roshi asks the student, "Show me your face before you were born." To comply with this seemingly impossible request the student must enter his "original mind." Perhaps a quest like this was unconsciously occurring to one of my psychology students (unversed in the lore of masks or Zen) who wrote in his dream journal:

> A dream that occurred many times as a child was one that involved masks on my face, hundreds and hundreds of different masks. Each time I pulled one off another remained. I could feel my own face underneath it all, but never could reach it. I can remember it bothered me for quite a while. Even now, sometimes, when I think about it, I wonder what a dream like that could uncover.

His last, perhaps not-so-naive question, is the same as the one asked by the Zen master. Does each mask imply the existence of others? Does the very fact of mask making imply the inexhaustible search for the identity of the self— of God?[14]

Modern attitudes to the mask have stressed its concealing role: the social mask one hides behind, the cosmetic mask with its painted expression, the sinister masks of the headsman or bandit, the ambivalent mask of the Lone Ranger.

But perhaps closer to the archaic meaning of the mask is that of the mask worn to carnival. When one enters "conceal-ment" behind the mask there is a paradoxical freeing of behavior. A transformation of character may take place, as hidden or suppressed parts of the self come to the fore. Ultimately the transformation is revealing rather than con-cealing. There is a glimpse of the inner cast of characters that inhabits each one of us.

I am in agreement with Carl Kerényi who defines the secondary functions of the mask as to conceal and to terrify. These are "degenerate" forms (far from their own genesis). The primary function of the mask is to unite the indwelling wearer (and the observer) with a mythic being, or as Jung would say, "an archetypal power." The mask, as we have found it in our own work, becomes a transformer of energy, a medium of exchange between ego and archetype. Thus in traditional societies one finds the taboos surround-ing the mask, its recognition as a power object, and the phenomenon of "possession by the spirit of a mask." One would not lightly put on a shaman's mask (or any power mask), for to do so would be to invite its spirit to possess you.

However, the making of one's own mask is a different story. The spirit invited to the possession is from within the mask maker. There is a legitimacy and appropriateness about the relationship. A dialogue ensues in which the ego ulti-mately must encounter the other powers within the psyche. The spirit of the mask presents (usually) the most important of these confrontations for the person at the present mo-ment: thus its healing role. It represents a concentration of psychic energy, and an offer of dialogue between ego and *other*.

The rigidity of the mask helps to bind the attention of the personality, or "collection of masks" (remember that Greek *persona* means "mask"), to this one face of the self that requires attention. This "arresting" quality of the mask is known as one of its recurring powers. We think of the

Gorgon's mask from classic mythology, which freezes the observer to stone, or the occult masks of African secret societies, the mere glimpse of which is said to cause instant death to the uninitiated.[15] The mask is held to be a power object in most traditional societies. But my contention is that its power resides in its impact on the psyche—of beholder or wearer.

Two examples from traditional societies led us to consider the structure of how masks may heal: the False Face Societies of the Iroquois of New York State and the Yaksha (demon) masks of Sri Lanka. The comparison is more interesting because, although the possibility of influence by either culture on the other is extremely unlikely, the similarities are striking.

A visitor to either culture would observe the following ritual stages: (1) Either serious illness threatens individual members of the community or an epidemic threatens the entire communal well-being; the illness may be "mental" or "physical" in our terminology. (2) Societies of masked dancers are summoned. The masks are twisted and grotesque, resembling demonic beings, or as one is told in Sri Lanka, "the sickness demons themselves." (3) A rite of exorcism or propitiation is staged, which resolves the illness on the symbolic or psychospiritual plane. The community is present or involved. (4) The patient recovers (or fails to recover) and the community simultaneously is revitalized by the ritual. (I suspect that even in the case of failure the importance of communal revitalization is not diminished.)

In both cultures the meaning of the masked enactment is accompanied by a myth of covenant between the supernatural and human realms. Two sets of stories, paraphrased below, are worth comparing. The first Sri Lankan story is as follows:

In the olden days there was a time when the demons of sickness (Yakshas, Rakshashas) were very powerful. They would wait for people on the roads, or even in the villages, and seize them. Many of these sickness

demons controlled fatal illnesses and people died in
great numbers. It got so bad the people complained to
the Lord Buddha. "Where is your karuná [compassion],
they cried, "we are grievously afflicted with the sickness demons, and they rampage freely over the land.
You must save us."

So the Buddha called the chief of the sickness demons
(Mahā-kola-sanni-yaksaya), who came in before him. You
must stop afflicting my people," said the Buddha.

"But," said the sickness demon, for he was wise and
crafty, "Lord Buddha, the people are lazy and given to
self-gratification. Some folk don't think much of us
sickness demons, I know, but it is we who keep the
people humble and pious. When they are sick, their
eyes roll heavenward and they begin to think of what
they have done wrong and to meditate upon spiritual
things and the nature of their attachment to the chain of
suffering."

"Hmmm," said the Buddha, and meditated on the
problem for some time. Finally he gave his judgment
to the great sickness demon: "You shall continue to
have the power to make people ill, but not to kill
wantonly. And if, when they become ill, they celebrate
the proper rites and sacrifices (which include the masks
of the great demons), they shall be healed."

Here is the second Sri Lankan story:

Now the birth of Mahā-kola-sanni-yaksaya, the Great
Sickness Demon, was as follows: Queen Asupalakumari
was pregnant, and her husband, the king of Visala-
maha-huvara, was journeying about the realm finding
the things she craved during her pregnancy. On his
return, a courtier, who hated the queen, told the king
she had been unfaithful to him. The king's fury knew

FIGURE 26. *Mahā-kola-sanni-yaksaya, the Great Sickness Demon, surrounded by eighteen small masks representing the diseases under the control of the demon (Drawing by Robin Larsen from a wooden mask, Singhalese, probably 19c, 1981).*

no bounds, and he levied a harsh judgment: The queen should be cut in half, one part to be hung on a tree, the other left on the ground for dogs to devour. The queen, who was innocent, flew into a rage at this judgment and uttered a terrible curse: "If the sentence is unjust," she said, "then the child in my body shall be reborn as a demon, and this demon shall destroy the whole town together with you, its unjust king."

When the judgment was carried out, it was as she said: The Great Sickness Demon, for it was he, sprang out of his mother's body, first nursed on her, then devoured her whole corpse to feed his strength. For a while he frequented cemeteries where he fed on corpses; then with a retinue of hideous followers, he ravaged the countryside. He infected the king with a deadly disease and then devoured the courtiers. Later, the Great Sickness Demon was subdued by the gods Iśvara and Sakra, who came in the guise of beggars. They extracted from the great demon the promise to accept sacrificial rituals using masks in exchange for restoring health to victims.[16]

Usually, on the masks at the sickness demon ceremony (Sanniya-Yakuma), only eighteen yakku (demons) are represented, along with their chief. In the myths, however, the Great Sickness Demon is described as having as many as 4,448 or 484,000 demon followers.

The Iroquois tell two myths of the origins of the False Faces. Both are included here, although abbreviated, as there are elements in each that refer to our theme. The first story follows:

As the Creator of the world was walking around inspecting his handiwork, a great Titan, in the form of a flying stone head, approached him. This demiurge disputed his creatorship, claiming the same office, and the two decided to have a titanic magical contest: moving a distant mountain toward them.

The Stone-Faced One tried first, but moved the mountain only partway. When the Creator's turn came, the Stone-Faced One got distracted for a moment (such was his nature) and looked away; when he turned again to watch, the mountain, rushing up, smote him in the face.

The Creator, contemplating the now-deformed demiurge, realized the being had great power and assigned him the task of curing diseases. Men would make his crooked mask and heal with it.

And here is the second Iroquois story:

As human hunters were camped in the deep forest, away from the habitations of men, they would catch sight of strange querulous spirit beings with twisted faces and long hair snapping in the breeze behind them. The hunters would return to their camps at night to find the ashes of the fire scattered about and the marks of some great dirty hand on the lodge post.

One day a hunter agreed to stay in camp while his partner went afield. During the day a strange twisted-face being came to him and picked up hot ashes and scattered them around. That night the hunter dreamed the being appeared to him and requested an offering of tobacco and mush. Later the hunters learned from the beings their songs and their method of curing by blowing hot ashes. They made masks of the spirits, the False Faces, which to this day are to be carved from a living basswood tree under ceremonial circumstances and, like masks of power in all traditional cultures, must be handled only in a sacred manner.[17]

Now what do these mythological tales, and the peculiar usages of masks in these societies, have to do with healing? In each tale we see a disturbance of balance, a righting or resolution, and a covenant between the supernatural realm (which

FIGURE 27. *Shak-a-de-o-wee,*
Iroquois False Face mask.
(Drawing by Robin Larsen,
1981.)

in animistic belief is causal) and the human, natural, and social worlds. Mask wearing is the sign of the covenant, the magical formula, the password for the aperture between worlds.

The masks may be quite specific for certain diseases. In Sri Lanka, each demon has his symptom picture, like the homeopathic remedies: *Pita-Sanniya,* who affects the gall and brings sleeping sickness, headaches, vomiting, and terrifying dreams; *Vedda-Sanniya,* who carries a hunter's bow and brings the plague; *Gini-Jala-Sanniya,* the fire and water demon, who brings fever and ague.

The task of the mask–manipulation therapy is to remind both the spiritual and the human worlds of their compact and to verify magically an ancient connection that modern medicine may be struggling to recover: the effect of the patient's spiritual state on his health. When a Navajo sand-painting healer places his patient in the mandala he has worked hours or days to prepare, he is trying to align psychospiritual forces in the patient, in himself, and in the universe. The priest in Sri Lanka who dons the mask of the patient's particular disease, and dances for him, is doing likewise. They are close to Paracelsus and Hahnemann's *similia similibus curantur,* like cures like.[18]

Illness brings its share of the grotesque into human life, grotesque masks are worn in its cure; and the restorative medicines of Asclepius came from horrific Medusa. When Perseus decapitated her, she bled two fluids: that which came from the right side brought death and that from the left restored life. Medusa herself (whose mask petrifies) was pregnant and, like Queen Asupalakumari, was cut in two parts. It was told that Poseidon had seduced her in the form of a horse (some say a bird) in Athena's temple. Athena, whose virginal priestess she was, was furious and transformed her into a nightmarish creature with a hideous mask. "She became a winged monster with gleaming eyes, huge teeth, protruding tongue, brazed claws and serpent locks, whose gaze turned men to stone."[19]

Strong passions and resentments are one source of illness, say the legends. Misunderstanding and cruelty make us sick. Put on the grotesque mask and, through voluntary acceptance of its message, achieve healing. It would not seem an overstatement to say these traditions recast illness as trials of spiritual growth. This is not exactly the same as "psychologizing" or looking for a psychogenic factor in all illness. It is, rather, the "meaning" dimension that is able to affirm suffering by seeing it in the larger context of understanding life. Ultimately this is a vitalistic perspective which sees "meaning" as a strong and subtle medicine, which infuses and regenerates the life force deep within the patient.

Psychologist Jerome Kagan's work has shown that the human face of whatever (recognizable) form is the pattern most likely to elicit responses from very young infants.[20] They also quickly come to recognize familiar faces and develop xenophobia for strange ones. When our daughter, Gwyneth, was only a few weeks old, she would stare in great fascination at the Tibetan demon masks that hang on the walls of our house. These are not exactly "Walt Disney" faces and are meant to be fierce and formidable, grins complete with tusks. But she liked them, would smile and laugh, and have incomprehensible conversations with them.

Unlike Kagan's "scrambled faces" they are recognizable "persons," with a certain character, and she seemed to have been responding to this dimension.[21]

If we try to locate the neurological structures that mediate such a deceptively simple human activity as mask making, we find they extend from the highest areas of the brain to the lowest. Of the cerebral hemispheres, the right (usually nondominant) is the specialist in nonverbal tasks: pattern recognition, imagery, and, especially, "places and faces." But this is the crown of the tree, and we must descend through the limbic system into dark prehuman roots in the autonomic nervous system (ANS). There we find the ancient responses: chills that run up and down the spine, gooseflesh, our hair (or feathers) standing on end, the color of a blush, and the grimace that originates in the viscera.[22]

The mask's ability to heal (or to arrest illness) may reside in its deep reach into the living nervous system. Only a small portion of this system may be contacted verbally; far more is programmed in images. If I ask you how you are, and you respond by making a face, I will probably understand your face without the mediation of words. And if you make the disgust mask (whose meaning is "I could regurgitate [disgust], but I won't") I may feel myself involuntarily make the same mask as well as experience a mild nausea, all without verbal cues. The vocabulary of the communication is imagery and sensation.

When we do warming-up exercises for our mask workshops, we ask participants to "make faces." Then, more psychologically, we ask them to indwell—put themselves inside—the attitude that accompanies that face. This makes us conscious of the neurological pattern that mediates that emotion, both its expression as behavior and its signal-communicational qualities.[23]

The human face attracts minute scrutiny for meaning among humans. The nuances of expression that signal, for example, "I am sincere (or insincere)" are extremely subtle. The meaning dimension emerges, then, as a primary modality for our understanding of masks. The mask resides closer to primary meaning, which is perceptual, preconceptual, and preverbal. Verbal definitions and logic refer to an order of secondary meaning which is learned and has formal referents and definitions.[24]

Words are not always the best vehicle for a mask to explain itself. In the spontaneous dramas with masks that emerge in our groups, we find that the masks "like" music and dance to "explain" themselves more fully. If there are words, these are often mythopoetic, liturgical, and highly charged with meaning. They may be concentrated formulas with a deep reference to affairs within the psyche of the person. Language within the field of primary meaning becomes poetry and magical incantation.[25]

To return to our mask stories, we may look at these as mythic structures by which the masks explain themselves. Two of them attribute the efficacy of the masks to a compact between divine and human powers (the first Iroquois and first Sri Lanka stories). The second story from each culture involves relationships between human and divine powers (i.e., the emergence of disease through human, not divine, violence). A child might ask the questions we often shrink from asking: "If God loves us why do we get sick?" The first stories reconcile us to the ways of the transpersonal powers, which are indeed mysterious.

A compact between the compassionate one and the mischievous one (trickster) reminds us of Job's sufferings, which are due, ultimately, not to the causes he thinks (such as his own sinfulness), but to a wager between transpersonal powers of which he was not even informed. Likewise compassionate Lord Buddha allows suffering (pathology) so we may retain our spirituality. The paradoxical nature of the universe is rendered through mythic personification and a symbol story that supports spiritual values.

The Iroquois False Face makers were also subtle metaphysicians, as the early Jesuits who went among them found. Their belief was that illness arose through the frustration of "desires of the soul." These innate and intuitive desires would manifest symbolically in the dream life of the patient. The False Face dancer might be a sensitive psychologist of dreams, as well as masked healer, skilled in recognizing important personal issues in their symbolism.[26]

In the great communal dream festivals, days of dream psychodrama would unfold, in which the goal was to help the dreamer realize his dream wishes. If these could not be attained "really," they were acted "symbolically," with actors and impromptu costumes.

What is the mental attitude necessary for such a performance? This has been described as the state of "as-if," the precondition for healing and symbolic awakening. Perhaps Campbell said it most lucidly:

> In the primitive world, where the clues to the origin of mythology must be sought, gods and demons are not conceived of in the way of hard-and-fast realities. The phenomenon of the primitive mask, for example, is a case in point. The mask is revered as an apparition of the mythical being that it represents, yet everyone knows that a man made the mask and a man is wearing it. . . . In other words, there has been a shift of view from the logic of the normal secular sphere, where things are understood to be distinct from each other, to a theatrical or play sphere, where they are accepted for what they are experienced as being, and the logic is that of "make-believe"—"as-if."[27]

In Sanskrit this is known as *anya-manas,* "the other mind," possession by a spirit.

FINDING OUR PERSONAL MASKS

In working with the masks experientially, we have tried to set up a simple, yet flexible structure that facilitates this quality: the "as-if," the open sense of wonder, the atmosphere that invites power to enter. (Is this to be readily achieved only in traditional societies, as it seems to those of us who romanticize them, with their ancient feeling for magic?) But there is usually hard work involved in ceremonies, as firsthand observation shows.

The ritual must be structured enough to contain and shape psychic energy and loose enough to allow it to flow freely from its own deep sources. At every step one is to dialogue with the images as they emerge. The images carry affect and are protean; they metamorphose as one tries to hold them. From this emerges the dialectic that accompanies every creative act. You may never render an image exactly from the guided fantasy to the completed mask; always more emerges, more than was intended, and often very "other." Many meanings—the riches of the creative psyche itself—flow in. In the psychodramatic stage you may confront these other meanings and see which are relevant, which carry the strongest feelings, which induce trance, or spellbind, and which do you prefer to avoid.

To answer these last questions, the discretion of the guide or workshop leader must be involved. How far can this person go, or how far should anyone go in a single instance of "confrontation with the unconscious"? (This is Jung's term, but apt in the sense that when we meet something that has been unconscious, there may be a confrontative quality to the meeting.) I believe that personal sensitivity and training as a therapist are indispensable for this delicate, yet powerful task. This is not to say that spontaneous healing does not occur or that anyone may not learn from the process of simply making a mask in a respectful manner, later dialoguing with or indwelling it. But the mobilization of masks for healing in the group context is a powerful ritual, and the personal issues that may emerge are of such a nature as to require both feeling sensitivity and therapeutic wisdom.

The workshop space and atmosphere must be safe, supportive, and open to exploration. If one can tolerate such paradoxes, it should be "seriously playful."

Where in the process does healing take place? It would be tempting to speculate that it happens in the grand moments of dramatic self-recognition that occur, or in the catharsis that may be provoked in simple dialogue with the mask (its reach into the neural "tree"). But we are equally willing to believe it could happen in the molding of the mask on the face (a strange personal act of "doubling"), or in the guided fantasy, or simply from partaking in a group ritual that is about healing.

A common figure that shows up in mask work is the spirit guide (see Chapter 9). We have heard guides speak with voices (other-seeming than the person's ordinary one) and deliver unexpected messages, even challenges to the waking ego. In Jungian terms this inner "guide" is the personification of the self: the life wisdom innate in the psyche of each person. Other figures such as the wise old man or woman, helpful animals, nature spirits, or personified wisdom figures from any age or culture may emerge.

Contrasexual masks often visit. The mask provides a vehicle for the anima or animus, or it may be a male dreamer's chance for the personal mother, the Great Mother, or his nixie soul image to tell him something that is overdue. A woman may encounter the personal father, an old patriarch, or even her young masculine hero, who is waiting for a voice and a face. Masks may also represent a race, an ancestor figure, or an element, such as fire. As among the Northwest Coast Indians, there are masks for natural phenomena like the sun and the moon, the sea, winds, the energy of young vegetation, and the falling-away wisdom of autumn or winter. Disease masks may croak their grotesque messages, but also at times speak surprisingly well and tell the ego a commonsense thing or two. Are illnesses the Jungian shadow on the biomedical plane, to be recognized and integrated? And are we to give them voices, make for them faces?

MASK DIALOGUES

Some "live" dialogues with the masks are recorded in this section. These are not as extensive as I would like, were I to attempt a full-scale exegesis of the mask work. However, in the context of this chapter, itself within the larger context of the book, I hope what I present will carry some flavor of this very special kind of conscious mythmaking. The dialogues carry their own quality of poetic incantation.

It is difficult, however, to summon the living atmosphere of an archetypal psychodrama being enacted in a group—a temporary community of healers and visionaries. The "feeling" atmosphere is palpable, and curious kinds of "knowing" seem to come to the masker who is working—playing—his or her mask, the therapist guide, and the group. The group is more lively than a Greek chorus—it will sing, drum, laugh, cry, hug, and heal by laying on of hands—but it also has the kind of wisdom and stateliness of the chorus. At

FIGURE 28. *Mask workshop: working before mirror.* (PHOTO BY ROBIN LARSEN.)

times it is like that "theater for divine onlookers" (see Chapter 2).

In the dialogues below, I am referred to as Stephen; mask makers are referred to by fictitious names. The major dialogues are related to masks that are included in Figures 29 to 35, to help you both see and "hear" the mask work.

Margaret has made an eerie, plain white mask with blood running out of the corner of the mouth, and fangs. It represents a type that we often call "the white witch." She puts on the mask in total silence (no accompaniment from group). The Mask says archly to the group: "I've come so she can see what she's doing."

I asked her, "Tell about yourself."

The Mask says, "I can't."

When a mask says something this declarative, I respect it and suggest a dialogue mode instead. I say, "Take off the mask, and talk to her as if she were a person."

Margaret says to the Mask, "I don't like you doing that. I don't want you to eat my friends. I know what you're thinking. Want to see what she's thinking? [Shows me the painted inside of mask, I ask if the group can see it too, which they do.] You're jealous . . . distracting . . . totally evil. [She has a moment of recognition.] I'm jealous, distracting, horrifying, evil . . . fiery . . . devouring . . . this side of me. [She is shaking—she turns back to the mask.] I haven't learned to accept you."

At this point I suggest Margaret try the mask on again. "I don't trust her," she says as she puts on the mask.

The Mask says in a changed tone of voice, "I'm coming out. You'll have to get used to me." She laughs a harsh, wicked witch laugh.

At this point we are face-to-face with something ambiguous and magical. The mask is, yet is not, Margaret. It seems horrible for her to own this shadow element as it presents itself. I try a different strategy: "I know that Margaret doesn't trust you, but I believe you're there for a purpose . . . find words to tell her."

The Mask responds, "I keep her from feeling how hurt she is."

I ask the Mask how it does that: "Do you discharge Margaret's energy? How?"

The Mask answers, "I do that. Just by being there, but right now it's real dangerous. I want something . . . and I want to stop trying to get it from other people."

To stop too rapid a self-disclosure, I suggest to the mask-wearing Margaret that an image will come to her that will help her understand what it is she wants, but not to tell us what it is now, just remember it. I ask her to take the mask off.

Margaret takes the mask off, shivers, and hugs herself. "I'm feeling frightened."

I ask her if she's feeling cold. "Oh yes," she says, shivering.

"Now I'm going to guess something," I say. "In real life, when do you feel this way? Isn't it after you've let her [the Mask] out?"

Margaret laughs painfully and says, "Yes."

"She steals your energy?" I ask.

"Yes!"

At this point I ask her to wear the mask and dance the image she got earlier of "wanting something."

"I want to be held," she says, "but I'm afraid I'll grab . . ."

The group comes in at this point to help with the dance, which has to do with wanting love and also, savagely, going right to the source—she is obsessed by the genital regions.

She says, "I'm grabbing!"

She is caught between acting out cruelty, and waves of desire . . . and remorse. T'ai chi ch'uan comes helpfully into play here as I dance wildly with her in a circle formed by the group. The demonic figure seems to come to the end of its strength. Margaret finally weeps deeply, spasmodically. We embrace, the group supports.

A male therapist who has recently been through a tragic love affair, in which he was treated most cruelly by a lover, is also a member of the group. His mask is embroidered with Anansi, the African spider-trickster figure, but there is a sadness associated with the feeling of having been fooled. This mask has to do with the shadow as trickster.

He feels a need to enter into a dialogue with the white witch.

"You gave me everything, and then took it away," he says. "You really took me for a ride; then you got me by the"—he pauses as he understands the connection—"balls! There, I've said it."

With the mask on he summons the depression he has been living with. The mask visibly amplifies the morose atmosphere. He tells his story to the group, and I suggest he interact with the witch in a tableau that expresses the meaning of what he has been going through. Both players seem to recognize there is some kind of sacrificial rite being accomplished. (The immortal words of Sophocles come to mind: "Who is the slayer, and who the victim? Speak!")

After the drama, both players seem relieved and somehow

FIGURES 29 AND 30. *Mask workshop: white witch and white witch with victim.* (PHOTOS BY ROBIN LARSEN.)

freed by the archetypal psychodrama. As usually happens, the group feels closer to the protagonists who have worked on a difficult and painful aspect of themselves, rather than the reverse (some kind of judgmentalism for betraying a flaw). This is the healing, therapeutic dimension of the mask work.

The following is an example unique in our experience in mask work. One brave woman came back to make a mask once a year with us, for five years. This example is instructive because it shows how truly one human soul may be inhabited by many masks (see Chapter 8) and how the kaleidoscopic masks of the self revolve over time in the same person.

In the first mask she made, Tina was working on a deep and painful issue. It was the emotional aftermath of having had an abortion, something she swore to herself when younger that she would never do. The recognition while wearing the mask in front of the mirror initiated a profound catharsis that lasted for several hours (the mask's role as a concentrator of energy).

The following year (see Figure 32) she recognized a masculine quality to the mask as she wore it. She had a feeling of bravado and independence: "I can cope with anything." It was while indwelling the conspicuous color green in the mask that she came to her major insight. "It's supposed to be the color of new life, but there's something about it I really don't like," she said. At this point, I mentioned that in Celtic mythology sometimes green is associated with death, which initiated the catharsis that time, as she realized she was dealing with the aftermath of the death of her father during the previous year. (Her young hero had emerged when she realized that without his reassuring presence, she was going to have to fend, much more, for herself.)

In the third year, Tina discovered something else was emerging. It was a powerful, primordial sense of selfhood. In this elemental, but beautiful mask, was a connection with the earth and feminine power; furthermore, her (one-eighth)

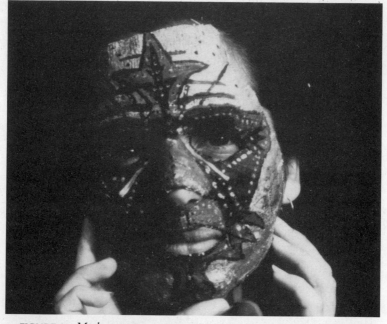

FIGURE 31. *Mask sequence: nature spirit.* (PHOTO BY ROBIN LARSEN.)

FIGURE 32. *Mask sequence: father's death.* (PHOTO BY ROBIN LARSEN.)

FIGURE 33. *Mask sequence: the shaman/healer.* (PHOTO BY ROBIN LARSEN.)

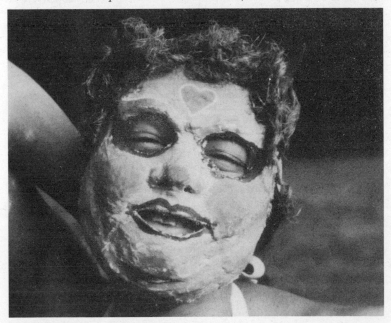

FIGURE 34. *Mask sequence: Mrs. Dowd.* (PHOTO BY ROBIN LARSEN.)

FIGURE 35. *Mask sequence: the beast.* (PHOTO BY ROBIN LARSEN.)

native American side began to emerge. In a workshop for
young shamans that we held in our community, led by
Michael Harner, she proved to excel as a "pointer" in the
bone game; a role requiring active clairvoyance or telepathy.[28]

The fourth year something totally unexpected took place.
We were doing a workshop largely composed of actors of
the Theater of the Open Eye in New York. Tina was our
assistant, but made a mask anyway. Not entirely unexpected by
her (she knew, usually, what mask was coming to her) but
to the vast amusement of the group we were visited by
"Mrs. Dowd" (Tina's name for this figure), who is archetypal, indeed. She is the fat lady in your church group who
bakes cookies for the social and then eats them all herself on
the way there. (This figure is a clown, whose job is to take a

shadow flaw and exorcise it by hyperbole; see Chapter 11.) Mrs. Dowd is shameless, but she laughs infectiously, and had the whole group with aching sides.

The following year, Tina had a big dream (briefly related below), which she brought up in her therapy with me. The dream seemed powerful enough to require the mask process, rather than normal therapeutic approaches.

> *I am in a beautiful garden, surrounded by flowers and all kinds of beauty. There is a swing, and I get on and begin to swing back and forth, higher and higher. There is a cliff nearby, but I don't mind. Right in the midst of my joy, a black hand with claws reaches up from the abyss and grabs my ankle. I awake screaming.*

The dream image I was to see some years later in a *Gnosis* magazine seems to imply a heedless bliss that invites a fall, or the terrifying power of the Lord of the Abyss. Tina took all weekend to make the mask, with some technical assistance from Robin.

At a climactic moment in the group I summon her wordlessly to the center. She sits facing her mask.

Tina says to the Mask, "You tried to kill me. You've been following me around for quite a while. I feel you all the time, in my stomach and my throat. Where have you come from, and why are you here?"

The Mask responds, "I warned you," and roars.

A Dionysian and bestial dance unfolds, as immense power seems to come into her, and the group. It is apparent that the demonic energy of the creature—not unlike the Nagual—is wild, but somehow accessible. The work with the mask in the group gradually seems to have a taming effect. She would take a while to integrate the elemental power of this dream being, now a mask, but the process had begun.[29]

This succession of masks shows a developmental series of encounters with aspects of the self as well as with what seem to be archetypal powers. Both are evidently required for us to find a center for wholeness in the midst of our own mythological chaos. Peeking into that turbulence of symbolic forms that surrounds the self, we indeed find our landscape, our animals, our guides and spirit lovers, our many masks of the self. The mask work allows us to encounter ourselves in intense, magical—but manageable—doses.

In some way the deepest meaning of the mask has to do with "finding our faces before we were born." The search for identity and a meaningful place in the universe we have found to be intimately bound up with healing. To make a mask is an excursion to that primordial zone where personal identity meets and merges with the more ancient powers of which it is constituted. This is truly a search for "roots" in the deepest sense, a reach into the field of life's very vitality.

Chapter 11

SYMBOLIC PLAY

Where the comic spirit has departed, the company becomes constraint, reserve eats up the spirit, and people fall into a penurious melancholy in their scruple to be exact, sane and reasonable.

—GEORGE SANTAYANA

This chapter looks at conscious mythmaking through humor and play. The forms I explore are the shamanic roots of circus, particularly the clown, or sacred fool; the symbolic world building of sandplay and how healing may occur in the midst of play; and, in a concluding section, an exciting kind of conscious mythmaking, "live fantasy," in which adults conspire together to create an imaginary universe—and then live in it.

It would not be appropriate to introduce these topics without mentioning the important influence of Johan Huizinga's *Homo Ludens: A Study of the Play-Element in Culture,* which reminded the modern intellectual world how serious a pastime play is for humans and introduced the term *Homo ludens,* "man who plays," as our worthiest title. This chapter will help you balance the weightier information from previous chapters—about initiations, underworld journey, and the contemplation of death—and, in fact, directs the reader to certain time-honored forms of mythmaking that lighten up these sobering facts of life. The clown, as we shall see, has made this his specialization—and humor really thrives on the contradictory, the inevitable, the unfair, and the unspeakable.

THE SHAMANISTIC CIRCUS

Circuses are traditionally performed in tents—not unlike a giant Siberian yurt, with its great central pole symbolizing the world axis—and within a ring or magic circle, which symbolizes sacred space. And everywhere in circus we see fragments of the most ancient religion in the world still being celebrated: sacraments to the body which is capable of behaving like a spirit. As someone twirls through the air defying gravity or juggles objects that seem to fly magically or dances on a rope, the horizontal plane which defines the ordinary movements of human beings is broken by the vertical. Within this magic circle, up, down, and all around are equal. Identities change, as in dreams, as costumes are put on or taken off; we cannot tell who is the acrobat, who the clown. And the ancient shamanic rapport between beast and human is apparent in this timeless world. The elephants dance, the bears frolic, the tigers obey.

French poet Theodore de Banville, writing of the English pantomimist-clown in 1880, observed that this figure had made a choice between possibility and impossibility.

He lives in the impossible, if it is impossible, he does it. He hides where it is impossible to hide, he passes through openings that are smaller than his body, he stands on supports that are too weak to support his weight; while being closely observed, he executes movements that are absolutely undetectable, he balances on an umbrella, he curls up inside a guitar case without it bothering him in the least, and throughout, he flees, he escapes, he leaps, he flies through the air. And what drives him on? The remembrance of having been a bird, the regret of no longer being one, the will to again become one.[1]

Mircea Eliade had not yet compiled his extensive material on the shamanic origins of magical flight, or the universal role of tricks and stage magic in shamanism, when this was written. And the ethnographic lore from which he assembled his evidence was still being generated. He would document the ancient origins of this urge to see the human being behaving like a spirit (or like a bird, who among physical animals best symbolizes the quality of spirit). But within the charmed ring of the circus, ancient rituals were still celebrated.[2]

Such peculiar terrestrial beasts are we, with mental wings, it seems. Flight was the preoccupation of our shaman ancestors long before Kitty Hawk. And if it is an act of hubris to fly physically rather than in spirit form, then we are in the age of Icarus and the sun may melt our waxen wings. The airliner is grand, but terrible indeed when it perishes. Evel Knievel, a modern hero whose earthy machine carries him aloft in a bright, symbolic arc, also enacts Icarus's fate fairly often. And after each plummet, he becomes the dismembered shaman, the wired-together six-million-dollar man with crystalline and platinum inner parts. The urge to see the body spiritualized, to fly, to break the tyranny of Newton's laws, to disappear, to metamorphose into something else, is in our hollow bones.

In an article entitled "The Shamanistic Origins of Popular Entertainments," drama scholar E. T. Kirby argued that in all illusionist art, from the stage magician to the sword swallower, to the clown, "he who takes blows," we find the themes of shamanism. As he said,

the performing arts that develop from trance may be characterized as the manifestation, or conjuring, of an immediately present reality of a different order, kind or

quality. . . . Shamanist illusionism, with its ventriloquism and escape acts, seeks to break the surface of
reality, as it were, to cause the appearance of a super-
reality that is "more real" than the ordinary.[3]

Thus symbolic play has ever been aimed at too ready a
mood of materialism; at Aristotelian logic, which measures
and judges the world too soberly; and at any view whose
boundaries are closed to the miraculous, the paradoxical,
and the unforeseen.

The following common elements in circus and shamanism
may be identified: acrobatics, pole or rope climbing; feats of
balance (the "master of equilibrium" motif illustrated not
only on the tightrope, but in the figure of Castaneda's Don
Genaro, dancing on the edge of the waterfall);[4] simulated
flying; costumes of all sorts; human-animal communication;
ventriloquism, magical appearances and disappearances; dismemberment (i.e., being sawed in half); survival of a life-
threatening ordeal (being shot out of a cannon); clowning,
puppets, masks; abilities while blindfolded (magical sight);
androgynous beings (the bearded woman or the effeminate
white clown); and freaks of all kinds (often treated as magical beings in traditional societies).

Children need no lessons to understand circus because its
reference is to that which lies deep in their bones as well, the
urge to participate in a half-remembered world of magic and
wonder. In the circus they also glimpse the terrible seriousness of adults at play, perfecting death-defying arts as simple-
seeming amusements. Behind the spontaneous and the
slapstick lie years, and maybe generations, of disciplined
endeavor. The circus ring symbolizes a bond to ritual no less
firm than that of a priest and his altar, and the mystery that
its hierophant (the ringmaster) celebrates is no less precise.

Is this the reference for our dreams of new religious forms
that include disreputable-seeming clowns and acrobats in
traditional sacred places (see Chapter 4)? The goal of the
circus arts, like the shamanic arts, is ever to aim at the

suspension of disbelief. Symbolically, the sense of sacred play is invited to inform our religious attitude. "Look," it says, "what seems impossible is possible. I show you magical things and make them seem easy, a trifle." The practical man in us knows there is a trick here. But he knows also the tremendous work that must have gone into this trick. This gives it a psychic reality; it is worthy of deep human endeavor to perpetrate this foolishness. The performer or clown invites our practical man to share in a ritual of carefully choreographed folly.

CLOWNS AND SACRED FOOLS

Perhaps in no area more than clowning are the archaic roots of circus revealed. The clown himself seems a hopeless atavism. Like a primitive or a child, he "messes up" what is supposed to go smoothly, he baits the ringmaster, bumps into the roustabouts. He incarnates all the mistakes that the performers must, in reality, never make. In traditional societies the precise function of the clown is to help the people see through too much solemnity in religious rituals. In many native American societies, clowns to this day attend (and mock) the most serious ceremonies of the religious calendar.

Among the Hopi and Zuni, for example, the clowns are priests with high office and specific types of ritualized clowning to perform. Often this includes dealing with everything left out of the formal aspects of the religion: sexuality and scatology especially, but also anything taboo, physical and mental deformity, grotesque traits of character, and perversity.

For example, the Newekwe society, one of the fourteen curing societies of the Zuni, specializes in public demonstrations of the most outrageous gluttony: eating not only the "inedible," but things designed to arouse disgust as well as astonishment. Different observers have reported the clowns delightedly eating wood, stones, clothing, garbage, and excrement of all kinds. Like the fabled circus geek, they bite off and devour the heads of mice and other animals, or fight over the carcasses of dogs.

Some of the late-nineteenth-century ethnographers who saw these clowns in action were horrified, failing to understand the shamanistic and esoteric implications of the strange acts. The Newekwe are healers, who specialize in curing digestive and stomach problems. Instead of putting the patient on a bland diet, they put themselves on a rough one; engaging in a public demonstration of the ridiculousness of gastrointestinal delicacy (provided one is mythologically and spiritually supported). The Newekwe also mock all aspects not only of their ceremonies, but the Christian ones as well, testing the white man's ability to see through his own tradition.[5]

"In its primal phase," wrote Kirby,

> clowning is identified with the representation of [the] diseased and deformed. The Aztecs had comic performances in which the ill and crippled were represented; "deaf, lame, blind, deformed, or sick people, or sometimes merchants, mechanics, or prominent citizens were mimicked, burlesqued and made fun of."[6]

He mentions that in Africa scrotal elephantiasis was burlesqued (thought to be a punishment for adultery) and among the Yoruba the six masks of the origin of the *Egungun* ceremony are a hunchback, an albino, a leper, a prognathic, a dwarf, and a cripple. I think also of the retinue of the Mesoamerican deity Quetzalcoatl, which also consisted of freaks, hunchbacks, and dwarves.

Psychologically, we could say that clowning has always addressed itself to the Jungian concept of the *shadow*. The grotesque, hidden, and unacceptable aspects of personal life are unveiled and shown to be universal. We recognize the outrageous braggart or buffoon (*bouffon*) as pure types and, if we are psychologically attuned, as classic elements in our own makeup. They are members of our "inner cast of characters" (see Chapter 8).

When we behold the pristine character of the fool on the stage, though, another ritual, sociological as well as psychological, is being performed. In the exorcisms of mental and physical disease, clown-shamans are often asked to enact for the community the soul of the disease, or its "personality." When the "sickness demon" has been thus personified and enacted, as in Sri Lanka (see Chapter 10), the illness itself may then be symbolically "laughed out of the community."

The clown—poor or outcast (the bum), too tall or too fat, or dwarfed—possessing some obvious deformity such as a huge nose or falsetto voice, and the accident-prone person, tripping on things, being hit by mops or flying pies, illustrate some basic qualities of human life that are far from satisfactory, yet beset us all. This aspect of the clown holds the funhouse mirror up to our "fallen" state, susceptible to "sin," the archaic meaning of which includes error and accident. This figure is referred to in Yiddish as the *schlemiel* and is very cleverly rendered by Woody Allen, whose specialty is the deeply introspective schlemiel.[7]

These observations may help us to understand the "contrary" clown tradition, then. Something in our psychology recognizes the arbitrariness of every willed human act and intention. We cannot will anything from ourselves without creating a "shadow." The role of the "contraries," such as the Heyoka society of the Sioux, is constantly to remind everyone of the absurdity of all human behavior. If the whole tribe gallops out of town, the Heyoka will be backward on his horse or going in the opposite direction. He sleeps in the day, rises at night, goes the wrong way round the ceremonial tepee. The Heyoka listens for puns and Freudian slips, and acts out the unintended meaning. The term *heyoka* is, in fact, an inversion of the familiar Plains Indian war cry *hoka-hey*.[8]

The members of this curious fraternity are selected not by

personal choice or the will of the group, but by lightning! Two great Sioux visionaries, Black Elk and Lame Deer, were Heyokas. At the time that he was known by John Neihardt, and later Joseph Epes Brown, Black Elk was almost blind. He told Brown this had occurred in a prank in which he was trying literally to act out a prophecy in which the earth would rise; Black Elk had laid a trail of gunpowder under the floor of the ceremonial tepee.[9] We might think of this as going a little too far, but the clowns among the Sioux believed themselves under supernatural injunction—from those marvelous mythic beings the thunderbirds—to perform these tricks as often as possible. Lame Deer said,

> It is very simple to become a Heyoka. All you have to do is dream about the lightning, the thunderbirds. You do this, and when you wake up in the morning you are a Heyoka. There is nothing you can do about it. . . . Having had that dream, getting up in the morning, at once I would hear this noise in the ground under my feet, that rumble of thunder. I'd know that before the day ends that thunder will come through and hit me, unless I perform the dream.[10]

The thing one must initially perform is usually something shameful, personal, and private, but the lightning may not be turned down.

A few years ago, in a syndicated newspaper, I read about a man from Long Island who had been hit by lightning sixteen times. Once it even happened in a room full of people where no one else was hit, and the lightning rolled in a ball down the table until it came to him. Naturally the article said nothing of Heyokas, nor did the poor man know anything of this obscure native American tradition. But I couldn't help wondering if his electrifying experiences had improved his sense of humor in any way and how many more times it would take to make him a clown, an inhabitant of a culture that offered him neither name nor myth of explanation.

The European commedia dell'arte psychologizes specific character defects and personifies them (Pantalone's aging goatish hypersexuality, for example). Exorcism is by hyperbole. The more we are able to exaggerate and thus to celebrate, the more laughter lends its healing solution to some of the most difficult aspects of our humanity.

The *bouffon* is a related transformation of this tradition. This clown is dwarfish and horribly disillusioned. He is permitted to be self-centered, sardonic, lustful, or vengeful. For most clowns in this tradition, their stage rendition has only come after the personally profound ritual of finding their own *bouffon* or their own angry dwarf to identify and enact.[11]

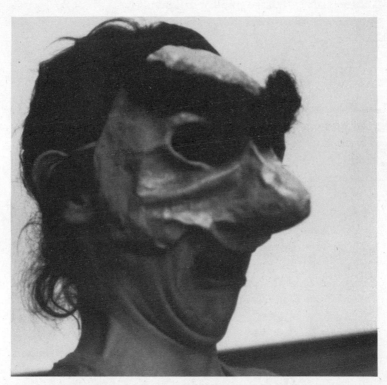

FIGURE 36. *"Bill," an Australian outback character, played by Heather Robb, mime.* (PHOTO BY AUTHOR.)

I have often thought, as I see this figure onstage or experience the healing laughter he or she occasions, "How nice to meet you like this, and not in fairer-seeming disguise in everyday life, as we so often do." In ordinary doings, the fair-seeming may be foul beneath. Here, in one kind of conscious mythmaking, foul is extracted from disguise and put on fair public display, even encouraged to strut around and make speeches. The laughter is the liberation bestowed by the revelation of the hidden element and our recognition of a universal personification of psyche, of which we all may partake at times.

In Chapter 12, I include exercises that invite you to find your own clown. These are among the most liberating and self-revelatory I have explored, and allow us first to recognize and then to laugh at our human limitations.

THE CLOWNS OF MANI RIMDU

In 1976, while studying masks in enactive ritual, my wife and I had a chance to observe and photograph the Mani Rimdu ceremony of Khumbu, Nepal. This Tibetan-Buddhist ceremony of the Nyingmapa tradition is unique, yet related to others of Tibet and Sikkim. It is loaded with shamanistic elements, especially those transmitted through the pre-Buddhist Bon religion. The masks of archetypal figures such as *Yamantaka,* the "conqueror of death," are included along with the central ones of the historical (and yet highly mythologized) figure of Padma Sambhava, who brought Buddhism to eighth-century Tibet through Khumbu, and *Khumbu-yul-lha,* resident divinity of the friendly little (19,294-foot) mountain next door, whose mask is worn and danced.[12]

But here I'd like to tell you about the wonderful clowns of Mani Rimdu, who kept us laughing for days, amid the hailstorms and high ceremonials of Thame monastery.[13] First there is *Mi-tshe-ring* the wise old fool, who messes up the "high masses of Tibetan Buddhism." Then there is *Rtogs-Ldan,* the Hindu Sadhu, or holy man, who never stops talking and *Bkra-Shis,* his straight man. There is Monkey, the Asian trickster-demiurge par excellence, and a few other clowns who are of lesser importance.

There is a wisdom to the tolerance of "controlled folly,"

FIGURE 37. *Mi-tshe-ring, Mani-Rimdu's wise fool.* (PHOTO BY ROBIN LARSEN.)

FIGURE 38. *Bkra-shis don-grub,
dummy servant to the clown
"sadhu" in Mani-Rimdu.*
(PHOTO BY ROBIN LARSEN.)

FIGURES 39 AND 40. (facing page) *Dur-bdag, helper of the Lord of the Dead
with detail showing dancer's feet and corpse-doll.* (PHOTOS BY ROBIN LARSEN.)

as exercised by the clowns in the solemn ceremonial. Observers of rituals that seem too time honored and sacrosanct are likely to go through a little inner rebellion at the seriousness of it all, perhaps even activate their inner trickster or resentful *bouffon*. It is a wise priest who legitimizes and externalizes the inner laughter. He has anticipated the refractory trickster he knows to dwell within each human. As a gentle adult will allow children to tease or play jokes, the religion endears itself to the people by its willingness to joke and let jokes be played on it. Those of us wise enough to revere the fool will see this as religion's strength rather than its weakness. Mi-tshe with all his mistakes is "the long-life man." The clown brings good luck. His archaic association, like that of *Ganesha* (the much beloved elephant-headed deity of India), is with fortune, luck, and coincidence. The people believed that to invoke Mi-tshe is to preclude the

ill-luck that may plague the most carefully undertaken human endeavors. The fool symbolically concentrates the unpredictable, ambivalent playfulness of the universe and binds it within the magic dancing circle of the Dharma.

For the Westerner, familiar with the lore of Zen, there are ironies in Mi-tshe's identity as Hwa-shang, an eighth-century Chan (in Japanese, Zen) master from China. We are used to the idea of the legendary self-possession and mastery of skills conferred by Zen. Zen carries a connotation in contemporary usage of a mystical mastery of life. It is an irony then to see Mi-tshe—Hwa-shang—unable to perform any action correctly. He is "un-Zen" in everything, the opposite of what one expects. It is said he lost the doctrinal debates with his opponent Kamalasila, who represented the correct view: that of the Buddhism brought to Tibet by Padma Sambhava, not that brought to China by Bodhidharma.[14] (Did Hwa-shang tire of theological debate, a Tibetan specialty, and rely instead on the Zen master's traditional use of clowning and the unexpected: the sudden blow, the wisely foolish paradoxical act?)

On the other hand Rtogs-Ldan, the Hindu sage clown, with his constant speechifying, makes us wish he would take the Zen clown's vow of silence. He abuses his sidekick (he is a "great man," like the Winnebago trickster), and like Hardy to Laurel, Abbott to Costello, or Pozzo to Lucky in Beckett's *Waiting for Godot,* he recreates the archetype of the righteous harangue (the pompous clown to the schlemiel). And do we hear echoes of a familiar inner dialogue: top dog to underdog (Perls), superego to id (Freud), or parent to child (Transactional Analysis).

And yet the abusive clown shows he is susceptible to exactly the same qualities he derides in his companion. He forgets the name of the monastery. With both cerebral hemispheres seemingly defective, he botches the correct (ritual) modes both of speech and behavior, somehow feeling immensely self-important all the while. The combination is irresistibly funny to the Sherpas.

Earlier in the ceremony the *durb-dags,* skeleton dancers representing guardians of the graveyard, had evoked the tragic mood; omnipresent and impartial, death seemed during their dance in its celebration, in the thin air of these terrible and wonderful mountains (see Figures 39 to 40). They had tossed about and cruelly stabbed a doll, which seemed to represent all the fragility of human life. Now the clowns are stabbing the doll, imitating the durb-dag, ludicrously miming the avatars of death. Bkra-Shis (the straight man) snatches up the doll and runs away from Rtogs-Ldan; he has grown fond of it, he says. The tension of the terror response to the *mysterium tremendum et fascinans* gives way to peals of laughter, and it is not hard to accept the blessing of the release.

The alternation of the two masks (the tragic and comic ones from ancient Greece, which have become the emblem of the modern theater) may cause a disorientation within the beholder, in which neither terror nor laughter prevails, but a third state, like the surprised open mind the Zen master induces with his stick blow or his riddle, the state of wonder.

In the lama's house where we are staying, there is a poster of Chairman Mao on the wall beside the tankas. I ask the lama about it, and he smiles sheepishly, "a kind of insurance policy," he indicates, and I remember that Tibet is only about twenty miles away as the *lammergeier* (the soaring Himalayan vulture) flies. Images of burned tankas and destroyed temples, tortured lamas, and the genocides of 1951 and 1959 come into mental focus.

This culture clings to the roof of a world that is all uncertain in its future, and in the ethereal beauty of sky, rocks, and ice, the Buddhist message of the precariousness of life returns amplified. Here it grins at us with a tusked demon's face, it wears a diadem of skulls and a mantle of entrails like a lady's fur wrap. We awoke one morning to the thin wailing of a *ryang-ling* (a human femur-trumpet). "All is impermanent, all is without a self," these eerie sights and sounds remind us.

★   ★   ★

"This is Buddhism?" our seven-year-old son, Merlin, asks sagely. For the last few months he has been used to the Buddhism of Sri Lanka, where the shaven, saffron-robed monks breathed a different decorum. Now he sees this pageant of converted demons, holy men with demonic manifestations, and the whirling black-haired zwa-nag. I explain these are Buddhist tantric magicians who supplanted the sorcerers of the Bon religion. He wants to know about the skeletons, the masks everywhere, the theta-rhythmic beat of the great two-headed drum. I falter at the size of his questions, then explain lamely about shamanism and its paraphernalia, here integrated into Buddhism somehow. "I like it better than Sri Lanka," he says, "there are masks and clowns."

A few hours later I hear Merlin talking to a Japanese balloonist we have befriended, and who is equally curious about the decorum of a Buddhism that differs from that of the forms he is familiar with: Zen, or even Nichiren, Buddhism. "It's Buddhist," Merlin is saying to the balloonist, "but there's shamanism too."

Comic interludes are not characteristically interspersed among the Tibetan sacred dances (Cham), although they do appear in the secular Lha-mo, and this may be an innovation of the Sherpa people, who claim the great saint Padma Sambhava (Lotus born) came to them with the Dharma first. But they are culturally and mythologically Tibetan, and constitute a unique still-living remnant of an ancient tradition.

But the great culture of Tibet is broken and the Dalai Lama in exile. Against the backdrop of these dismembering horrors, the warmth and humor of the Tibetan people shine. (Once during some personal time with a representative of the Dalai Lama, I was all too ready to launch into a general condemnation of the Chinese invasion. The man I was with, who had fled on foot through the icy passes, with so much personal harm and loss, shamed me by his lack of rancor.)

Laughter contains the same vibratory and tension-releasing

effects as weeping. Here at Thame, one could easily both cry and laugh; the Sherpas show us laughter, healing laughter, and it cleanses from its opposite, the sorrow of life.

SANDPLAY AND HEALING

As we were preparing to leave Thame monastery, a sand drawing was being created as part of a healing ceremony. This event surprised us because we had associated this ritual mainly with the Navajo.[15]

Among the Tibetans, or the Navajo, a lama, priest, or medicine man will work for hours to make a symbolic space, a frame of reverence, out of the commonest substance of the earth. Major features of the mythic cosmogony will be represented in the colored sands, so that the sand mandala becomes a microcosm. It is through this symbolic identity with the universe, with what *is* or with the Tao, that the ritual will work its magic.

In mid-life, his friendship with Freud over, Jung entered into a depression; and who was to heal the great healer? Not knowing what else to do, he went to the beach of the Zürichsee and began to play in the sand. Jung later believed it was through this "sandplay" that he reestablished his contact with his inner roots, regenerated his psyche, and reconnected with the validity of his own personal path.[16] He did not have the cultural support of the traditional societies, but still this earthy medicine worked its traditional magic. The homeopaths say of their remedy *silicea*—nothing more than an energized bit of sand—that it is deep and powerful.[17]

More recently, Dora Kalff developed sandplay as a powerful therapeutic tool. Her "free and sheltered space" of the sandtray and playroom is the frame of reverence, the rainbow-boundary of the Navajo within which the soul plays and sees itself in a reflection; remember that in the mirror's glass is melted sand.

At an international transpersonal psychology conference I

attended, many distinguished presenters noted that sandplay provided lasting and major therapeutic change for their patients—adults as well as children.[18] Most mentioned their indebtedness to Kalff and Jung for opening their eyes to the value of this method and helping to develop its procedure.

Kalff indicated the sandbox should be of a specific size, which she arrived at by years of experimentation: 19½ inches by 28½ inches by 3 inches deep. "The measurement of the box," she wrote, "exactly corresponds to what the eye can encompass." Close by on shelves are

> hundreds of little figures made of lead and other metals: people—not only of various types and professions of modern times, but also figures from past centuries, negroes, fighting Indians, etc. . . . There are also wild and domestic animals, houses of different styles, trees, bushes, flowers, fences, traffic signals, cars, trains, old carriages, boats; in short everything which exists in the world as well as in the fantasy of the child. . . . The child chooses objects which he especially likes. He forms hills, tunnels, plains, lakes and rivers in the sand, just as they are in his world, and allows the figures to act as he experiences them in his fantasy.[19]

Kalff insists that freedom characterize the play within this space and that the therapist facilitate, more than guide in a highly structured way. The tableaux and dialogues that ensue may be recorded by the therapist with a tape recorder or on a notepad or by photographing, which enables developmental sequences of sessions to be remembered. Kalff noted that people who wish to pursue her specific method must study it in depth and, preferably, receive training from a qualified sandplay therapist.

Cecil Burney, an American psychologist with Jungian and Kalffian training, pointed out the powerful implications of this method for personal mythology.[20] The "player" will make a world in which he or she will place the self (like the

FIGURE 41. *Child with sand tray*. (PHOTO COURTESY OF LUCY BARBERA AND ARYA MALONEY.)

cosmogony of the Navajo or Sherpa). But the symbolic features of the landscape will be a personal land-nam, with private associations and loaded with feelings (see Chapter 4). And yet, almost always, to the accustomed eye of the sandplay therapist, there are the archetypes: the world mountain of our aspirations, the island self, the mystery cave of transformation, the beast as initiator, the protean self (as identities change and are substituted), and the hero journey.

I first experienced the power of sandplay in the office of my Jungian analyst more than twenty years ago and, since then, have found it of great value in my own therapeutic work. I can only add two comments to Kalff's observations: the method works as well with adults as with children, and the "hip" symbolic imagination of today asks for inclusion in the form of *Star Wars* characters, a whole line of mythical beings such as dragons and hyppogryffs (if you don't know what that is, ask a kid), and elf and dwarf protagonists from

Dungeons and Dragons. Tolkien figures such as Gandalf and Hobbits are a must, as well as superheroes of all sorts, flying saucers and spaceships, and other contemporary iconography.

I also include images that have to do with more ordinary and domestic things: nuclear families, babies, bottles, food, picnic baskets, beds, and sleeping bags. I also recommend old people, doctors, tombstones, churches, crosses, and so forth so that players are able to include these elements of ordinary reality in their "play" as well. Like dreams, sandplay presents the images and events of daily life in a kind of magic mirror. We may look at life from a different perspective. In this regard, sandplay is also good for breaking therapeutic impasses. As in dream, so in sandplay we may intermingle symbols, something from daily life with the mythic: "That's me and my dog there, and we're going through the forest, and there's Yoda sitting in a tree."

Although I utilize sandplay in my therapeutic work, it is not my primary therapeutic modality, but is often integrated with many other approaches. To enrich and deepen this discussion, I interviewed two sandplay therapists, Lucy Barbera and Arya Maloney, for whom sandplay is their most frequently used modality. They work largely, but not exclusively, with children; sometimes they work individually with adults or in the family context. However, in the following dialogue, the emphasis is on work with children.[21]

The sandplay experience seems to be accompanied by a characteristic shift in perspective, a distinctive alteration in one's sense of scale. This establishes a new context in which people, events, and our responses to them shift subtly in relationship to one another. In discussing the therapeutic effect of this perspective shift, Barbera observed, "There's a world in the sandplay tray. One child saw the room and the figures and said, 'I can make a whole world in here.' It's empowering, for a child to have a world at his or her fingertips."

Kalff's prescribed size for the sandbox is adhered to by many sandplay therapists. As Barbera explained, "We tried to follow her dimensions. It has to do with being able to see the whole 'world,' the whole situation at a glance. You can take it all in."

From the immediately apparent "controllableness" of this little world arises a sense of freedom: we needn't, after all, work so hard to hold it all together. Maloney described this release into the flow of the play, which often seems to happen at the threshold of the sandplay room: "When the children come in, they go up and down and look at all the objects and figures before they start. It's kind of a trance."

Barbera added, "There's something else directing them— you can see it in their body language as they walk around, pick up one figure, then another—the way they go moving through the space. Something else is directing them other than their minds. It's more like a kind of 'soul operation.' "

The sandtray becomes not just a little, circumscribed world, but a border realm, through which an adventurer may cross over into worlds beyond. In a sense, it becomes itself the portal that permits our passage, or it can become a window through which we can safely look without passing, a window through which we ourselves can be seen, or it can become a magic mirror. Barbera recalled, in one series of sandplay sessions, "a kind of crystal wand that came with one of the hero figures. This one boy used it in just about every tray he did, and he said, 'You know what this is a sign for?' I said, 'No.' He said, 'It's a mirror to see the gazebo [a center of tranquillity in his "world"]. It's to see yourself, it's to see everyone.' So it was like a mirror. The sandplay creates a way to see."

This *seeing,* as we have observed, has to do with consciousness, and with opening awareness. Visual artists have long been fascinated by this alteration not only of perspective, but of what we think of as an overall state of consciousness, achieved through manipulation of scale in artwork.[22] As Alice down the rabbit hole or through the looking glass, we find old habits of eye-mind-body communication no longer sufficient; we are almost forced to reexamine and reorganize. But in our sandplay world, unlike Alice, we are more sheltered, we have secret helpers, we may move beyond the powerlesness of the child. There seems to be an interaction, on a subtle level, of new ways of seeing (from above, like a god, or from within, like a tiny germ) with something like *siddhi,* special powers, granted, as it were, by our magically attained condition of hugeness or minuteness. Insights reveal themselves in unexpected ways, as we find ourselves creators and masters of a whole new world. Sandplay therapist Burney pointed out that we receive a kind of empowerment that continues and increases as more sandplay work is done.[23]

Maloney observed, "The actual healing occurs silently; there's something about certain constellations manifesting themselves in the tray, this sense of 'Ah, that's it!' . . . In nearly every tray there's a witness figure, it's a persistent theme," a theme that recalls the cultivation of the internal silent witness well known to both Eastern and Western meditative disciplines. Maloney contributed an even more explicit image: "Sometimes it's a figure standing outside the box or on the rim, sometimes it's within. In one child's sandplay there are always these birds, sitting and watching everything." Here we encounter one of those images, not uncommon in this work, which startles us with a little *frisson* of recognition: In the Mandukya Upanishad, we read, "Two birds, inseparable friends, cling to the same tree; one of them eats the sweet fruit, the other looks on without eating."[24]

At such moments in our work as therapists, a psychic bell rings, alerting us: We have indeed stepped across some kind of border into a realm where different laws may prevail.

Out of all the other possible modalities, other kinds of imaginative games, what is it with sand and a wooden box that is special? It is one of the commonest, and least conscious, of gestures—this dipping of our hand into sand, to play. Sand is among the commonest of substances, at once veriest matter and yet—with its crystalline refractiveness—

does it partake, somehow, of the nature of light? White sand spilling through our fingers in sunlight has ever had the power to entrance our vision, as if we held for a moment a million little mirrors of spirit fire.

Barbera said, "I've often seen a child just sit in front of a sandtray and let the sand run through his fingers, without doing anything with the figures. One child working with John Hood Williams did this and then he looked over at John and just said, 'Sand.' I thought it was beautiful."

In my own work with sandplay, I've seen that happen often, particularly when a child is shy about starting a process of self-revelation. As Barbera noted, sand is by nature "a 'grounding' substance. I've seen kids use sand ritualistically. They'll create a picture, then sprinkle sand in certain places . . . it's very important."

We see the importance of these "certain places," and the importance of the preciseness with which the sand marks them, when we are privileged to watch the painstaking creation of the healing sand mandalas in certain Hindu or Buddhist tantric rites, or in Navajo sand painting. Burney reminded us of the ancient associations to *sand:* He related the word to *send,* as in "send a message"; also he connected it to dream in the figure of the "sandman," who in fairy-tale lore brings sleep—and dreams.

Maloney said, "You can do dreams in the sandbox; or start where the dream leaves off and carry them on."

"I've also done work where you do a sandplay," Barbera continued, "and then treat it like a dream, as if the sandplay images were dream images. It's very powerful."

We have, by this very act of sitting down to play with sand, evoked the liminal zone of the seashore where we played as children with sand and pebbles and dreams, while the waves of the limitless ocean teased and reshaped and ultimately overwhelmed our little creations. In sifting sand we mimic the artistry of the elements, of wind and time; and we participate in one of humankind's most ancient acts of magic, still common with sorcerers and priests in all parts of the globe. Such acts set loose the mythic imagination, inviting its transformative invasion.

We spoke earlier of the silent witness, and the way in which "the actual healing occurs silently." There is a quality of silence, of being alone in one's own world, of privateness, in sandplay. And with this privateness, there is often implied a kind of secrecy: there may be secret helpers who augment one's power; secret tunnels with secret entrances; secret graves; secret treasure; and secrets kept, secrets lost, and secrets found. "One of the things that happens is kids get a chance to bury figures," Barbera said, "they disappear but you know they're there; then they get them again later. There seems to be a real release in doing that. . . . The theme of treasure being discovered comes up again and again. It's a very simple thing. Of course, there's a treasure, it's there, you can find it. It's often very carefully placed."

"We also have a lock and a key [in our sandplay collection]. That gets a lot of use. Sometimes, for example, they'll set up a bridge, they'll lock it, you need a key to get across. (Bridges are important too.) But often a lock will be placed somewhere, and the key carefully hidden somewhere else; maybe bury it and even plant a tree over it. You can lock up certain kinds of images, but then you know how to get to them again, you know where the key is."

We know most poignantly from work with abused children how potent are these locked-up images. Child or adult, in the sandtray world we possess the power to lock away certain experiences, like destructive genies in bottles, or the power to choose to retrieve the safely hidden key and set them free to fly away on their own adventure or to serve us.

Within the safe confines of the sandtray, we can play at confronting what most terrifies us; we can open the cages or prisons—after all it is only play—that lock up our lives. We can address our biggest questions to those who are big enough to answer them.

Maloney described "one kid who had a real archetypal mandala. He had what he called 'the four kings of the earth.'

In front of each king was a tomb. The black square, 'the main guy,' was between them all. Later he indicated it might be 'God.' "

Such a configuration suggests an advanced tray; it may require a lot of uncovering, a lot of work, to get to the point where "God" or the "devil" appears in transparent guise, in the midst of the court of heaven or hell.[25]

In our therapy center there was, for a while, some construction going on, and a truly horrible little piece of garbage was unearthed: black, with nails and junk embedded all together, sharp and ugly looking. I followed my intuition and put it on the shelf. Sure enough a child gravitated to it like a magnet. He asked me, "What is it?" I said, "Oh, just an evil thing." It appeared in every sandplay he did after that (he was a child who was having a lot of trouble with being "bad"). He would surround "the evil thing" with guardian figures: trolls with clubs, beasts and inhuman monsters of various kinds from the Dungeons and Dragons set. It played a pivotal role in a number of adventures for him. Afterward, I reflected on the role of evil in fairy tales and epic adventures; it often is what actually gets things going. When the nineteenth-century Hindu saint Ramakrishna was asked why evil was permitted in the universe, he replied, "It thickens the plot."

This brings us to another theme of profound importance in sandplay therapy: that of having a thing or place of our own. When we are children, we spend what is for many a tiresome lot of time learning about all that is someone else's—often older "someones," who have been here longer and made prior claim: this is older sister's room, that is Daddy's toolbox, we must not play on Mother's desk. So it is most important in sandplay when, as Barbera reminded us, "Children identify with an object, that is *their* object. It is very much connected with them, and they get it out every time." Simple as this may seem, it injects a special potency into certain sandplay events. This is consistent with what is called "object relations" in neopsychoanalytic theory, but in sandplay we see it set off in a much richer way, given a heightened dimensionality by the mythic coloration of its setting. Maloney acknowledged the occurrence of classic Freudian scenarios, remembering "one where the baby is up on the roof . . ."

"All alone up there?" I asked.

"Just baby, up on the roof," Maloney affirmed, and noted this exposure to be a counterpart of the previously discussed burial motif. For many children there is an implied abandonment in the arrival of a younger sibling. The child feels peripheralized or, on the other hand, may wish to exile new baby to the roof. Sometimes babies are buried. "One sandplay, though, had a 'crucified baby,' " Maloney continued (more in a Jungian vein). "First it appeared in a manger. Then he had it outside, put it upside down in the sand for a while. It's a difficult concept, crucifixion, but in the sandplay you can touch it, handle it."

Barbera developed the theme of a private place with another story: "One boy was working something out in a very difficult family situation. His mother had a very hard time letting him be, and when she came to the sandplay room she would always ask him to explain [what he was doing, despite the therapist's asking her not to]. One time she came into the room and saw his play. There was his little gazebo in the center, in the midst of chaos, and he said, 'There I can feel safe.' That time she got it. She finally glimpsed what was happening and started to cry, seeing how strong his need for that place was."

Although we won't go into it in this discussion, sandtray work with adults is also intensely revealing and has applications for both individual and group work. Particularly in his work with whole families, Maloney noted, "the dynamics come out right away, in very interesting ways."

Barbera commented, "Some adult sandtrays are very beautiful."

One cannot properly discuss sandplay without images. To convey more vividly the way a sandplay scenario unfolds its

FIGURE 42. *Sand tray: hero approaches church.* (PHOTO COURTESY OF
LUCY BARBERA AND ARYA MALONEY.)

FIGURE 43. *Sand tray: serpent and two swans.* (PHOTO COURTESY OF
LUCY BARBERA AND ARYA MALONEY.)

levels of meaning, the discussion that follows refers to the situation depicted in Figures 42 and 43.

Maloney set the stage: "The goal is to reach these two swans. There is a gold one and a glass one. If you touch the glass one there is poison and you die instantly. There is a snake who alone is able to neutralize the poison by drinking it. The church protects the two swans. There is a battle. There are all kinds of dangers and traps. You have to get to the real swan (the gold one) and either avoid or detoxify the other one."

In this interesting tray there is danger and there is healing. One hero stands in front of the church. Another hero lies on the ground to the right; he encountered the toxicity of the glass swan, which would seem to be a brittle form (glass) of what symbolizes the highest value (gold). The swan song is associated with death and thus with transformation.[26] In Vedic tradition Brahma rides a swan; in the art of greater India the swan is related to, and interchangeable with, the *paramahamsa,* the wild gander who flies beyond and who connotes solitude, healing, breath, and spirit. The swan also belongs to Aphrodite: ugly at hatching, as in the story of the ugly duckling, it matures into extraordinary beauty. That it is a *gold* swan alerts us to its association with authentic value and imperishability.

The serpent acts in a way we do not expect. Instead of poison-inflicting, he saves from poison. This is like the ancient adage of healing that says: That which wounds shall also heal. (Remember the two fluids from Medusa's neck and the serpents of the Asclepia, which are auspicious and associated with healing; see Chapter 10.)

As with the mask work, there are sometimes truly luminous moments in sandplay. A character or figure will speak, or the player, from his vantage above the whole world, will speak in an essential language that reminds us of magical incantation or high poetry. Burney told of a man who had barely finished high school and who worked most of his life as a mechanic. At one of these essential moments, contemplating a sandtray he had made, he said, "Through tricks comes healing. From the gifts of friends comes perception, from the unknown man comes knowledge, and through suffering comes truth. And this is me (in the center) with my burden, trying to find time for myself."[27]

In another sandplay in the series, the same man used a figure of the Virgin Mary saying, "She's not just my mother, she's the mother of everyone." Dealing with the death of his father, who had died with many unresolved issues of rejection, he said, "Here the wisdom of the heart is winning out over the hollowness of death."

In these moments of clarity, reflecting on the big picture of one's life that is paradoxically evoked by the "little picture" in the sandbox, the invisible healing spoken of by Maloney takes place. The pictures need not be interpreted aloud for the client, or "analyzed to death." The nonverbal hemisphere with its resident mythic images both creates and beholds—with recognition—the symbolic world within its momentary frame of reverence. What we have seen is that a series of moments of encounter and recognition such as these can actually improve our adequacy as individuals—in Campbell's sense—in the very midst of our encounter with the fearful wonder that is life.

As Burney concluded,

Schiller once wrote that humans are only truly free when they are at play. Play enables the energies of the psyche to be released and transformed. There is a parallel in Sanskrit to this element of play. "Lila" is said to represent divine play. Divine play is a part of all of us. In our seriousness, we sometimes lose awareness of our ability to play. One lesson to be learned from the Sandplay process applies to all of us: What we need is a serious psychology of play and a playful psychology of seriousness.[28]

THE DESIGN OF THE LABYRINTH

Many a parent has looked on in adult wonder as their child (or children) engages in the fantasy game called Dungeons and Dragons.[29] This successful game was developed about fifteen years ago; and to me it points to the returned presence of what I have called "the living landscape" on our imaginal horizon. Up until the mid-1960s even the work of Tolkien was known only to an esoterically inclined few. Since then the attention attracted to his work has been phenomenal. In his wake has come a communion of perhaps somewhat lesser, but inexhaustible, creative minds: the literary fantasists of the "sword and sorcery" and more recent genres. It seems children are not the only ones to gravitate toward faerie.

What used to intrigue me was the complexity of fantasy that ten-year-olds—clustered about my son—would put into their game: characters with definite strengths and shortcomings would be generated by each player, their magical talents and resources enumerated, and a master player—the dungeonmaster—would invite them into an incredible realm of terrors and wonders. There would be imprisonments in tenebrous dungeons and, of course, escapes; encounters with magical beings created by the dungeonmaster; horrible deaths in subterranean pools of acid, with a good likelihood of resurrection if your friends possessed the will and the magic; and all kinds of mythological creatures including cyclopes, demons, magic wielders, priests, alchemists, witches, shape changers, and the inevitable dragons. Usually there would be a goal for the quest being enacted: a treasure, the rescue of a maiden or the rescue of a good wizard imprisoned by a bad one (like Gandalf by Saruman), the gaining of a magical talisman, or the destruction of evil in some form.

With my penchant for things mythic and my knowledge of their persistence, I should not have been surprised at the prevalence and popularity of Dungeons and Dragons and the fantasy genre. But still it unfolds against a world that does not believe in its fundamental premise: the reality of magic. The paradox gets my attention: mythic imagination is alive and well in the nurseries of a demythologized society.

Something its founders call Live Adventure Quest is an adult form of fantasy play.[30] In a country landscape that is relatively sequestered and yet open to the improvisation of environments (caves of mystery, enchanted castles, and magic pools), the planners—like the dungeonmaster—set up a series of symbolic encounters, trials, resources, and magical beings. The players who agree to come (approximately sixty to a hundred adults, and maybe a few children) must design their own character and his or her resources, special qualities, and a convincing costume. There may be actual combat, which is symbolically enacted with foam swords and spears, but there are also magical weapons: potions of transformation, spells, and magical traps.

As I researched this game and talked to many players, some marvelous insights were precipitated about conscious mythmaking. The structure and symbolic props are specific enough to compel a definite adventure, but essential to the play and vitally apparent in it is a principle of indeterminacy, leaving room for the unforeseen and the mysterious conspiring of chance (which may be the factor that brings back some players year after year). Moreover, the players being adults (presumably with their "children" still very much present within), subtleties and psychological twists appear that I have never yet seen, even with very bright children at fantasy play. None of the players knows for sure who or what they will encounter from the constellation of possible situations and beings, including the other questers. (Just like "real life"?) Possibilities are provided for personal growth: a character realizes that his chosen approach to life, say as a warrior, has its limitations and problems and may experience a conversion to peacemaker or healer.

In 1989, I was privileged to sit in on planning meetings and to interview planners as well as players in this fascinating example of creative mythology. (The denouement was, of course, to play the game in full costume, and "in character," for the three days.) Billy Joe (or Hwyllion), master planner for the current year, has given considerable thought to the interplay of what we shall call *make-believe* or *pretend magic* and *natural* or *real magic*. His words provide a felicitous introduction to the material that follows:

> The primary reason that most players attend these games is one of entertainment and enjoyment. We share a common interest in myth, fantasy, and play, and come together for an environment to explore and play in. While personal growth and therapeutic value often are encountered in the game, we are not selling this as a therapy technique. Most likely, the growth, the inspiration, and the therapeutic value we experience is the direct result of the fact that this is a game of "make-believe," an escape from ordinary reality as we know it.

> Sometimes the spontaneity and synchronicity of our quest game does invoke a very real kind of magic other than the "pretend" magic of spells or potions. This is the magic of just the right thing occurring at just the right moment, the magic that allows a particular action or interaction during play to strike a personally meaningful chord, the magic that allows us, for a suspended moment, to experience this mythical land as a tangible alternative reality. As Jamie Mandolare pointed out after Pike One [an earlier game]: "God likes to play too."

> It is this "natural magic" that draws us into creating and participating in this kind of game to begin with. We have set the stage for a magical psychodrama with a complete cast of mythic characters: heroes, villains, warriors, healers, dragons, demons, wizards, gods, goddesses, spirits, and fairy folk. When a character takes counsel from a particularly impressive and in-

spired wood god, say, the result can lead to deep personal insights and growth. The experiences we undergo during the quest can be *very* real depending on the degree to which we accept this "nonordinary reality." By the same token, the game format safeguards those with reservations about loss of boundaries, because it's the player who regulates the depth of his or her experiences.

This introduction to the game meets the criteria Campbell specified for mythological celebration: the suspension of Aristotelian three-dimensional logic and the introduction of an "as-if" quality that invites power to enter. Unlike the children I have interviewed in regard to their Dungeons and Dragons experiences, this mythically attuned adult is able to define and differentiate real and make-believe varieties of magic. The make-believe magic is the deliberate agreement that symbols shall connote suspension of the ordinary rules of time and space. Thus a water balloon hurled by a sorcerer is agreed to contain a "shrinking spell," which will reduce the recipient to diminutive proportions. But the imaginally shrinking person has an experience known only to himself or herself, which nonetheless evokes childhood and a mythical state beyond, filled with his or her own personal Lilliputian fantasies. He or she emerges from the experience—say when the spell, by agreement, has worn off or by another potion—with an ineffable sense of wonder at the scale of things we so easily take for granted (and here is the real magic).

Another place where real magic shows up in these games is in the coincidences that Jung referred to as "synchronicities." For most of us scientifically socialized moderns, the unfoldment of experiences follows a relatively Aristotelian or Newtonian causality. Things occur because other things "made them happen," in ways that are consistent with physical reality as we know it. For this view, events such as dreams by distant relatives of a personal tragedy befalling a loved one in wartime, or something like the apparition of a grandfather to a woman living 10,000 miles away in India, must be "mere coincidence," or as Freud thought, delusional reconstructions *ex post facto* based on wish-fulfillment. The concept of "synchronicities," however, as outlined in a seminal paper coauthored by physicist Wolfgang Pauli and Jung, postulates a meaning dimension interconnecting "physical" and "psychological" events. This notion also is consistent with many of the underlying assumptions of Eastern religions, especially Taoism, which have always conceived matter to be transparent and at times almost purely symbolic.[31]

Interestingly enough, the principle is not only the underlying presupposition of the *I Ching*—or *Book of Changes,* an ancient oracle book from China—but is embedded in systems of magic and divination the world over, thus it is a perennial feature of mythology. In fairy tales, as we have seen (Chapter 4), there seems to be a conspiracy between the inner logic and development of the hero and that which he or she encounters on a quest. Often, as in the recent bestselling fantasy series *The Belgariad,* the characters must periodically consult books of ancient prophecy to know where they are going in their mythic adventure, and along the way, seeming coincidences that appear are actually manifestations of the prophecy.[32] Thus we find again the idea of a spiritual ecology, which begins as far back as the shamanic world view. The spiritual and natural worlds are interactive and interdependent.

We follow this process further now in a dialogue between the players of the live fantasy game. Planning and work meetings began in midwinter, some taking place in full costume and character, with planners arriving on snowy evenings by lantern light. The following dialogue took place on an afternoon in the spring, following a weekend of working together in the wooded hillsides and fields of our farm in New York (that year's game site), preparing a dragon's treasure cave, a magical labyrinth, an enchanted portal, and sundry fairyland traps and scenarios. We were gathered together in the upper story of a hexagonal, rustic cedar gazebo that would host a congress of fairy folk during the game, while its lower floor would house the fantastic glassware and devices of an alchemist. Taking part in this discussion were four experienced players who were involved in planning the forthcoming game. Jeffrey—who would double as the alchemist and his magically addled brother, Mad Tom—is, in his "regular life," a student in a nurse-practitioner program and has a degree in biochemistry. Billy Joe and Jules are artists and silversmiths, partners in professional life as in game play. James Lee, Billy Joe's brother, is a sculptor and healer, a student of massage therapies. Also present was my son, Merlin, in college at the time; he was new to the game but assisted with the work of set and prop construction. It has been my observation that players and planners as a group are notably creative people, with a diversity of skills in fine crafts and theatrical arts. Your attention is also called to the way in which their essential preoccupations reflect those of this book. An impressive level of artistry is evidenced in the details of the game, in such items as artfully carved sorcerer's staves, in the "antiqued" parchments and graceful calligraphy of magical scrolls, in handmade coins and jewelry hoarded by the dragon—itself a splendid sculpture about the size of a horse, which would hang suspended in a grotto between cliffs, writhing its long neck, breathing fire, and speaking in an electronically amplified voice.

My role in the following dialogue, as a novice player (sorcerer's apprentice?), was to elicit responses that show how some of these experiences unfold from within the players. Because synchronous events had had no small effect on the planning phase of the game, I opened with the question: As labyrinth designers, what is the role of synchronicity?

Billy Joe responded, "Synchronicity is the glue—that is, the magic. What you can do is set up innumerable devices and interweavings of possible paths, but those are like little springboards for each individual's—"

Jeffrey finished for him, "—possibility chambers."

Right away, my ears pricked up. "Say that again?"

"There are possibility circles," Jeffrey explained, "you walk somewhere, and in that place, possibilities are intensified. Sometimes you are presented with certain spells, or transformations. . . . What I did with my character, who was transformed [in a previous game], was that he was really tough, rough, and ready, a kind of a thief"—Jeffrey turned to Billy Joe—"I stole from you on my way out, with you going into a fit [this was an aftermath of an encounter with a dragon], a really nasty character."

Billy Joe gestured expressively, remembering the scene: "I was writhing on the floor, and he ripped me off! I trusted him!"

Jeffrey went on, "The way the transformation vision came was that I picked up this piece of paper that told me to go to a cave or a field. I chose the cave and stumbled in . . ."

"By chance?" I prompted, and Billy Joe took the cue.

"*When* people stumble in—and *how* they stumble in— There were all kinds of different possibilities set up. It could be a little shrine in the woods . . . and we throw in some coins or baubles. You can cross at different times in front of that shrine at different points of the day and always those objects are different. People are coming in and putting stuff on there—sacrifices and offerings—more than they are taking it off."

Jules added, "They'll create their own myths." Jules, with Billy Joe, made the coinage for the game, elegant little pieces of several metals, including silver, with mystic symbols cast on their faces. The mere handling of these coins is evocative of divinatory magic.

I asked Billy Joe, "Were you intending to lay a symbolic trap for Jeffrey?"

"A lot of people encountered this possibility chamber," Billy Joe said. "Players were instructed to sit down, read this scroll, and meditate."

Jeffrey continued, "My character was a very snarly, crude guy. He would set people up to be accused, start rumors, take money. I chose a packet with a note. My note said, 'Do you want to learn something about your path? . . . You are a self-centered person whose life is getting worse. . . . You must change your ways.' I was asked to visualize a goddess, deep within the earth, and make my peace with her as I sat and meditated. It made a powerful impression, emotional too. My character vowed to change his life."

"This was a therapeutic thing, then, that deepened your awareness," I commented. "But it wouldn't have worked in the same way if you hadn't been in that particular role."

"Which makes it more synchronistic," added Jules.

"It does make it more synchronistic," I agreed. "Because the role seemed to invite what happened to him," a role decidedly unlike Jeffrey's actual character. A longtime, active player, Jeffrey sometimes plays several very different roles in one game. Synchronicity becomes, in a sense, a partner in the action, visible in this often uncanny, apparent complicity between the "possibility circles" structured into the game and the player's choices of the moment. At such junctures the game becomes another kind of magic mirror held up to real life.

Jules told another story of character transformation: "There was a player in my group one year who was kind of a rogue and a thief and a no-good. We wound up going on a holy mission, and at first he said, 'Well, I'll go with you but I'm not really involved.' But through the interactions of our group, and this very sacred quest, he became transformed into someone who wanted to work for the good of the community. His original intent had been to amass as much material wealth as he could, but after he had changed his perspective, he kept finding bags of treasure, and wealth was pouring into his lap."

As I listened to these players talk and thought about instances of synchronicity I have encountered in mask workshops and other symbolically evocative circumstances, I began to ruminate as follows: In today's world the mythic is in a kind of exile from ordinary human commerce. Synchronous events may happen, but they have to break through our secular concepts and the barriers set up by our culture, somehow. (I should add here that I had the opposite experience during my travels in India, Sri Lanka, and Nepal, where the mythic imagination appears to be alive and well; synchronicities seemed to unfold at an almost alarming rate.) When, however, one creates a space into which the mythic may be invited—a temenos or a spirit trap, such is our symbolic deprivation—live myths rush in like atmosphere into the vacuum of a bell jar. Hence the efficacy of rituals, any rituals, in our time.

I was fascinated enough by the symbolic "traps" used in the games to make an inventory of the ones planned for the 1989 event. I also include a list of mythological creatures and characters for the reader's interest.

SYMBOLIC TRAPS

Labyrinth with Cyclops
Land of the Dead
Gate between Worlds
Dragon Cave
Cave of Skulls
Oracle
Highwaymen's Camp
Dream Circle
Magic Shop (potions, books of spells)
Tavern
Lightning-Struck Tree
Healing Pool
Power Circle and Shrines

MYTHOLOGICAL CREATURES

Sphinx, traveling, with riddle
Nymphs, Fauns, and Woodland Sprites
Fire-Breathing Dragon (winged, hovering at mouth of cave, and speaking)

Cyclops
Magical Hag
Ancestor Figure
Huge Hard-to-Identify Beast

CHARACTERS

Alchemist
Healer
Mages
Thieves
Shopkeepers and Innkeeper
Gamekeepers and Scouts
Bard
Travelers
Noblemen and Noblewomen
Magical Green Man
Soothsayer
Astrologer
Fairy Folk
Warriors and Knights

During my interviews I pursued specific themes that seemed to relate to other aspects of my ongoing meditation on mythic imagination. "One of the things I'm interested in," I explained, "is the inner cast of characters, and how one can enter a role that is the opposite of his usual self, or maybe an exaggeration of his ordinary characteristics."

Jules responded with the story of "a character called Ravenlock who came to the game and just wanted to kill— that was his mission. Circumstances prevented him from doing that the first year. . . . The next year he did; he got in with marauders who sacked all the parties throughout the day. Interestingly, the following year he came back as a member of a healing order that permitted no violence at all."

I found that an interesting sequence. "So that would be a pair of opposites that reveals itself in the characters: You might play a fool or a saint—in Oriental community theater they have some figures who are both at once" (as Mi-tshe-ring described earlier in this chapter). I wondered if this alternation of character type was a frequent pattern—people playing one character and then the opposite the next season?

"Oh sure, in fact people often do," Billy Joe said. "In a similar story to Jules's, one fellow came as a knight who was for the good of mankind—noble but kind of obnoxious. He was doing things for the benefit of the community: he went to vanquish a demon." Billy Joe declaimed, pompously: " 'I shall vanquish this demon for the good of the community and for the good of humankind, and blah, blah, blah.' But he got possessed and turned to"—in a nasty, groveling sort of voice—" 'Yes, master, what can I do and who can I kill?' The next year he stayed more with the peculiar character he had become than the one he started as."

As a psychologist, I found myself interested in these latter issues. If Jung and Heraclitus are right, it would seem all too easy to fall into "pairs of opposites" within. Too much of the ego ideal, and we invoke the shadow. Too much ruthlessness and we come face-to-face with the need for ethics. The interesting thing about the fantasy game is that it gives people the opportunity to explore their inner characterology in a playful "as-if" mode, rather than in real life, where it may indeed come out to their detriment. (Do we sometimes forget that, with the cold eye of eternity on us, all life is "as-if" and get caught up in some of our ordinary roles much too seriously?)

In the games, players are often given the opportunity to die. As we have seen in Chapter 6 (see also the creative mythology exercise, "The Funeral Exercise," in Chapter 12), this may be an edifying experience, one that occasions taking stock of one's life and perhaps adjusting one's values. In the fantasy game, dead persons may move among the adventurers as spirits, to participate in subtle ways—talk to mediums, influence oracles, and speak to other spirits. (Their

FIGURE 44. *Darvon Vradka, who is unnaturally aged because of a failed attempt at creating life. He forgot to disconnect a magical umbilicus and failed to include the seed of soul material (jet) needed for the success of the experiment. He comes here to Van Etten (the game site) to reclaim the lost life energy from his magical son. He is played by Nick Hogan, one of the original founders of the game.* (PHOTO COURTESY OF BILLY JOE THORPE.)

FIGURE 45. *The demon Dercas, with his cloak of many colors, and his minions. Left to right: Root Melder, the alchemist who freed the demon; assistant demon; Dercas; and assistant demon.* (PHOTO COURTESY OF BILLY JOE THORPE.)

condition is announced to other players by a white headband that denotes their incorporeal state.) Like the angels in the Wim Wenders film *Wings of Desire,* the player attains a spirit's-eye view of the human condition, which may impart its own peculiar revelations.

Billy Joe remembered several "ghost tales," among them one of "a woman who traveled in Jules's party, who was a priestess of the goddess and a diviner, and she would look into her cup and get messages. I happened to be an astral mage who could become invisible any time by pulling a white hood over my head [a standard game device for indicating invisibility]. I took a number of opportunities to give her specific visions. She'd look in her cup and all of a sudden I'd be there. At the time when specific things would happen, that would be a time to do a divination. I could see her making the preparations and come through the woods and be there. Something that wasn't a planned aspect of the game ended up becoming employed because it was easy to do and felt appropriate. That was synchronicity in terms of how we connected."

This brought up the issue of "complicity with synchronicity" again. Because the game is occurring simultaneously among a large group of people scattered over a considerable piece of ground, I wondered whether the planners deliberately designed intersections or temenos places.

Billy Joe described the way in which the planners try to simply provide openings, or felicitous junctures, making use of the common elements of fairy tale and romance: "People naturally gravitate toward a healing pool or well. . . . One year there was a place in a maze called The Well. It was a reflection well, and when you looked in, different possible visions would come to you. They would come via choosing a card in a [Tarot] deck. Take a card, and you would 'see' what was happening to you. The first person to hit that well was a man who was really concerned with karma and the afterlife. The card said, 'What you see in the well is a reflection of all your past lives and hidden moments.' He said, 'Wow, that's heavy,' and realized it was overwhelming knowledge. He died from "too much knowledge." Then he had to go around as a spirit for the rest of the game, but he used his knowledge for the good of all the other players . . . he used his information to keep the game running.

"There was one fellow who came several years in a row as the same character. He was very attached to that character, and I had questions as to whether he was going to be willing to let go of that character—because everything we do in the game is on the honor system—if it's your time to die, you know it is. . . . I wondered if he would make that choice straight. When his time came, it was unmistakable: he fell down, and by total synchronistic chance, the King of the Land of the Dead—which was a specific area in the game that you went to when you died—happened to come up out of his own realm and stand across this pond. And as soon as this character went down, he called out, 'Asilomar, Asilomar!' The dead man looked over, and there was the King of the Dead, who asked, 'Is it your time to come to me?' And the man said, 'Yes, it is my time to come.' And so he went and became a spirit guide.''

As I continued to go over my notes and tapes, I realized that the material could form a book in its own right, so many were the tales of wonder. However, sufficient has been presented to amplify and illustrate some of the major themes of this book: seeing through, the living landscape, maps, labyrinths, death as a teacher, and spirit guides. For the reader with an interest in this zone occasionally there are newsletters that may be obtained and that can lead to further references to this field.[33] As adults with one foot in the mythic realm, the group of players conclude this section.

James Lee, creator of the dragon for the 1989 game, summed up: "In what we call the ordinary world, we live in a culture which is preconditioned to think such things [as synchronicities] really don't happen. I think when we come out of a game we realize that our ordinary lives are not so ordinary but—when we let them be—surrounded by myths."

Billy Joe amplified his brother's statement: "When they [these often unrecognized nonordinary events] happen out of context—in the grocery store—there's something nonmythical about it. But when you set up this game which is really an intensive, centralized, concentrated, archetypal thing, not only do you recognize the events in their broader mythological context, but there's creative mythology, this sort of magnetic attraction that pulls that power into it and makes it operate like clockwork."

Merlin added, "In playing the game, entering the labyrinth, you're making a conscious choice—maybe not totally conscious, because there's an element in the game also of not knowing—but you do choose consciously to go into the space and to relinquish conscious control of the situation."

And Jules gave us the last word: "Because you can't control it once you're in: it will go where it will, and it will go to a good place."

Chapter 12

CREATIVE MYTHOLOGY EXERCISES

This final chapter introduces creative mythology exercises that Robin and I have developed over years of workshops, thus offering you a chance to experience something of mythic power at work. These are not intended to be done all at once, but one or two at a time, with each one followed by reflection or journal writing. We invite you, like the many visionaries in this book, to partake of a firsthand experience in creative mythology. Having led you thus far in learning why the mythic imagination is an endlessly intriguing subject, I am willing to let you have the last word.

It is customary to give the reader who is about to undertake something personally unusual, such as exploring other dimensions of the mind, a warning. I will not say, "This could be dangerous to your health," or "Do this only under the care of your family physician," and so on. Our time is the age of the specialist, and in an endeavor such as self-exploration we do not need an additional bureaucracy of the soul, rather permission for each and everyone of us "to enter the forest, where it is darkest," as I have described. However, to engage in these exercises is no less dangerous than life itself. All kinds of unexpected things may emerge. The exercises are not intended as a mental-health program, or a cure-all for major life problems, but as an aid to self-exploration for people who judge themselves qualified.

People who wish to venture beyond boundaries they themselves feel are safe are encouraged to do so with a helper, probably a trained psychotherapist with whom you feel comfortable. Explore adventurously, but wisely!

A Note to Group Leaders: You may use these exercises with groups, but you must use your own discretion in the application of an exercise to a particular group. We also appreciate being credited if you use one of our exercises.

GENERAL INSTRUCTIONS

These experiential exercises are included to assist you in a structured way to explore some aspects of your personal myth. Little is required to begin this process, but two principal aids will be useful throughout.

1. **Creative visualization.** This is best accomplished while you are physically relaxed and unhurried. Begin by going through your body, part by part, until it feels relaxed and peaceful. Imagine your mind to be a blank screen on which images may appear. Some people may like the idea of crystal gazing, looking into a deep well, or looking into a magic mirror. Use whichever of these works best for you. If you don't readily experience mental images, imagine "as-if" you were. Listen also for "imagery" from other sense modalities: auditory, kinesthetic, or simply a kind of mental "knowing" that a story or image is unfolding.

2. **Personal mythology journal.** Keep a personal record of the exercises and experiences you explore. Use a loose-leaf notebook with dividers, so you can work flexibly within the journal. Use separate sections as described below. Include simple drawings, even if you don't feel

art is your forte (if you look through the journal even a few weeks after you begin, you will see the point of this). Create poetry (without worrying about its formal qualities, unless you are a poet), especially to capture feeling qualities of a dream or image. Render some things in prose; for example, write down your first dream, then draw a scene from it, or a map, and then render it in poetic form (consider also musical renditions if so inclined). Compare how each of these modalities feels to you in connection with the same subject.

Journal Sections

1. **Dreams.** The only way to keep an adequate dream log seems to be to have your notebook beside your bed. The dream can best be written *immediately* after waking. Recall of details is most complete then and less so the longer you are awake. Write the general theme or plot of the dream, then fill in details. Include even things that may seem unimportant to you. The dream need not be complete. Often even small fragments are helpful. Date your dream entries. If other details come to you during the day, add them to your journal. If you have a strong feeling about what the dream means, include that.

The following questions may help you get a more complete picture of the dream.

Where does it happen?
Who is there?
Who are the central characters?
What is discovered, lost, changed?
What is the feeling atmosphere?
Unusually strong colors, objects, perceptions?
Incongruities or contradictions? (For example, a figure who seems to be at the same time two people you know.)

Note: Don't try to go out of your way to "analyze" each dream. Rather, just notice its feeling, tone, and theme. You may even find overt messages, puns, or double entendres. For whom might the message be and from whom? Be attentive to dreams you feel are "big" dreams or guiding dreams.

2. **Fantasies (daydreams).** Where do you go when you "wool-gather"? Try to see where your mind goes on its "time off," when you are not employing your conscious attention. Try to learn a way to watch your fantasy without interrupting it. When you feel the fantasy has naturally finished, write it down, asking yourself the same questions outlined for dreams. Notice whether you are the central character or someone else is. How are you different in the fantasy from ordinary life? Look for obvious elements of wish fulfillment, compensation, or anxiety. Fantasies also often contain creative impulses. What potentially productive activities do you find in fantasy? How might you actualize them?

Notice *when* and *where* you fantasize. How often? How vivid and rich are the fantasies? Are they visual, auditory, both? Olfactory? Notice colors, textures, physical feelings that may be involved, emotions, strong feelings, impulses, and the like. Does the fantasy recur? Does it seem stuck, or is it going somewhere? How can you resolve the impasse the fantasy presents?

3. **Personal mythology exercises.** These exercises are presented in this chapter. In this section of your journal you may record encounters with an inner guide, a shadow, allies, and so forth. Try to date your entries. Use pictures, poems, and incantations.

4. **Daily log section.** This section resembles the more usual form of a diary; record daily events, insights, meaningful

experiences, "synchronicities," disasters, feelings, and moods. Biorhythm charts may also be kept to observe periodic fluctuations of bodily, mental, and emotional states.

5. **Creative work section.** This section relates to creative endeavor; writing, drawing, planning a house, or making music. You may also work out self-actualization, feelings of growth, and life objectives. Fantasies that involve long-term attention, poems, novels, musical ideas, inventions, personal projects, biography, and philosophical readings and thoughts may be developed in this section.

Note: Every now and then read your journal, go from section to section, see if images, symbols, and myths cross the (artificial) boundaries you have set up. Do your mythic preoccupations show up in your dreams or daily life? Note such coincidences further. Use the creative work section to extract useful symbols, ideas for creative projects, works of art, stories, and legends.[1]

In addition, people may wish to explore personal mythology with others. This can be very rewarding for couples, families (children love imaginal games), or personal mythology groups that meet to explore together. Participants may simply wish to meet to share their journals or to accomplish a particular structured exercise together.

CREATIVE MYTHOLOGY EXERCISES

The Inner Guide
Finding One's Allies: Animal, Vegetable, and Mineral
Seeing into the Shadow
Meetings with Gods and Goddesses
Ancestral Roots
The First Dream
The Hero Quest or Soul Journey
The Alternative Life
Creating a Clown
The Funeral Exercise

The Inner Guide

This exercise may be done before all others, especially if you feel your guide might be helpful to you in some of the other exercises (he or she usually is).

Relax your body part by part until you feel deeply relaxed. Let your breathing become very slow.

You are standing before a door that is the doorway to your deep unconscious. Visualize the door in some natural place. Is it in an old building, a cliff, or the base of a tree?

Allow this door to become more and more vivid and real for you, until you can see every nail and rivet, or whatever is its construction. When it has become very clear, you find yourself deliberately reaching out and opening it. Enter with a sense of excitement.

As your eyes become accustomed to the gloomy interior you find yourself at the top of a spiral staircase that goes down, down inside your psyche. I don't know whether your personal spiral staircase goes clockwise or counterclockwise, but whichever way it goes, begin your descent with a sense of excitement and anticipation, you are going inward to meet your guide. The stairway will make seven complete turns before you are there, so without hurrying, you imagine yourself going down and around, down and around, moving at a rate that feels comfortable to you, but continues to move.

At the bottom of the staircase you will find yourself in the dwelling place of your inner guide. The chamber will reflect his or her qualities in style and decoration, but it will be very comfortable. Your guide may be human, male or female, or even animal or part animal, or even resemble a spiritual or totally imaginary being.

When you encounter your guide try to meet the guide's eyes, ask him or her if he or she is your inner guide. Watch and listen carefully that you receive a confirmatory answer before you proceed. If this is not your guide, ask if you can be taken to the guide. (If so, you may follow this figure until you come to the guide. Once again repeat the ritual of introduction, "Are you my guide?" Wait for confirmation.)

Your guide may seem familiar to you or unfamiliar, perhaps, in appearance only. You may ask your guide how long he or she has been with you.

Ask your guide now if there is anything he or she needs you to do to make things even better or clearer than they are now to facilitate his or her work of guiding you. Listen carefully for the answer.

Then you may ask the guide if it is all right for you to call on him or her in this way when you need his or her assistance. Ask if there is any special ritual needed or is it all right to follow the procedure you used to come here today.

Now you may ask the guide if there is anything else you need to know before returning to the ordinary world. Listen carefully for the reply.

Take your leave, thanking the guide for being with you and for this meeting, and begin to retrace your steps upward, moving up and around, up and around seven times, until you are back once again standing just inside your door. Take a moment to reflect on what has occurred, believe that you will remember it clearly, and return to the outer world.

Homework: Write in your journal about your encounter with the guide. Try to feel if you have sensed his or her presence in your life at various times and in certain situations. Write down anything the guide told you, warned of, or encouraged you to do. Be prepared to take his or her advice fairly seriously. If it is not appropriate to act on something literally, see if there might be a symbolic enactment that you can do.[2]

Finding One's Allies: Animal, Vegetable, and Mineral

Our Stone Age ancestors knew that the natural world was full of their allies—minerals, plants, and animals. Because they lived in such intimacy with nature they knew that parts of it were friendly and other parts unfriendly. In homeopathy, naturopathy, and herbal healing we also learn about plants or substances that affect us, or talk to us. Before each part of this exercise, relax and visualize.

MINERAL ALLIES

You are in a place without vegetation, only sand, rocks, and minerals scattered about, maybe some water. Feel yourself settle into this place in a way that is comfortable for you.

Now imagine that the minerals and stones and everything are alive. They are quiet and much slower than you are, but they are conscious. Slow yourself down to their level of awareness.

Out of all the minerals in this place there is one right now that might talk to you. Perhaps it will seem to glow with light or energy from within. Take time to experience this now.

Bring back in your imagination some piece of this mineral to the center of your little space. Is it stone, crystal, or metal ore? Do you know its name? Now begin to explore what the meaning of this mineral might be for you. Is it a part of your own makeup? Or is it something that you need? Allow yourself to experience a relationship to it.

Homework: Try to find a physical version of your mineral ally. Carry it around with you, put it in a medicine bundle or shrine if that seems appropriate. Study its geological or chemical properties. Allow yourself to visualize its age. Crystals are especially potent and traditionally have been used in ceremonies of all kinds.

VEGETABLE ALLIES

Next you are going into a place that is like the Garden of Eden. Every kind of plant and flower grows there according to its own inner laws. First just allow yourself to walk in this garden, among trees, shrubs, creepers, vines, flowers, moss, and lichen. Experience the richness and aliveness of this place.

Allow your sense of awareness to extend to the life around you. The plants are vibrating faster than the minerals; feel their wordless aliveness, the personalities and qualities of the different plants.

Some plants may be your allies and some your antithesis, some plants are poisonous, some are thorny, and some are insignificant seeming. Allow yourself to go past superficial qualities to the one plant you need to encounter as an ally now.

Experience its form, the way the life moves through it. What are the pharmaceutical properties that may lurk in its leaves or roots? Can you allow yourself to experience the deva of this plant as a living being? Encounter this being and understand what this plant holds for you now, or at other times in your life.

Homework: Study more about this plant ally that has come to you in an imaginal state. Look it up in an herbal dictionary or encyclopedia. Study a pharmacopoeia to learn of its medicinal properties. Learn about the family and genus of the plant, what additional uses it might have.

ANIMAL ALLIES

One way to invite your animal is to move around with relaxed breath and allow yourself to flow into animal movements. Is there a repetitive motion or particular style? What sounds do you want to make? Let the animal just "come to you." Are you a wolf, a snake, or a bird? What kind? Are you male or female, young or old? Enact your animal until you feel you have really given it life and shape with your body.[3]

After you have determined your animal ally, you can do the following exercise. Sit with a straight spine and imagine the different levels along it, allowing yourself to be drawn effortlessly to a particular level that needs—for now—the most attention.[4]

The levels are the base of the spine, behind the genitals, the solar plexus, the heart, the throat, the forehead, and the crown of the head. Once you have located the level that needs the most attention, allow yourself in imagination to go there. Invite your animal to come to you in visionary form. Allow it to move by itself and assume that you understand its language and can speak with it.

Now sit once again, bring your animal down into your level within that has the special dwelling or nest for this animal. Allow it to go into that space. Feel you can talk with it. Ask it if it needs anything from you now.

Last, allow yourself to experience other animals if they are present. Do they have anything to add to your dialogue?

If you wish you may call a parliament of the animals to consult with them all together. Are any sick or in need of special attention? If so ask the parliament what to do, or how to help. Are any of the animals angry with each other? Allow them also to interact with each other.

Homework: Write in your journal about this animal. Include the animal in a poem or incantation that speaks of your visionary encounter with it. Let the poem come to you naturally, with its own rhythm; maybe there are animal sounds within it, among the words. Don't be afraid to use these onomatopoetic devices.

Study your animal in books or encyclopedias that discuss its habits. Try to relate the animal's special qualities to areas in your life that need specific attention: endurance, seeing in the dark, keen vision, or strength, for example.

Seeing into the Shadow

Before you decide to do this exercise, you should first have established your relationship to your guide. Ask your guide if it is now appropriate for you to go and encounter the shadow.

You may descend from the guide's chamber that you have already visited, or imagine yourself with the guide in a dark wood, or at the entrance to a cavern, whichever you prefer.

Once you are firmly with your guide you may begin the adventure. Be prepared to meet the unexpected, to be surprised, or even confounded, because you are about to enter that realm where the light of consciousness does not—under ordinary circumstances—go.

Move through your forest or cave together with a feeling of commitment to meeting the shadow. You are curious but also serious and willing to meet the unknown.

As you approach the shadow you may avert your eyes rather than look directly at him or her or it. Be respectful. Ask the shadow if it is willing to speak with you. Clear your mind, simply be open and receptive. Learn whatever the shadow has to teach you. Is the shadow willing to share its personal history with you, when it came to be?

What special needs might the shadow have? Is it appropriate to bring a gift? Ask your guide how to behave with the shadow, especially if there are difficulties or problems that arise within.

Again, take your leave with some sense of ritual and bring back whatever you have learned from the shadow. Write in your journal. If you are in therapy you may also bring what you learn to therapy. You may also go back to your guide to ask for further advice.

Meetings with Gods and Goddesses

Pick a god or goddess with whom you feel you have an especially important connection or problem. (You may consult an astrological chart or horoscope to help identify an area of concern or conflict, i.e., problem with Mars, Saturn, etc.) First make contact with your guide. The guide will take you to the temple or shrine of this god.

Imagine the journey taking a little time. You are walking through a landscape, climbing Mount Olympus, approaching a sacred grove, entering a cave, or crossing the river of the underworld. Let your guide point out to you what things you will pass to reach this zone. Is it appropriate to bring a symbolic gift or token? The proper attitude for meeting with a god or goddess is reverence, even if it is a deity with whom you have been having trouble.

Approach the deity with your guide, present your gift or token if you have one, and ask if there is anything he or she wishes to say to you. Listen with an open mind and heart for the answer. If it seems appropriate, ask the god or goddess to bless you with a gift or token in return. Ask if there is any other god or goddess you should visit now or later. Is there any service they require of you?

Follow the same path, without hurrying, as you retrace your steps.

Homework: Write in your journal of this encounter. Use poetic language to describe what you experienced. See if there's some kind of homage or devotion, particularly of a symbolic kind, that this encounter now requires of you.

Ancestral Roots

Pick out older members of your family who have been influential to you. You may include people you have not known personally, but whose stories and influence are familiar. Try to describe each person's life myth in a few sentences; for example, "She always wanted to see her children have a better life than she did." Or, "He always was moving around, never could settle down." Or, "Her real love was animals." Don't be afraid to include things that are negative if they are important: "He never appreciated his family, only his drinking buddies." The important thing is to get the central themes of this person's life.

Are there common themes between people or generations going back? Were some children influenced by their parents' myths, which they tried to live out in their own lives? Do some branches of the family have a theme in common? Are there conflicting myths (i.e., independence versus dependence on others)? For this exercise, a family tree is helpful.

Begin with deep relaxation to visualize clearly. Imagine that there is an ancestral "being" in you, someone very ancient, an "old one." Allow this image to develop, until you feel a kind of living presence. He or she may personify as a particular person: grandfather or grandmother. Mine, for example, is ancient, like the hills, and very earthy. Feel that you can receive aid and answers from this being. Ask or visualize what myths are the most important for him or her. In what ways is your life a manifestation of his or her themes?

What is the mythology of your ancestors? Are your roots Celtic, Norse, African, Middle Eastern, native American or a mixture of several? Find and read myths from any traditions that were important to your ancestors. Do you resonate with parts of them? See if you can identify a patron or mythic being who has a connection or relevance for you. For example, my background is Norse and I have always been fascinated by the figure of Odin, especially his shape-changing and shamanic qualities and his search for the runes of wisdom. Several of my ancestors have been involved in what seem lifelong quests for "the runes of wisdom."

Devise ways of communicating with this patron, the ancestral being, asking him or her for guidance with life tasks. Later you may ask other relatives about their feelings of ancestry and relationship to particular ancestors.

The First Dream

Relax yourself and visualize going back in time to the earliest dream you can remember. Take just a minute to remember some details of your life at the time. How old were you? What was your home like, the room in which you slept? What was important for you, back then? Then imagine the dream from beginning to end. Finish as best you can and come back to the present.

Write the dream in your journal, or better, write it in poetic form. The poem should capture the feeling quality of the dream.

In what way does this dream capture something basic in your life? Does it relate to now as well as then? If there is something frightening or frustrating, or if the dream finishes in an unsatisfactory way, give yourself permission to redream it, so that it comes out better. You may personify your little child self at the time and come to (your own) aid as an adult helper, if needed.

See if this dream contributes anything to your understanding of your own personal myth. It usually does.

The Hero Quest or Soul Journey

It is understood at the outset that heroes come in two
varieties—male and female—and that this journey is pointed
toward the "deeper" variety of hero quest hinted at in
Chapter 5 in which the hero encounters important aspects of
himself or herself. Yet playful and even whimsical aspects
are included as well. Don't hesitate to lie or exaggerate—
about your endowments or the dangers, for example, if the
story seems to require it. We'll worry about the truth later.

YOUR BIRTH

You—like all of us—are the divine child. You have been
sent here from a distant star where all vibrates in harmony
with the source of creation. But here you are in this fallen,
still-unformed earth, between heaven and hell. Perhaps the
world needs someone like you.

Take several minutes to relax and visualize yourself close
to the realm of perfect harmony. Then let your inner guide
show you how to enter a wonderful body and mind that can
accomplish great things. Find your strengths and weaknesses,
all heroes have them.

Imagine the conditions of your birth. Are there prophe-
cies? Wonders? Who are your parents? What is the setting?
Try to feel or visualize the kind of world you will be born
into.

THE WORLD OF WONDERS

Feel yourself rise far above the conditions of incarnation and
birth for this little hero. Now, as a cosmic principle, your
goal is to mature him or her through the labyrinthine path
of experience and encounter. Allow the "kind of world" to
come in more strongly. Is it this world or another—with its
own place or time? Does the world have indwelling deities,
natural wonders, or dangers? Imagine what they might be

and how the hero below will encounter them. Is the world a whole planet or simply a small community, or even a family? Imagine what the world needs and what the hero needs.

Return to your identity as hero down below. Visualize your resources more strongly now. What are the powers with which you were born? What helpers might materialize along the way? Do you have allies among the supernatural dramatis personae of your world? Do you have enemies?

What is your quest? Will you recover a treasure? Find a talisman long hidden? Rescue someone? Slay something? Heal the community? What stands in your way?

THE JOURNEY

You are a growing child hero. What happens to you along the path? Are your powers helpful or inappropriate? How does the world respond to you?

You are setting out on your quest. Do you carry weapons or have special powers? Do you have allies? Do you have companions? Visualize your goal—but allow what will unfold specifically along the way to come by itself as your fantasy deepens.

What happens first? After each of as many stages or adventures as you require—with a suggested maximum of six—write a few notes in your journal. Let yourself be surprised with each event, obstacle, ordeal, or discovery; do not try to make them conform to any prearranged form, see what starts to unfold for you as you proceed.

Allow yourself to succeed—or to fail—in your quest. Do you bring something back? Is there some kind of effect from what you have done? Imagine more than one possibility. Take a moment to see how, for better or worse, it affects the whole world.

RETURN

What do you bring back to the community? Who notices what you have done? How do people feel about it?

Notice how you feel on your return. Especially imagine how your body feels. Is there any growth or change you note? Do you also greet old friends, family? How do they feel about your journey?

Find out what you do next. Will there be more quests? Or are you content to settle down to a quiet existence? See if you have a version of "he or she or they lived happily ever after."

DYING AND TRANSITION

Imagine your old age. What have you learned? Experience your preparation for death? Allow yourself to die and pass out of your body. Rise up again to the perspective above the whole life and look at it in broad outline. What have you learned? Write your epitaph—keep it to one sentence.

The Alternative Life

Imagine yourself walking along a misty road; it is evening.[5] Allow yourself to enter all the sensations of walking, breathing freely, and enjoying your surroundings. Gradually you approach a bridge. Things are very indistinct as you do so. You know that on the other side of that bridge is the landscape of another lifetime. Set foot on the bridge and begin to walk slowly across. It may help if you count slowly from one to ten as you cross the bridge.

As you step off from the bridge look down at yourself. What kinds of shoes are you wearing? Sense your body; is it male or female? What kinds of clothes do you have on? Now begin to look around. Are there other people? What kind of setting are you in? Is something going on? What is your place in it? Allow yourself to be pulled into what is happening.

You may move forward or backward in the life with a sense of freedom. Look at the conditions of your birth, your parents, and your home. Are there any significant details of your early life? You may also move to the time of your death to experience that. After you have died, how do you feel about the whole life? What was your myth? Did you manage to live by it authentically? If not, in what ways did you fail?

Homework: Bring yourself back slowly to this lifetime; your memory of what you have experienced will remain clear. Write of your experience in your journal. Compare that life with this one. Are there any similar themes or myths that you are working through? Try to describe them.

Creating a Clown (*Bouffon*)

Take a few moments to think about your own limitations, problems, things that continuously trip you up.[6] Out of these pick one or a cluster of traits that you think could be expressed.

Imagine yourself growing shorter. Temporarily, you will come to embody just these (negative) aspects of yourself in a very pure way, letting everything else go. Do you have any peculiar physical attributes that also relate to or express this fault or flaw you are working with (a hunched back, lameness, a large nose, . . .)?

Now imagine what your voice will be like. (Sometimes a falsetto is very funny.) Find a voice that expresses your character. Pick a couple of phrases that express your feelings and that you use over and over again. Allow yourself to mutter, mumble, and soliloquize. You may harangue an invisible audience of people you don't like or want to tell a thing or two.

Walk around. What is your gait? How do you carry yourself; do you have any unusual mannerisms? See what they might be. Given a character like you, what kinds of experiences might show up to trip you up, what kinds of experiences arise that bring your flaw(s) to the surface?

Another way to work with this character is to get a commedia dell'arte mask, say Pantalone, or Capitano. You may also use a Halloween mask or make a mask. Find a private place with a mirror. Put on the mask, walk around, get into the character, find your voice. You may carry on a constant monologue. What do you say? Tape-record it.

Note: The above exercises may be done in imagination, or acted out. If the latter, try to set up an audience of friends who are sympathetic to what you are doing. Use costume, makeup, or mask.

Homework: Write in your journal about this clown. What kinds of self-knowledge unfold from working with him or her? In what ways can the clown help your daily sense of humor?

The Funeral Exercise

Imagine yourself to be at your own funeral. While your body is in the casket, you are above the whole scene, looking at it all with clarity, detachment, and compassion. Who is there? See if you can sense what they are thinking and feeling.

Who delivers the eulogy? Allow yourself to hear what the person says in some detail. Allow this part to go on for as long as you need to hear everything he says about you.

Afterward, what do people talk about? Is there something like a Jewish *shivah,* in which people tell about you, both good and bad? Try to hear what they say.

Finally go to your own grave or cremation. Experience dissolution and a great peace and contentment. Imagine your own epitaph—keep it to one simple statement, a sentence, or a short poem.

Homework: This exercise can bring up strong feelings as well as a valuable perspective on your life. If experiences come to you, write them in your journal, talk them over with a friend. If you are in therapy, you may find it helpful to discuss this exercise and your experiences with your therapist.

MAKING A PERSONAL MASK

This process requires at least two people and is not for children. The materials required are surgical plaster gauze and ample amounts of petroleum jelly. For decoration, you will also need acrylic paints or poster paint, glue, hair or feathers, shells, bark, and literally anything that seems to express the quality of your mask.

First, the materials should be prepared and laid out nearby. Surgical plaster is to be cut in strips, some straight, some curved, usually about 2 inches by 4 inches and smaller.

FIGURE 46. *Two-day mask workshop format.*

Warm water should be available to soak the gauze, and you will need lots of paper towels.

One person lies down while the other person sends him or her on a visionary journey to find a mask. This is a version of The Inner Guide exercise, and you may use him or her. One can also ask the guide to help in the envisioning or encountering of masks. The person who is acting as the helper instructs the other one to "come back with a mask."

After he or she finds the mask, he or she endeavors to "hold" the expression of the mask while the surgical plaster is molded over the face. The helper must be sure to use lots of the petroleum jelly thoroughly to cover the face, especially eyelashes and eyebrows if plaster is to be put over the eye. Beards can be covered with kitchen plastic wrap or left out of the mask. A linen or paper towel can cover the hair up to the hairline. The helper must be very careful not to get the petroleum jelly in the other's eyes. He should also be extremely careful to leave plenty of space around the nostrils and mouth and to keep the plaster out of the nose and mouth so that the person laying down can breathe easily. Some masks are half-masks, others are full-face—or beyond in the form of scaffolding or protuberances. Elaborate decorating, whether structural or with paints or glue, takes place after the mask is removed.

The mask will dry as you work, providing a curious sensation to the indweller (the person "holding" the expression). It should be sturdy and have several layers around the outside for strength.

When the mask is firm to the touch it is ready to be removed, and the person wiggles his or her face inside the mask until it comes loose. The helper stands behind and uses gentle motions to detach the edges of the mask from the skin and hair.

In our workshops masks are usually left out to cure overnight, or in some cases, structural work may be done right away if there is some hurry. Electric hair dryers can be used after removal to help masks to dry. The masks should not be painted until dry; this includes all structural attaching, molding with the plaster, gluing and so forth—although some decorations may also be added after the mask is painted, larger decorations are customarily done before. Masks may also be painted, decorated, or simply "sized" (for comfort) on the inside. Finish by attaching elastic ties through slits in the reinforced rim of the mask, so it may be worn.

The process may be inverted before painting or decorating: the two people switch roles so that they both end up having a mask. That way both may decorate and work with the masks at the same time. A curious bonding occurs with mask making, so that each person has a new, special relationship to the other.

Psychodramatic work may be done after the mask(s) are complete. People sit in a circle around a mirror. The mask wearer tries on the mask in the center, right in front of the mirror so that he or she can see himself or herself in masked condition.

Usually one person works at a time, with one facilitator sitting to the side or the whole group acting as facilitator (examples of mask work are found in Chapter 10). Masks generally like music and dance. The facilitator(s) should have an open, serious, yet playful attitude toward what may unfold. The person "working," that is, playing, will usually know when he or she is "finished." Sometimes it is appropriate to design further tasks or dialogues to be enacted with the mask.

To Mask Makers

A few notes in conclusion to those who may use masks in healing. Masks are best treated among us, as among our ancient ancestors, as power objects. They act "as-if" they were persons, or entities. If they can heal, they can harm. They can, it seems, "act up" when ignored or treated carelessly. (We have seen masks surrounded by strange coincidences, even sometimes, apparent poltergeist activity.)

For these reasons, we recommend storing the masks in a safe (and even ceremonial) manner or, if it seems indicated, burn them or bury them in a natural place to dispose of them. Some masks like to be displayed; let them, by all means. But ask the mask!

SUMMARY

Experiential exercises are fun to do and psychologically revealing to the person as well as the group. If done carefully and respectfully, they can be potent as well as revelatory. It is usually worthwhile to make some kind of record (journal entry or drawing) to bring you back to the meaning of the experience. They should only be done in groups that have a "safe" feeling to all participants and a prevailing sense of confidentiality as well as supportiveness.

Epilogue

Ultimately the significance of a book such as this one is found in the psyche of you, the searching, imagining, living human reader. My role has been, in keeping with the mythos of Aquarius, my birth sign, to pour the water—the flowing life stuff—from one jar—the rich imaginally opened minds of my sources—into another jar—you the reader's own mythic imagination. My presupposition has been that there is a common structure and a rich potential resonance in our imaginations, but I have also lived long enough to know that among the similarities that make us mutually human, there are a thousand differences.

Myths, as I have pointed out, are infectious, and it is their very nature to jump from mind to mind. When a person has been seized by a myth form, it is tempting to share it. But as Campbell showed, myths become "overdone" when the poet moves to prophecy and the visionary becomes an evangelist. It is fortunate that our myths are not all alike, the differences in personal mythology providing some of the richest leaven for the human experience. We all share experience of hands and fingers, yet our own fingerprints are discernibly different from those of anyone else on the planet. Not only this book, but all of human experience hovers between the poles of this pair of opposites: the collective and the personal.

If this book does manage to realize the full potential I have envisioned for it, I may only come to know it in a gradual form when people tell me, not that they agreed with everything I said, or that they would now like to join a movement, but that it has touched their lives in some significant way or initiated a personal awakening. The message that has affected us most strongly in the mythic revival is that the hero really does have a thousand faces. The vision of meaning that emerges from this recognition has spiritual implications, but no religion attached, because the very point is to relativize all forms that hint at realities beyond the physical. There is a certain clarity of metaphysical vision that may then come to the personal quester, when he or she has realized this Archimedean point of vantage beyond the chaos of conflicting myths and paradigms. Paradoxically, the human soul must see itself in many ways to understand its single grand adventure.

FOREWORD

1. Joseph Campbell, *Myths to Live By*.
2. A. David Feinstein and Stanley Krippner, "Personal Myths and Dream Interpretation," *Dream Network Bulletin* (May 1982): 1, 6.
3. Joseph Campbell, *The Hero with a Thousand Faces*.

INTRODUCTION: THE MYTHIC IMAGINATION

1. *The Mabinogion* and a part of it called *The Red Book of Hergest* chronicle the doings of "the children of Llyr." It is the pre–Anglo-Saxon Welsh national epic, or cycle of myths. For a readable version see Evangeline Walton, *The Children of Llyr*. The tradition of child theft may be found in W. Y. Evans-Wentz, *The Fairy-Faith in Celtic Countries*.
2. Gary Larson is the nationally syndicated cartoonist of "The Far Side." See Gary Larson, *Beyond the Far Side;* and Gary Larson, *The Far Side Gallery*.
3. Later I would find the Winnebago trickster cycle, as retold by Paul Radin, in which not a trickster's nose, but an even more prominent appendage would achieve similar feats of independence, even to the point of fertilizing a chief's daughter on the far bank of a river. Heracles does something similar in a bawdy version of one of the side adventures during the quest for the Golden Fleece (see Robert Graves, *Hercules, My Shipmate*). Freud thought, of course, there was a secret identity between the nose and the phallus.
4. *Stereotypes* is the term coined by journalist Walter Lippmann for simple-minded perceptions and cognitions. *Archetypes* is Jung's psychological explanation for perennial ubiquitous patterns of thought.

5. In my undergraduate work at Columbia College, I was given the opportunity to study with excellent teachers (Fred Keller, Ralph Hefferline, even B. F. Skinner for short periods) and came to know the simple maze of the rodent mind (or behavior I should say), but I had little introduction to the grand labyrinths and multidimensional spaces of the human mind. This was changed by a wonderful little course—worth a whole curriculum—called "Metaphor, Symbol and Myth," taught by Robert Gorham Davis, to which I was referred when I complained about the lack of instruction in Freud, Jung, and other depth psychologists in the psychology department at the college. "That stuff," I was told, "is really literature."

6. Calvin Hall, "What People Dream About," *Scientific American* 184 (1951): 60–63.

7. W. B. Yeats, "Magic," *Essays and Introductions* p. 38. Yeats was really talking about visionary and clairvoyant experience, but I believe what he said also applies to big dreams and major healing insights in therapy.

8. Joseph Campbell, "Mythogenesis," in *The Flight of the Wild Gander,* 77, 80.

9. Clyde Kluckhohn, "Recurrent Themes in Myths and Mythmaking," in *Myth and Mythmaking,* ed. Henry Murray.

10. The theme of the "grand man," or "universal human," is found throughout Swedenborg's writing. It also appears in Indian Jainism, where the form of the universe is represented as a cosmic person.

11. Adolf Bastian (1826–1905) contrasted *Elementargedanke* (elementary or archetypal ideas) with *Völkergedanke* (ethnic ideas). Adolf Bastian, *Ethnische Elementargedanken in der Lehre vom Menshen,* Vol. 1 (Berlin, 1895), ix. Bastian's contribution has been discussed by Campbell in several works, among them *The Hero with a Thousand Faces,* 18 n. 18., and *The Flight of the Wild Gander,* 44ff.

12. See Robert Ornstein, *The Psychology of Consciousness.*

CHAPTER 1: THE ROOTS OF PERSONAL MYTHOLOGY

1. As Campbell would often say, what we call Greek *mythology* (with all its archaic quaintness) was actually Greek *religion* for its followers. The same is true with Oriental and African mythologies, which are really religions. Campbell's implication was that there is

a kind of unconscious superiority that Westerners assume to other, especially third world, religions.

2. Joseph Campbell, *Creative Mythology,* vol. 4 of *The Masks of God,* p. 4.

3. C. G. Jung, in foreword to *Symbols of Transformation,* xxiv. This was really kind of an "afterword," because it was written in 1950, thirty-seven years after the original publication of the book as *Wandlungen und Symbole der Libido.*

4. William McGuire, ed., *The Freud/Jung Letters,* no. 106 Freud, p. 169. Freud also said, "I am glad you share my belief that we must conquer the whole field of mythology"; see no. 158 Freud, p. 255.

5. In the same letter, Jung recommended that Freud look into the mythology of Dionysus, the dying and resurgent god, whose symbol was also the phallus. He mentioned that in ancient Egypt the symbol was worn by women during festivals, and pulled up and down by a string. Jung evidently thought Freud would enjoy the reference! McGuire, *Freud/Jung Letters,* no. 162 Jung, p. 263.

6. After a fruitful, eight-year collaboration, their friendship was to break up badly in 1913, as each perceived how radically different the essential values and outlook of the other were.

7. This is spelled out in Sigmund Freud, *The Future of an Illusion.*

8. Freud's view is consciously aligned with Darwinian determinism and is convergent with the philosophy broadly called positivism. Jung's ideas resemble Emersonian transcendentalism and "the perennial philosophy," as Aldous Huxley called it, which presupposes a unified spiritual field underlying all phenomena.

9. McGuire, *Freud/Jung Letters,* no. 286 Freud, p. 469. Also: Freud to Jung: "Why in God's name did I allow myself to follow you into this field [mythology]? You must give me some suggestions. But probably my tunnels will be far more subterranean than your shafts and we shall pass each other by"; see ibid., no. 280 Freud, p. 459.

10. Ibid., no. 282 Jung, p. 460.

11. William Blake, "All Are Men in Eternity," Kazin, ed., *The Viking Portable Blake,* 486.

12. Perhaps the clearest ancient formulation of the role of the faculty I have chosen to call mythic imagination is found in Plotinus's "Enneads." Another ancient root is in the Gnostic tradition, which extended beyond the Hellenic to the entire Middle East. The Gnostics believed that valid religion was only to be found in personal ways of praising God, rather than collective worship.

This led to their extermination by the early Church fathers. See Elaine Pagels, *The Gnostic Gospels*.

13. Morton D. Paley, *William Blake*, 41.

14. Samuel Taylor Coleridge, *Poems and Prose*, selected by Kathleen Raine (Middlesex, UK: Penguin, 1957), 190. See also my concept of the primary and secondary imaginations as used in Stephen Larsen, *The Shaman's Doorway*.

15. Coleridge's poem "Kubla Khan" was never finished, for as he feverishly transcribed it an annoying visitor, known for all posterity as "the man from Porlock," called. Because of the vividness of the personal mythology presented, the poem is reproduced here for the reader's interest.

Kubla Khan
In Xanadu did Kubla Khan
A stately pleasure dome decree:
Where Alph, the sacred river, ran
through caverns measureless to man
    Down to a sunless sea.

So twice five miles of fertile ground
With walls and towers were girdled 'round:
And there were gardens bright with sinuous rills,
Where blossomed many an incense-bearing tree;
And here were forests ancient as the hills,
Enfolding sunny spots of greenery.

But oh! that deep romantic chasm which slanted
Down the green hill athwart a cedarn cover!
A savage place! as holy and enchanted
As e'er beneath a waning moon was haunted
by woman wailing for her demon-lover!
And from this chasm, with ceaseless turmoil seething,
As if this earth in thick fast pants were breathing,
A mighty fountain momently was forced:
Amid whose swift half-intermitted burst
Huge fragments vaulted like rebounding hail:
And 'mid these dancing rocks at once and ever
It flung up momently the sacred river. Five miles meandering
with a mazy motion
Through wood and dale the sacred river ran,
Then reached the caverns measureless to man,
And sank in tumult to a lifeless ocean:

And 'mid this tumult Kubla heard from far
Ancestral voices prophesying war!
  The shadow of the dome of pleasure
  Floated midway on the waves;
  Where was heard the mingled measure
  From the fountain and the caves.
It was a miracle of rare device
A sunny pleasure-dome with caves of ice!

  A damsel with a dulcimer
  In a vision once I saw:
  It was an Abyssinian maid,
  And on her dulcimer she played,
  Singing of Mount Abora.
  Could I revive within me
  Her symphony and song
  To such a deep delight 'twould win me,
That with music loud and long,
I would build that dome in air,
That sunny dome! those caves of ice!
And all who heard should see them there,
And all should cry, Beware! Beware!
His flashing eyes, his floating hair!
Wave a circle round him thrice,
And close your eyes with holy dread,
For he on honey-dew hath fed
And drunk the milk of Paradise.

Coleridge, "Kubla Khan," in *Poems and Prose,* 88.

16. Yeats has told how he passed through a period of creative depression, finally "asking" his personal helping daemones for aid, and receiving—through his wife's automatic writing—the mysterious archetypal system revealed in W. B. Yeats, *A Vision.* It is the system that then permeates all of his later poetry.

17. Yeats, "The Mandukya Upanishad" in *Essays and Introductions,* 482.

18. Yeats, "The Celtic Element in Literature," in *Essays and Introductions,* 185n. The entire essay is about the passing of the "ancient religion," of a mythologized nature.

19. "Are we solely dependent upon archaic texts for the evidence of the power of myths?" said Joel Covitz. He continued, "But is not every psyche a myth creator and always a myth creator even today? After all, by assuming that every individual is in

search of his own myth, or inner structure of his individuation, we are also postulating that a myth-making process is going on in each person's soul." Joel Covitz, "The Jewish Myth of A-Priori Knowledge," *Spring* (1971): 50.

20. Jung, *Symbols of Transformation,* xxv.

21. C. G. Jung, *The Practice of Psychotherapy* 197.

22. As a historical note, it should be mentioned that David Feinstein, who recently completed an interesting book with Krippner on the subject of personal mythology, was also at that meeting, as was Cecil Burney, later president of the International Association for Transpersonal Psychology. Another important pioneer of the personal mythology movement is *Psychology Today* editor Sam Keen, who was already doing workshops on personal mythology, some of them with Campbell, in the 1970s. Keen's book, written with Anne Valley Fox, has just been republished. Sam Keen and Anne Valley Fox, *Your Mythic Journey* (Tarcher). Another important American contributor to the field is Jean Houston, who also taught with Campbell, and for at least two decades has been writing about psychology and myth. An American Psychological Association symposium on personal myth was also held in 1989.

23. Campbell, *Creative Mythology,* 3.

24. Ibid., 6–7.

25. Harry Levin, "Some Meanings of Myth," in *Myth and Mythmaking,* ed. Henry A. Murray, 111–112.

26. Edward C. Whitmont, *The Return of the Goddess,* 150.

27. Roland Barthes, *Mythologies,* 9

28. Stanley Keleman has told me he is currently completing a book based on his and Campbell's work together, tentatively titled "Myth and the Body."

29. Stanley Keleman, *Living Your Dying,* 74.

CHAPTER 2: THE RELEVANCE OF MYTH TO EVERYDAY LIFE

1. "Phenomenology," an introspective approach to philosophy, was introduced by Edmund Husserl (1859–1938), a Czech philosopher.

2. A structured introspection in psychology was developed by Wilhelm Wundt and his student E. B. Titchener. See P. D. Ouspensky, *In Search of the Miraculous,* for a description of Gurdjieff's self-remembering. See also Ornstein, *The Psychology of Consciousness.* For biofeedback, see Barbara Brown, *New Mind, New Body.*

3. James Joyce, *Ulysses*. James Joyce, *Finnegans Wake*. Ezra Pound, *Cantos*. T. S. Eliot, *Four Quartets*.

4. After decades of studying Eastern religions and "spiritual psychologies," Jung nonetheless urged us modern Westerners not to become literal imitators of them. Rather, he thought we should learn from them an essential technique, to use in a way suited to the unique psychic configuration of our hemisphere. He called his distillate "the self-liberating power of the introverted mind." This simple yet brilliant formulation reevokes the age-old notion that we free ourselves from compulsion through self-knowledge. C. G. Jung, "Psychological Commentary," in *Tibetan Book of the Great Liberation*, ed. W. Y. Evans-Wentz.

5. S. Larsen, *The Shaman's Doorway*, 27–32.

6. This is the old James–Lange theory of the emotions (independently arrived at by William James and Danish psychologist Carl G. Lange around the turn of the century). Emotions involve the proprioception of our whole self responding to an experience. This includes genetically programmed, "instinctive" responses, including our "gut" reaction and the expression on our face.

7. Paranoia, in fact, has a special relationship to mythmaking, as I explore in the next chapter. Myths that are consciously held may be seen through, even providing a new way of seeing for consciousness. Those unconsciously held (the unexamined life) become literal truths or facts. And of these opaque structures it may be said that no greater block to conscious experiencing, and hence to personal freedom, exists.

8. Even behavior modification specialists with their powerful techniques of operant conditioning are often helpless when they find themselves pitted against one of these intrinsic patterns. (I stress the negative here because I am describing unconscious behavioral mythologizing.) For example, Keller and Marian Breland, a husband-wife psychologist team, train all kinds of animals for circuses using behavioral techniques. They began their work with the assumption they could train any animal to do anything. Experience taught them the reverse; that learned behavior worked best in cooperation with an instinctual behavior such as food washing in raccoons. It does not work well or persist when placed in "competition with instinct." See also Jerome Kagan's comments on the implications of this finding for behavior theory, in Kagan ed., *Psychology: An Introduction*, Chap. 3.

9. Conscious mythmaking is equivalent to Stage 5 in the system developed in S. Larsen, *The Shaman's Doorway*, esp. 35–36 and chap. 4. A valuable example of this alignment of ritual space and

visionary quest is found in A. Meier, *Ancient Incubation and Modern Psychotherapy,* and Henry Reed, "Dream Incubation, a Modern Reconstruction." See also Chapter 9 for more on this subject.

10. Eric Bentley, *Theater of War.*

11. Charles Darwin explores this in *Expression of the Emotions in Man and Animals,* a little-known but important book.

12. The dramatic devices of classic drama—*catharsis* (emotional release), *anagnorisis* (tragic recognition), and *metanoia* (change of attitude) seem to show forth a recognizable psychological structure to this learning process.

13. Adolph Bastian (1826–1905) was a German scholar of anthropology whose idea of elementary versus folk ideas was influential on Campbell's thought. See Joseph Campbell, *Primitive Mythology,* vol. 1 of *The Masks of God* 32–33.

14. Whitmont, *The Return of the Goddess,* 210.

15. Ibid., 241.

16. Campbell, *Myths to Live By,* 45. Some readers will ask why I like the terms *mythic* and *ritual.* Psychology indeed has studied these phenomena, and there are perfectly acceptable designations in the literature that seem to describe the same thing: E. C. Tolman's "cognitive structures" and Leon Festinger's cognitive maps, which function as behavior-determining forms and the literature on social role behavior. Robert Kelly's "personal construct" theory is a clinical reformulation that shows how ingrained personal belief systems may limit a person's perception, hamper personal autonomy, and induce neurotic fear. And Jung's term *complex* (a feeling-toned area of personal conflict that affects and may disrupt cognitive functioning) once and for all is abroad in the world. (Cabbies in New York City will tell you their mother-in-law has one.) It is simply the antiquity and venerability of "myth" and "ritual" that make them, for me, preferable to these perfectly acceptable and equivalent, modern terms.

17. Jean Piaget and B. Inhelder, *The Psychology of the Child.*

18. Henry A. Murray, the Thematic Apperception Test, and Henry A. Murray, the Children's Apperception Test, in which the adult or child is asked to tell a story based on a picture that they are shown.

19. C. G. Jung, *Archetypes and the Collective Unconscious,* analyzes a number of patient's mandalas. C. G. Jung, *Psychology and Alchemy,* also contains visual materials from patients. See also Margaret Frings Keyes, *The Inward Journey.*

20. Jung, *Archetypes,* 382; also fig. 49.

21. Wolfram von Eschenbach, *Parzival.* In this version Parzival

fails to ask the question because his mother has told him not to ask too many questions. He is disconsolate when he fails the test and is ejected. The remainder of the story concerns his attempt to regain the castle—which he does—finally fulfilling the test.

22. Jung's experience is retold in C. G. Jung, *Memories, Dreams, Reflections*, 12, 22, 26f., 41, 174.

23. See also Whitmont, *The Return of the Goddess*; Sylvia Perera, *Descent to the Goddess*, Penelope Shuttle and Peter Redgrove, *The Wise Wound*, and Rix Weaver, *The Old, Wise Woman*.

24. G. Stanley Hall had both Freud and Jung as houseguests during their visit to Clark University in 1909, and was an early sponsor of psychoanalysis. Later Hall grew closer to Adler's perspective.

25. Marie-Louise von Franz, *An Introduction to the Psychology of Fairy Tales*.

CHAPTER 3: SEEING THROUGH THE IMAGINATION

1. Heinz Werner, *The Comparative Psychology of Mental Development*.

2. John Zubek, ed., *Sensory Deprivation, Fifteen Years of Research*.

3. One of the more dramatic breakthroughs in animal language showed that chimpanzees and gorillas were capable of lying, hence of imaginative fiction. See Francine Patterson, "Conversations with a Gorilla," *National Geographic*, October 1978, 154, no. 4: 483.

4. An important book that explores this is Mike Samuels and Nancy Samuels, *Seeing with the Mind's Eye*.

5. James Hillman, *Revisioning Psychology, Dream and the Underworld*. See also the work of a scholar of Islamic mysticism, Henry Corbin, *Spiritual Body and Celestial Earth*, Bollingen Series XCI.

6. C. G. Jung, "Paracelsus as a Spiritual Phenomenon," in *Alchemical Studies*, vol. 13 of *Collected Works*, 162–163. Paracelsus's own imaginal world was an incredibly rich mythology of beings and forces. Along with the medieval alchemists, he felt there was a *lumen naturae*, a light in the world of nature—and not less importantly, in man—which guides our visions of discovery and inner transformation.

7. Charles Johnston, *The Yoga Sutras of Patanjali*, 110.

8. Ibid., 24.

9. From "The Laocoon Group." See Alfred Kazin, ed., *The Viking Portable Blake*.

10. It should be remembered that William Blake and Samuel Taylor Coleridge were contemporaries and friends who exchanged ideas and images on the nature of the creative process.

11. W. B. Yeats, "Autumn of the Body," in *Essays and Introductions*, 193.

12. Stephen Dedalus appears in both *The Portrait of the Artist as a Young Man* and *Ulysses*; he is named after the Greek mythical craftsman Dedalus, who fashioned the Labyrinth on Crete and other wonders.

13. Roberts Avens, *Imaginal Body: Para-Jungian Reflections on Soul, Imagination, and Death*, 64.

14. Hillman, *Revisioning Psychology*, 123.

15. Silberer was a Viennese, a contemporary of Freud and Jung, and an insufficiently known contributor to some of their early ideas. Herbert Silberer, "Report on a Method of Eliciting and Observing Certain Hallucination Phenomena," in *Organization and Pathology of Thought*, ed. D. Rapaport. Contemporary psychologist Wilson Van Dusen, following some of Silberer's methods, observed this mirroring to be especially true of hypnagogic events, hallucinationlike phenomena right at the borders of sleep. These are not easy to catch and the inner observer is in the same position as a naturalist studying some shy wild species of creature. Van Dusen referred to them as "fragile fringe phenomena." He said, "When the hypnagogic is obviously being autosymbolic of one's state at the moment, it is just of that precise instant." Wilson Van Dusen, *The Natural Depth in Man*, 87.

16. Van Dusen, *The Natural Depth in Man*, 88.

17. Wilson Van Dusen, "The Natural Depth in Man," essay in *Person to Person: The Problem of Being Human*, ed. Carl Rogers et al.

18. C. G. Jung, *Psychological Reflections: A New Anthology of His Writings, 1905–1961*, Bollingen Series XXXI, 26, 27.

19. Stanislav Grof, "Theoretical and Empirical Basis of Transpersonal Psychology and Psychotherapy: Observations from LSD Research," *Journal of Transpersonal Psychology* (1973): 20.

20. Patricia Garfield, *Pathway to Ecstasy*, 56. See also Elsie Sechrist, *Dreams, Your Magic Mirror*.

21. Martha Crampton, "The Use of Mental Imagery in Psychosynthesis," *Journal of Humanistic Psychology* (Fall 1969): 12–13.

22. Emanuel Swedenborg, *The Intercourse between the Soul and Body*. See also his *Spiritual Diary*. Both books contain references throughout to the concept of the person as "spiritual receptacle."

23. Wilson Van Dusen, *The Presence of Spirits in Madness*. Also reprinted in his work, *The Presence of Other Worlds*.

24. Chogyam Trungpa, "The Six Realms of Existence," in *Consciousness, Brain, States of Awareness, Mysticism,* ed. D. Goleman, 266.

25. William James, *The Varieties of Religious Experience,* 417.

26. Independently, in 1978, psychologist David Feinstein formulated his own, almost identical, concept of "mythic assimilation." David Feinstein, "Personal Mythology as a Paradigm for a Holistic Public Psychology," *American Journal of Orthopsychiatry* 49, no. 2 (1979).

27. G. Kelly, *The Psychology of Personal Constructs.*

28. Feinstein, "Personal Mythology as a Paradigm," 208.

29. Jerome Bruner, "Myth and Identity," in *Myth and Mythmaking,* ed. Henry Murray, 276.

30. Campbell, *Primitive Mythology,* 4.

31. Campbell, *Creative Mythology,* 185.

32. Karl Pribram, "Problems Concerning the Structure of Consciousness," in *Consciousness and the Brain,* ed. G. Globus et al. Along with David Bohm, Pribram is the originator of the holonomic theory of consciousness and brain functioning. In a hologram, one may find representations of the whole in any part. Can spiritual realities—or religions—work this way too?

33. Hillman, *Revisioning Psychology,* esp. chap. 1.

34. Claudio Naranjo and Robert Ornstein, *The Healing Journey.*

35. Mircea Eliade, *Shamanism,* 88.

36. John G. Neihardt, *Black Elk Speaks.*

37. M.-L. von Franz, keynote address delivered at a meeting of the International Transpersonal Psychology Association in Davos, Switzerland, summer 1983.

38. Campbell, *The Hero with a Thousand Faces,* 25.

CHAPTER 4: THE LIVING LANDSCAPE

1. Hillman, *Revisioning Psychology,* 13.

2. Bruner, "Myth and Identity," 277.

3. C. G. Jung, "On the Nature of the Psyche," in *The Structure and Dynamics of the Psyche,* 211.

4. Sigmund Freud, *A General Introduction to Psychoanalysis.*

5. Marie-Louise von Franz, on the concept of *frevel,* "pseudo-courage, which is infantile daring out of unawareness or lack of respect. See Marie-Louise von Franz, *Shadow and Evil in Fairy Tales,* 143ff.

6. "Land-nam," a concept formulated by Ananda K. Coomaraswamy. Quoted in Joseph Campbell, *The Way of the Animal Powers,* Vol. 1 of *Historical Atlas of World Mythology,* 123.

7. Avens, *Imaginal Body,* 69.

8. The black box theory of the behaviorists implies that nothing *inside* the human being may be analyzed or described, only what goes in—stimulus—and comes out—response.

9. European psychology has always had its Gestalt psychologists, interested in the patterns of consciousness. Robert Desoille in France (the directed daydream) and Hanscarl Leuner in Germany (guided affective imagery) began exploring and developing their own methodologies for working with mental imagery. Those other indefatigable German researchers, Schultze and Luthe, were teaching people autogenic training, a program of training inner responses, including visualizations, which they said led to not only recovery from neuroses and anxiety, but also a self-mastery comparable to that bestowed by Yoga or biofeedback, and the ability to self-hypnotize to achieve specific outcomes. See Jerome Singer, *The Inner World of Daydreaming;* Robert Desoille, *The Directed Daydream;* and Hanscarl Leuner, "Guided Affective Imagery (GAI): A Method of Intensive Psychotherapy," *American Journal of Psychotherapy* 10, no. 4 (1969).

10. All are from Tolkien's first popular book, *The Hobbit.*

11. Behind the fey and innocent-seeming landscape of the trilogy lies a self-coherent mythological world of considerable depth and self-consistency. This mythology is outlined in detail in J. R. R. Tolkien, *The Silmarillion.* The cosmology he creates is very believable and familiar somehow. In this regard, Tolkien's personal mythology verges on being collective or "transpersonal."

12. Gary Gyjax, *Advanced Dungeons and Dragons,* 4th ed. (Lake Geneva, WI: TSR Games, 1977).

13. The old rhyme of Bilbo that Frodo remembers just as the adventure begins. J. R. R. Tolkien, *The Fellowship of the Ring,* 110.

14. Marie-Louise von Franz, *Lectures on Fairy Tales.* Also see von Franz, *Interpretation of Fairytales,* and *Shadow and Evil in Fairy Tales,* 119.

15. See von Franz sources cited in note 14.

16. Von Eschenbach, *Parzival.*

17. See Black Elk, *The Sacred Pipe* has the story of White Buffalo Woman. This book also contains Black Elk's account of the seven rites of the Oglala Sioux.

18. This is usually recounted as "Sir Gawain and the Loathly Bride"; her name is Dame Ragnell.

19. Lawrence Kohlberg, "Stage and Sequence: The Cognitive

Developmental Approach to Socialization," in *Handbook of Socialization Theory and Research,* ed. D. A. Goslin; and on shocks, Stanley Milgram, "Behavioral Study of Obedience and Disobedience to Authority," *Journal of Abnormal and Social Psychology* (1967): 371–378.

20. T. W. Adorno et al., *The Authoritarian Personality.*

21. Frederick Perls, *Gestalt Therapy Verbatim.*

22. The *I Ching,* "Oracle 51: Chen—The Arousing, Shock, Thunder" 210. As an aside and a personal note, while I was revising this chapter in the fall of 1989, I threw this hexagram just before leaving for a research trip in California. The oracle was brought to mind two weeks later when I participated in the Bay Area earthquake on October 17, 1989 in which I partook! Nonetheless my research went on. "The shock terrifies for a hundred miles around, indeed." I am not suggesting—but neither would I rule out—using the *I Ching* to predict earthquakes.

23. The quote is from Phillip Staniford, "Inside Out: Anthropological Communication of Alternate Realities," *Phoenix, The Journal of Transpersonal Anthropology.* Vol. 1, no. 1 (Summer 1977). See René Daumal, *Mount Analogue.* Also Frank Waters, "Symbols and Sacred Mountains," *Phoenix,* 6, nos. 1 and 2 (19): 59.

24. Phillip Staniford, "The Sacred Mountain," *Phoenix,* Evans-Wentz's lectures were published in W. Y. Evans-Wentz, *Cuchama and Sacred Mountains* (Athens, OH: Ohio University Press, Swallow Press, 1982).

25. C. G. Jung, "The Practical Use of Dream-Analysis," in *The Practice of Psychotherapy, Collected Works,* vol. 16, paras. 323–324. See also his "Analytical Psychology and Education," paras. 127ff; and "Dreams and Story of a Mountaineer."

26. Robert Masters and Jean Houston, *The Varieties of Psychedelic Experience.*

27. Bernard Aaronson, "Psychosynthesis as System and Therapy," *American Journal of Clinical Hypnosis* 10, no. 4.

28. Ibid.

29. James Hillman, "On Peaks and Vales," in *On the Way to Self Knowledge,* ed. Jacob Needleman and Dennis Lewis. This is one of Hillman's classic essays.

CHAPTER 5: DEPTH MAPS OF THE PSYCHE

1. *Root metaphors* is psychologist Erik Pepper's term—it is analogous to Chomsky's "deep structure" of language.

2. Freud thought Jung was too involved with the "manifest content," the surface, of dream symbols and that Jung did not recognize the sexual roots of all things psychic; Jung thought that Freud stopped his investigations with the personal, not the deeper, collective zone of the unconscious. See McGuire, *Freud/Jung Letters,* no. 280 Freud, p. 459, on depth psychology.

3. Campbell, *The Hero with a Thousand Faces,* 30.

4. Ibid.

5. See Joseph Campbell, *Occidental Mythology,* vol. 3 of *The Masks of God,* 88.

6. Ibid.

7. Ibid., 90.

8. Ibid., 91.

9. This account was paraphrased from Campbell's rendition of the story, which was extracted from scholarly translations of different versions of The Gilgamesh Story. See also N.K. Sandars, ed., *The Epic of Gilgamesh,* Campbell, *Occidental Mythology,* 87–92. See also N. K. Sandars, ed., *The Epic of Gilgamesh.*

10. Samuel Noah Kramer and Diane Wolkstein, *Inanna Queen of Heaven and Earth.*

11. Roger Woolger, "Death and the Hero," *Arche* 2 (Autumn 1978).

12. R. D. Laing, *The Politics of Experience,* 166.

13. Stanislav Grof, "Beyond Psychoanalysis," IV (Preprint of talk presented at the International Conference on the Voluntary Control of Internal States, Topeka, Kansas, 1970), 34.

14. Ibid.

15. William Blake, *The Marriage of Heaven and Hell.*

16. Campbell, *Myths to Live By,* 214–215:

The first [function of myth] is what I have called the mystical function: to waken and maintain in the individual a sense of awe and gratitude in relation to the mystery dimension of the universe, not so that he lives in fear of it, but so that he recognizes that he participates in it, since the mystery of being is his own deep being as well. . . .

The second function of a living mythology is to offer an image of the universe that will be in accord with the knowledge of the time, the sciences and the fields of action of the folk to whom the mythology is addressed.

The third function of a living mythology is to validate, support, and imprint the norms of a given specific moral order, that namely of the society in which the individual is to live. . . .

And the fourth is to guide him, stage by stage, in health, strength, and harmony of spirit, through the whole foreseeable course of a useful life.

17. Neihardt, *Black Elk Speaks,* 25.
18. See Eliade, *Shamanism,* for a discussion of vertical movement and its relation to the sacred.
19. For a discussion of the shaman's androgyny, see Eliade, *Shamanism;* see also S. Larsen, *The Shaman's Doorway,* chap. 4.
20. The work of psychologists such as Carl Rogers and Jerome Frank seems to support this conclusion. In several studies, simply meeting with the client, especially in the initial sessions, and regardless of the therapist's orientation, provided an amelioration of symptoms. See Jerome D. Frank, *Persuasion and Healing.*
21. Eligio Stephen Gallegos, *The Personal Totem Pole.*
22. Daniel J. Levinson's *Seasons in a Man's Life,* follows a sequence comparable to the one presented in Gail Sheehy's popular work *Passages.*
23. See Stanislav Grof, *LSD Psychotherapy.* The Jungian analyst Roger Woolger presents similar findings in his well-written study *Other Lives, Other Selves.*
24. Roger Woolger, "Imaginal Techniques in Past-Life Therapy," *Journal of Regression Therapy* 1, no. 1 (Spring 1986): 35.
25. Grof, *LSD Psychotherapy,* 290.
26. In *LSD Psychotherapy* Grof summarizes the implications of a comprehensive perspective for Depth Psychology:

These observations from LSD psychotherapy regarding effective mechanisms of therapeutic change clearly indicate that none of the existing psychological schools covers the entire spectrum of and provides an adequate explanatory framework for all the processes involved. . . . Depending on the nature and level of the experience, the system that offers the best maps might be Freudian psychoanalysis, Rank's psychology, the theoretical constructs of C. G. Jung, Tibetan Buddhism, alchemy, Kabbalah, or some other ancient cartography of consciousness, the mythology of a particular culture, or a particular spiritual system. [But, he cautions] a rigid adherence to any conceptual framework is ultimately antitherapeutic.

CHAPTER 6: INTO THE SHADOWLANDS

1. James Hillman, *The Dream and the Underworld,* 29.

2. Hillman, *Revisioning Psychology*, 82–83.

3. To see through Freud's peculiar religion it is important to note that soul is free to experience endless and inexhaustible possibilities (true "polymorphous perversity") in ways that body is not. (People are always getting the two mixed up.) We are capable of imagining the "unimaginable" so that we may perhaps conceive of it beforehand and, therefore, avert it. (Hence imagination's polymorphousness can be shown to have Darwinian "survival value.") But more than "reality function," it seems to me psyche uses pathology's images to speak of its own mutations. We may experience many inner deaths and rebirths. Parts of us can decay and fall away. Sometimes we are in ferment, or self-fertilizing. Sometimes we make love to ourselves; personifying ourselves into two partners, we may find ourselves in an intimate inner version of the forbidden act of incest, or sodomy, or even of bestiality.

4. For those who doubt the power of this dynamic, try the following experiential improvisational exercise. Divide a room of adults, or children, into two categories: "angels" and "demons." Give everybody a chance to experience both roles. Observe which is the more dynamic and evocative. Unfortunately for the sake of sanctity, the glee of an authority-given permission to experience wickedness usually outdoes by far the saintly rectitude of angelhood.

5. See S. Larsen, *The Shaman's Doorway*, chap. 1; Eliade, *Shamanism;* and Grof, *LSD Psychotherapy*, particularly his discussion of "Perinatal Matrix III." In *The Practice of Psychotherapy* Jung discusses this phase of dismemberment, using alchemical metaphors:

The painful conflict that begins with the nigredo or tenebrositas is described by the alchemists as the separatio or divisium elementorum . . . or as dismemberment of the body, excruciating animal sacrifices, amputation of the mother's hands or the lion's paws, atomization of the bridegroom in the body of the bride. (p. 197)

6. Jung, *Archetypes*, 9ff.
7. Ibid., 262ff.
8. See ibid., 29ff., for a discussion of this.
9. See Margaret A. Murray, *The God of the Witches*.
10. The *sushumna* is the central axis of the spine, through which,

according to Yogic theory, the soul makes its final departure at death, or through which it rises in the *kundalini* experience.

11. See also S. Larsen, *The Shaman's Doorway*, 82.

12. Mother Goose nursery rhyme in *Book of Verse, Childcraft*, vol. 1, 9.

13. In actual practice, both interpretations must be held open for discussion. In this image it is not hard to see through each level to find the other: women's transpersonal rage is also her rage—particularly around women's issues. I refer women readers also to Sylvia B. Perera, *Descent to the Goddess;* Whitmont, *The Return of the Goddess;* and Shuttle and Redgrove, *The Wise Wound,* an excellent discussion of the menstrual implications of feminine and shadow issues.

14. Buffie Johnson, *The Lady of the Beasts*, 3.

15. Heraclitus, DK. Fragment 26. Quoted in Avens, *Imaginal Body*, 109.

16. Richard Kastenbaum and Ruth Aisenberg, *The Psychology of Death*, 154.

17. Ibid., 166.

18. See Kenneth Ring, *Life at Death*, 119, 199, and 211; and his *Heading Toward Omega.*

19. Raymond Moody, *Life after Life*, 64.

20. Kastenbaum and Aisenberg, *The Psychology of Death*, 149.

21. From personal notes taken from a lecture by Elisabeth Kübler-Ross at International Transpersonal Association conference, Davos, Switzerland, 1983.

22. See Elisabeth Kübler-Ross, *On Death and Dying.*

23. Masters and Houston, *The Varieties of Psychedelic Experience*, 188ff.

24. Grof's theory places mass murderers, sadistic dictators, and people who think that a new world can only come to birth in a bath of blood, at Perinatal Matrix III (the agony of expulsion down the birth canal) in their psychological development. Could such people be encouraged to act out their growth pains symbolically rather than actually? Terrorism and its attempt to tear apart the fabric of ordinary daily reality for its victims—the desire for "breakthrough" at all costs—show their derivation from this portal matrix. Here the (hypothesized) instinctual control matrix of the I-thou, "what I do to you I do to me," the universal ethical principle, is suspended and the pathological pattern supervenes. He who gives death to innocent others seeks, in a tragically paradoxical way, his own birth.

25. Although he does not credit her for it, Freud may owe this

insight to Sabina Spielrein, who in 1912 published a paper on the psychoanalytical importance of the "death instinct," with references to death in mythology. See reference to Spielrein's "Life and Death in Mythology" in McGuire, *Freud/Jung Letters*, no. 310 Jung, p. 498.

26. See Campbell, *The Way of the Animal Powers*. The theme is explored throughout the book.

27. See G. I. Gurdjieff, *Beelzebub's Tales to His Grandson*. For a more readable presentation of Gurdjieff's ideas, see P. D. Ouspensky, *The Fourth Way* and the character G. in Ouspensky's *In Search of the Miraculous*.

CHAPTER 7: BEASTS AND BIRDS OF THE MIND

1. Paul Shepard, "The Ark of the Mind," *Parabola* 8, no. 2 (1983): 54.

2. Joseph Epes Brown, "The Bison and the Moth: Lakota Correspondences," *Parabola* 8, no. 2 (1983): 6ff.

3. Campbell, *The Way of the Animal Powers*, 193.

4. The May 1983 issue of *Parabola* was dedicated to remythologizing and respiritualizing our relationship with animals.

5. Barry Lopez, "Renegotiating the Contracts," *Parabola* 8, no. 2 (1983): 15.

6. Emanuel Swedenborg, *Arcana Coelestia*, 8 vols.

7. Josephus Flavius (ca. A.D. 37–100), quoted in Raphael Patai, *The Hebrew Goddess*, 117.

8. Ibid., 124.

9. See Patai's discussion of the masculine and feminine aspects of the Hebrew deity, ibid., chap. 3.

10. Charles Allyn Williams, *Pre-Christian*, part 1 of *Oriental Affinities of the Legend of the Hairy Anchorite*.

11. Max Brand, *The Untamed*. This is a popular novel.

12. Cleve Backster, cited in Peter Tomkins and Christopher Bird's *The Secret Life of Plants*.

13. Rupert Sheldrake is an English biologist whose theory of morphic resonance has been greeted with both enthusiasm and skepticism from different quarters of the intellectual community. See Rupert Sheldrake, *The New Science of Life* and his *The Presence of the Past: Morphic Resonance and the Memory of Nature*.

14. Campbell, *The Way of the Animal Powers*, 47.

15. Swedenborg, *Arcana Coelestia,* no. 143.

16. John Worcester, *Correspondences of the Bible: The Animals.*

17. From "The Song of Amergin": the version excerpted is essentially John MacNeill's translation, rearranged by Robert Graves and discussed in *The White Goddess,* 215–227. According to Graves, Celtic bards "pied" or scrambled their incantatory poems to conceal their power from the uninitiated.. Gwion Bach (or Taliesin) includes the core lines of Amergin's poem within his longer "Cad Goddeu." See note 19.

18. Taliesin is also associated with the child–shape changer Gwion Bach, an earlier transformation.

19. Gwion Bach, "Cad Goddeu," translated from *Book of Taliesin,* in *The Mabinogi and Other Medieval Welsh Tales,* ed. Patrick K. Ford, p. 183ff. "Cad Goddeu" is usually translated literally, "The Battle of the Trees," but is sometimes called "Taliesin's Riddle." See note 18.

20. Lee Sannella, *Kundalini: Psychosis or Transcendence.* Arthur Avalon's, *The Serpent Power,* is the classic text. See also Gene Kieffer, ed., *Kundalini for the New Age* and W. Thomas Wolfe, *And the Sun Is Up.*

21. A number of mythologies around the world, as well as children's locker room drawings, exhibit flying penises—often with wings, in a clearly Freudian mythology. The flight motif is evidently connected with that organ's tendency to rise—sometimes without obvious stimulation. As H. Zimmer is rumored to have remarked, "Just the idea is enough."

22. Num. 22:28–31.

23. Robin Larsen, "Spiritcatcher's Notebook," part 1 (Ph.D. diss., Union Graduate School, 1977), 4.

24. See the discussion of the enactment of vision, especially as it relates to Black Elk in S. Larsen, *The Shaman's Doorway,* chap. 2.

25. Interestingly enough, the eagle is also the symbol of John the Evangelist, a detail which I became aware of after I quoted John in illustration of the above dream. While the other three evangelists are represented by the zodiacal figures of bull (Taurus, Luke), lion (Leo, Mark), and man or angel (Aquarius, Matthew), the visionary John (Aquila, the eagle) breaks the temporal plane of the zodiac, soaring into a symbolically freer sphere (that of the extrazodiacal constellations). See Herbert Whone, *Church, Monastery, Cathedral: A Guide to the Symbolism of the Christian Tradition,* 70ff.

26. Campbell, *The Way of the Animal Powers,* 79; Jung, *Archetypes,* 336–337.

27. In some early Christian crucifixion images, the serpent (Nehushtan) appears on the cross in place of Christ's body; the unicorn is a medieval addition to Christian iconography. Both unicorn and serpent evoke the regenerative power of Christ.

28. See also R. E. L. Masters's interesting treatment in *The Goddess Sekhmet*.

29. See Gallegos's *The Personal Totem Pole*. See also Michael Harner, *The Way of the Shaman*.

CHAPTER 8: THE INNER CAST OF CHARACTERS

1. The Gospels of Matthew, Mark, and Luke all repeat a series of accounts of Jesus' exorcistic healings: these can be located through the indexes of most Bibles, which list them under "Miracles." Mark tells the story of "Legion" with the best storyteller's style and supplies all the intriguing details: Jesus is met by a madman who runs wild and naked, "who had *his* dwelling among the tombs; and no man could bind him, no, not with chains: Because that he had been often bound with fetters and chains, and the chains had been plucked asunder by him, and the fetters broken in pieces: neither could any *man* tame him. And always, night and day, he was in the mountains, and in the tombs, crying, and cutting himself with stones" (Mark 5:1–4). The "unclean spirits" recognize Jesus as "Son of the most high God" and beg him not to send them far away; they suggest he let them enter a herd of swine, which is nearby—no less than 2,000 pigs (an interesting reference to the goddess and the underworld). So Jesus does, and the swine, now demon-possessed, rush into the sea and drown. The swineherds are terrified by these events (and, we suspect, dismayed by the loss of their charges). But the man is returned to his "right mind," allows himself to be dressed, and sits calmly to hear Jesus teach.

2. See Neihardt, *Black Elk Speaks,* and my discussion of the enactment of this vision in *The Shaman's Doorway,* 103.

3. See the discussion of this in S. Larsen, *The Shaman's Doorway,* esp. 53ff.

4. Later formulations of this theory have the figures within each other, as in the "anima of the animus," and the "animus of the anima." Some modern Jungian writers have reformulated this concept, saying that each sex has both figures within, but the

contrasexual one is perhaps more important in personal psychology because of its qualities as unknown and opposite. See also John Sanford, *Invisible Partners*.

5. When demonically charismatic people seize the world stage (and it seems they do, at an uncomfortable pace for the rest of us), we are all tested ethically to our very utmost, and must come to terms with our own inner fragmentation. Hitler on the world stage frightens the most thoughtful of us into self-examination: Do I have a dictator inside? What allows him to come to power, or prevents him from doing so?

6. Stephen Larsen, *Myth and Consciousness* (Ph.D. diss., Union Graduate School, 1975), 370.

7. Frank Baum, *The Wizard of Oz,* 110.

8. In *The Wizard of Oz* (but also in J. R. R. Tolkien, *The Lord of the Rings;* C. S. Lewis, *The Chronicles of Narnia; Star Wars;* and even *Star Trek*), we see the perennial psychological utility of having a cast of characters with different qualities: a wizard, a dwarf, an elf, a Hobbit; an intellectual, a feeling type, a visionary, a practical man; a hero, a princess, a vagabond, two robots—with notably different characters—a Wookie. Somehow the whole adventure revolves around the kaleidoscopic interplay of different characters.

9. Jung, *Symbols of Transformation,* 419.

10. Psychiatrist R. D. Laing, Jungian analyst John Weir Perry, and others have postulated that when acute psychosis is allowed to run its course in a safe and sheltered space (not resisted with antipsychotic medication), it will often come to its own natural end, usually producing all sorts of mythological and cosmic imagery along the way. See Laing's, *The Politics of Experience* and his *The Divided Self.* John Weir Perry's, *The Lord of the Four Quarters; Myths of the Royal Father.* Dr. Perry founded Diabasis House, a withdrawal-and-recuperation center in California for people to run through their psychotic episodes.

11. Jung, *Symbols of Transformation,* 255.

12. Ibid., 420.

13. See also Philip Zabriskie, "Goddesses in Our Midst," *Quadrant* no. 17 (1974).

14. Campbell would often say of Yahweh, or Jehovah, the Jewish tribal deity, "His only problem was he thought he was God." (But so have a lot of other people.) What Professor Campbell meant by this was that the Judeo-Christian tradition has failed to perceive the difference between their culture-bound images and some cosmic absolute. This tradition has been less willing than others to see that its own religious images, just like everyone

else's, cannot begin to describe the Absolute in its totality. In Campbell's view, this misconception has led to a number of ethnocentric problems: from the notion of a "chosen" people, to the most remarkable acts of spiritual barbarism toward other traditions by Christian missionaries.

15. When Ronald and Nancy Reagan were known to have consulted an astrologer, the scientific community especially was outraged and indignant at what they thought was a type of medieval thinking in the highest office in the land. From the point of view of a somewhat amused bystander, it was a conflict of mythic paradigms. While clear thinking is undoubtedly required for the highest office of the land, the president would do well to consult his or her nondominant hemisphere sometimes, to dream and vision a better America, as well as think about it.

16. Once a professional colleague referred to me as a "genital type," and I think I may have bristled visibly before my conceptual apparatus took over and I realized he was paying me a compliment. While I was working on this chapter, a friend, bioenergetic analyst Ron Robbins, shared with me his own discomfort over the classic Lowenian (bioenergetic) character types based on psychosexual distortions. His own typology is more humanistic: dreamer, creator, communicator, analyzer, inspirer, solidifier, and achiever. See Ronald Robbins, *The Rhythmic Cycle of Change*. Robbins believes that at any one point in our career we may exemplify these figures.

17. In the Hindu-Buddhist tradition human beings are in some ways greater than the gods because they are capable of growth and transformation. The myths are full of tales of the very foundations of heaven being shaken by some human—or demon—ascetic whose meditative concentration becomes so profound it imperils the very gods with a new power to restructure the universe.

18. I recorded this quote during a lecture I attended at the C. G. Jung Institute, Zürich, in 1976.

CHAPTER 9: THE INNER GUIDE

1. For one veteran researcher's confirmation of this therapeutic effect, see Stanislav Grof, *Realms of the Human Unconscious; LSD Psychotherapy;* and *Beyond the Brain*.

2. See Masters and Houston's excellent chapter, "The Guide," in *The Varieties of Psychedelic Experience*.

3. McGuire, *Freud/Jung Letters,* no. 125 Freud, p. 197.

4. Ibid., no. 50 Jung, p. 96.

5. Freud in 1911 was finishing his book on primitive religion, *Totem and Taboo.* But in an ironic way Jung was already pulling down the totems and violating the taboos of psychoanalysis, especially the primacy of the sexual theory and the inner guidance notion that Freud distrusted so profoundly—Jung's "religious-libidinal cloud," as he called it.

6. McGuire, *Freud/Jung Letters,* p. 485 n. 2.

7. Ibid., no. 288 Freud, p. 472.

8. Ibid., p. 483.

9. Psychoanalysis refers specifically to the Freudian school; analytical psychology designates the Jungian.

10. Jung, *Archetypes,* 216.

11. C. G. Jung, *Word and Image,* 188.

12. The only myths Freud would admit for our age were Narcissus's and Oedipus's bitter and disillusioned tales, in which the self and the family take the place of the gods, for once and all (if there were any god, as we have seen, it would be Eros–Thanatos, he of the portal). Then there is that curious piece of creative mythology Freud made up by himself, the myth of the "primal horde." Not content with Oedipus's classic age for his myth of origins, he recast the story in a time of such nebulous antiquity it is clearly *illo-tempore,* "the dream time" of the ancestors, in which nonhuman primate or protohuman males again and again slew and devoured their patriarch parent to possess their mothers. It is their antique collective guilt that figures so importantly in the Oedipal and incest taboos. To take seriously Freud's view of how ancient behavior influences modern psychology shows him, as well as Jung, to be the originator of a theory of "the collective unconscious," and Freudian premises to be closer to the scientific mythology of Lamarck than to Darwin.

13. Jacob Needleman's address was delivered at a meeting of the East Coast Association for Transpersonal Psychology, Stony Point, 1983. See also Needleman and Lewis, *On the Way to Self Knowledge.* The foundations of Transpersonal Psychology may be found in the correspondence between Anthony Sutich, a man tragically paralyzed below the neck, and Abraham Maslow toward the end of Maslow's life. See accounts of their conversations and correspondence in the first issue of *The Journal of Transpersonal Psychology.*

14. The Senoi method was originally outlined by Kilton Stewart, in his monograph "Dream Theory in Malaya," which appears

in *Altered States of Consciousness,* ed. Charles Tart. See also *The Shaman's Doorway* in which I devote a chapter to the Senoi method and compare it with the dream theory of the American Iroquois. See also Strephon Kaplan Williams, *Jungian-Senoi Dreamwork Manual.*

15. Carl and Stephanie Simonton's method of creative visualization as a way of dealing with life-threatening illness has been well documented. See Carl Simonton and Stephanie Simonton, *Getting Well Again;* also Jean Achterberg, *Imagery in Healing.*

16. Jung, *Archetypes,* no. 101, 49. The quote is paraphrased from the general discussion.

17. See S. Larsen, *The Shaman's Doorway,* chap. 2, for a comparison of the dream lore of these two widely separated traditional cultures.

18. See Leuner, "Guided Affective Imagery"; and Desoille, *The Directed Daydream.*

CHAPTER 10: CREATIVE MYTHOLOGY

1. P. M. Matarasso, ed., *The Quest of the Holy Grail* 52–53.
2. Campbell, *Creative Mythology.*
3. Pagels, *The Gnostic Gospels,* 19.
4. Ibid.
5. Jung, *Psychology and Alchemy.* See also Jung's *Alchemical Studies* and *Mysterium Coniunctionis.*
6. Stephen Larsen, "Swedenborg and the Visionary Tradition," *Studia Swedenborgiana* 3, no. 4 (1980). In the late eighteenth and throughout the nineteenth centuries, especially in America, students of the Swedish scientist and visionary Emanuel Swedenborg (1688–1772) were following his example by keeping dream journals and spiritual diaries. Swedenborg himself had found little consolation in orthodox dogma and claimed to have had his own spiritual awakening in mid-life. He turned away from a brilliant career as one of Europe's outstanding scientists, to become a visionary who claimed that he had an ongoing revelation of spiritual realities and journeyed regularly—in spirit form—even to heaven and hell (an idea that was not well received by the Lutheran orthodoxy of eighteenth-century Sweden). In Swedenborg's radical (for the eighteenth century) theology, heaven and hell are not chambers of cosmic reward and punishment, but spiritual dimensions to which the soul naturally gravitates by its own momentum. We are in heaven or hell long before we die, said Swedenborg,

and it is our own personal choice that has put us there. Swedenborg's earlier version of Jung's individuation was called by him "regeneration," and described as a journey of personal spiritual growth and development throughout a lifetime. It is quite evident in perusing the historical impact of Swedenborg that his most significant influence was on the creative arts and literature, especially the postimpressionist movement of the Nabis, the visionary painters of the Hudson Valley school, the poets Blake and Yeats, and New England transcendentalism, including its adherents Emerson, the Jameses, and Thoreau.

7. In *The Shaman's Doorway,* I presented the notion of a dialogue between myth and consciousness as the crucial one for our time. I suggested Five Stages of Mythic Engagement between these two faculties, implying particular historical and cultural relationships, and specific limitations for each stage, especially the first four. These are, briefly, and in order, (1) Mythic Identity (in which consciousness is drowned in myth, as in possession or schizophrenia), (2) Mythic Orthodoxy (in which consciousness is "locked into" a specific body of mythic forms, as in traditional religious belief), (3) Objective Phase (as in the desacralized reality that accompanies our modern science), (4) Suspended Engagement (as in the spiritual disciplines of Yoga or Zen, which seek to demythologize the self—in a different way than science—through a disillusionment of consciousness), and (5) Mythic Engagement and Renewal (which relates to the creative techniques discussed here).

8. Baudelaire's poem "Correspondences," which some say has never yet been translated adequately. For the reader's interest I include a recent translation by Robin Larsen, which appears in Robin Larsen, ed., *Emanuel Swedenborg: A Continuing Vision,* 340:

Correspondences

Nature is a temple from which living pillars
Now and then allow disordered phrases to emerge;
Man comes there among forests of symbols
Who observe him as if familiar.

Like long echoes that mingle from afar
In a profound and tenebrous unity,
Vast as night and radiance,
So perfumes, colors, sounds correspond.

There are perfumes fresh as the flesh of infants,
Sweet as oboes, green as prairies
—And others, corrupt, rich and triumphant.

Expansive as infinite things:
Amber, bergamot, incense, and musk,
Singing the rapture of spirit and senses.

9. This problem is nowhere so evident as in the collision of creationism, and the scientific-evolutionary perspective in American education, which was never fully resolved, it seems, by the Scopes trial. People seem to vacillate in an either-or mode, rather than learn to see with metaphoric vision. The concept of metaphysical vertigo has also been taken up in Larry Dossey, *Recovering the Soul*.

10. Joseph Campbell, *The Inner Reaches of Outer Space*, 17.

11. Ibid.

12. A version of this chapter was first published in *Parabola*, Stephen and Robin Larsen, "The Healing Mask," *Parabola* 6, no. 3 (1981): 78.

13. What Campbell himself had in mind was that myths themselves are "the masks of God."

14. Although masks are not common ritual paraphernalia in our society, I have seen masks appear in dreams many times in my dream sample; they are often imbued with a mysterious or numinous power and immediately attract the attention of the dreamer. I do not go into these in detail here because the subject, while interesting, would be a digression from conscious mythmaking, that is, how to use masks in healing.

15. The *Kumang* mask used by certain African secret societies every seven years is described by Leo Frobenius in *Kulturgeschichte Afrikas*. "The ceremony is conducted at the base of a ginipa tree, from whose wood the mask is carved [like the Iroquois basswood False Face masks]. The feathery shape of the masked dancer appears from his pit at the base of the tree. Already men are dropping dead from the power. The masked figure changes size, from as small as a one-year-old child to as large as a palm tree. Later he will prophesy for the next seven years." In Andreas Lommel, *Masks*, 20.

16. The Sri Lanka stories are paraphrased from several versions collected during my visit to Sri Lanka. See also Paul Wirz, *Exorcism and the Art of Healing in Ceylon*.

17. The Iroquois stories are paraphrased from accounts in anthropological journals. See also W. M. Fenton, "The Masked

Medicine Societies," *Annual Report of the Smithsonian Institution* (Washington, DC: 1940); and W. M. Fenton, "The Seneca Society of Faces," *Scientific American* 64 (1937).

18. Paracelsus, a.k.a. Theophrastus Bombastus von Hohenheim, wrote, "What makes a man ill also cures him." See C. G. Jung, "Paracelsus as a Spiritual Phenomenon," Samuel Hahnemann (1755–1843) was the founder of homeopathy, which is based on the principle of "like cures like." The remedy should imitate the illness, jarring the body's vital force into its healing response.

19. Medusa's description reminds us of the "terrible woman" from world mythology: India, Kali; Bali, Rangda; and Cundrie of Celtic literature. This account is from Robert Graves, *The Greek Myths.*

20. P. H. Mussen, J. J. Conger, and J. Kagan, eds., *Child Development and Personality* 101ff.

21. We also know that the characteristic human emotions of rage, joy, love, and so forth have their "masks." Darwin, in *The Expression of Emotions in Man and Animals,* was among the first to show the deep-rooted morphogenesis of some of our "faces." Ethologists have now documented in much more detail the subtle languages of facial expression used by canids and primates. Wolves' facial and body language, for example, is far more important than vocal communication. See Michael Fox, *Behavior of Wolves, Dogs, and Canids.*

22. Ornstein, *The Psychology of Consciousness.*

23. William James and Danish scientist Carl G. Lange, at the turn of the century, each proposed the theory of emotion that now bears both their names: the James–Lange theory. In this theory emotion is really the proprioception of bodily changes already produced by built-in neurological response patterns. (If you meet a bear in the woods, you don't run "because you're afraid," you find yourself startling and running away first, and then you realize how afraid you are.) See William James, *Principles of Psychology,* vol. 2. Years later, the influential method of mimesis developed by Stanislavsky gave a first and a second corollary to the theory: one may induce a psychoemotional state by physical imitation of it, and having done so, one may induce similar changes in the emotional state of the observer (audience) through perception.

24. See the discussion of primary meaning in S. Larsen, *The Shaman's Doorway,* chap. 1. The term first appears in the essays of Coleridge and subsequently is taken up by W. H. Auden. The recognition (Greek, *anagnorisis*) and emotional release (*catharsis*) of classic drama are successively deeper psychoemotional events that

unite the audience and actors in an experience of the common structure of human meaning. When we see the familiar theatrical emblem of the two masks—tragic and comic—we see the poles or boundaries of a spectrum of human feelings, which the masks enclose: the subject matter of the theater.

25. The meaning response in the human psyche is explained in this way by Gestalt psychology and holism: the organism in confrontation with wholeness seeks meaning. "Who am I?" "What is the meaning of my life?" These are questions big enough to refuse to let us go, even when we would rather let go of them; and the process of this confrontation provokes our sense of incompleteness and fragmentation. We are "broken on the wheel of life." But even partial answers are glimpses of one's place in a larger conscious whole. Awakening to meaningful belonging is equivalent to healing. Our feelings about ourselves and our relationship to life affect our vitality at its deepest levels. They reach from the crown to the roots of the living tree.

26. S. Larsen, *The Shaman's Doorway*, chap. 2. See also A. F. C. Wallace, "Dreams and Wishes of the Soul," *American Anthropologist* (1958).

27. Joseph Campbell, "Historical Development of Mythmaking," in *Myth and Mythmaking*, ed. Henry A. Murray, 33.

28. The game is one that Harner has adapted from a game played by South American Indians, probably the Jívaro, although the game is actually rather widespread among traditional societies. The group, say forty people, is divided into halves. One side "hides" or conceals four bones; the other, through a kind of spirit seeing, must determine which of two pairs of hands, contains two marked bones. There is no indication where the bones are, and the concealing group tries to distract the opposing side. Tina proved eerily infallible. Years of subsequent experience taught her that her paranormal gift operated often. See Harner, *The Way of the Shaman*.

29. It has been my finding, as previously mentioned, that if I can get the person to indwell and act out the terrifying monster in the dream—or even the power of a tornado or tidal wave in a different kind of nightmare—a bridge is made, a rapprochement between ego and "other." The power can be brought to dialogue and be engaged.

CHAPTER 11: SYMBOLIC PLAY

1. Cited in John H. Towsen, *Clowns*, 142.
2. Eliade, *Shamanism*.

3. E. T. Kirby, "The Shamanistic Origins of Popular Entertainment," *Drama Review* 5–15.

4. Carlos Castaneda, *A Separate Reality: Further Conversations with Don Juan,* 125ff.

5. These clowns are described in many places. See Barbara Tedlock, "Boundaries of Belief," *Parabola* 4, no. 1 (1979): 70.

6. Kirby, "The Shamanistic Origins of Public Entertainment," 148.

7. Yiddish is a truly marvelous language of psychological types, including many subtle deformations of personhood, the schlemiel being only one type. See Leo Rosten, *The Joys of Yiddish.*

8. The term *hoka-hey* refers to the triumph one will have over one's enemies, and includes the obscene reference (which obtains in various forms in other traditional societies) that the victorious males may "mount" their victims.

9. Joseph Epes Brown, "The Wisdom of the Contrary," *Parabola* 4, no. 1 (1979): 54ff.

10. Richard Erdoes, *Lame Deer, Seeker of Visions.*

11. See also Par Lagerkvist's rendition of this figure, in *The Dwarf;* this character, like Aaron the Blackamoor in *Titus Andronicus,* is a villain so thoroughly evil, vengeful, and saturnine as to become clownlike; humor through exaggeration. See the "Creating a Clown" exercise in Chapter 12.

12. We trekked in high Nepal in 1976 in the area jointly designated Solu-Khumbu, which is the access to the highest mountains on earth. Thame monastery is about thirty to forty miles, over mountain passes, from Tibet. The area is culturally Tibetan.

13. The classic documentation of this ceremony is found in Luther Jersted, *Mani Rimdu.* Jersted, an anthropologist, was on the legendary 1963 American West Ridge Climbing Expedition on Mount Everest when he gathered much of this material.

14. See glossary entry in Jersted, *Mani Rimdu,* 169.

15. It was even stranger to notice the physical resemblance of the Tibetans to the high plateau–dwelling Pueblos and Navajos of North America. (We had seen the sand painting in India, too.) But if "geographic diffusion" is to explain the similarity over the 10,000 miles that separates them, we must look to ancient times, and the Siberian land bridge. Independently, we might have to explain the persistence of such precise rituals of healing, in cultures which have come to differ widely. And if it was simply belief that was being manipulated, why did not other, simpler, culture-bound healing rituals supplant the making of these silicone mandalas, with their complexity and recondite symbolism? Also, as I thought

to myself at the time of our visit there, Khumbu is not exactly the beach, or the Painted Desert. Mandalas are also used in the mask-wearing healing rituals of Sri Lanka. See Chapter 10.

16. See Jung, *Memories, Dreams, Reflections*.

17. The remedy *silicea* is associated with lack of stamina, dread, and a passive approach to life. It is the major structuring element in plant and animal tissue that gives it firmness and the ability to "stand up." See James Tyler Kent, *Lectures on Homeopathic Materia Medica*, 1904, 925.

18. The conference was held in Davos, Switzerland, in 1983.

19. Cecil Burney kindly made available to me Dora Kalff's paper of 1980 in which this quotation appears.

20. Cecil Burney, "Exploring Personal Mythology through Sandplay," *Association for Humanistic Psychology Newsletter* (April 1982): 13–15.

21. The dialogue presented here is from my interview with Lucy Barbera and Arya Maloney of Stone Ridge, New York, on February 19, 1989.

22. Among artists of the present century, we think first of the surrealists, of course, like Alberto Giacometti (1901–1966) for his *The Palace at 4 a.m.;* and makers of miniature worlds in boxes, like James Cornell (1903–1972). We would also include the sculptors David Smith (1906–1965), with his monumental constructions, and Hans van de Bovenkamp, whose recent work includes tiny, highly reflective worlds on miniature tables or giant tables so large we must climb up a ladder to reach the playground of mysterious objects on top. The table calls to mind the sand mesa of South American shamanism.

23. Cecil Burney, Ph.D., who died in 1987, was one of the most influential of American sandplay therapists. At the American Psychological Association Symposium on Personal Mythology held in 1980, he discussed sandplay as a viable and important mode for understanding personal myths. He had studied with Dora Kalff, who developed the sandplay method with which I am most famil-iar. Kalff is Swiss and claims part of her original inspiration for this creative therapeutic method came from Jung. The acknowl-edged originator of sandplay therapy is the British psychologist Margaret Lowenfeld. Lowenfeld and her students have contributed greatly to the field of sandplay therapy.

24. Translated by F. Max Müller. See reprint of 1890 edition of his translation of the Upanishads, vol. 1 N.Y.: The Christian Literature, 1897 p. 38.

25. We recognize in the "four kings" the great princes who

attend the High King in the cosmic center: the four archangels passed from Hebraic tradition to the ceremonial magic of the Islamic and Christian West, the rain-bringing Tlalocs who preside over the four quarters of the Central American world mountain embodied in its pyramid temples, the animal powers who stand at the compass points of the North American medicine wheel, and the four kings, or *Ging-pa,* who dance the same seasonal and spiritual round in the masked ritual of Mani Rimdu in Himalayan Nepal. The deeper we probe in our psychomythic spelunking, the more assured we become that the visages that loom out of the shadows will be familiar ones.

26. The origin of the word *swan,* according to one scholar, is the Latin *sonare,* "to sound," which derives from a Sanskrit root meaning "sound." Thus the connection of the name with the myth that the swan sings (*sonare*) before he dies. It has to do with purity and the idea of the original sound behind phenomena. See Whone, *Church, Monastery, Cathedral,* 161ff.

27. Burney, "Exploring Personal Mythology through Sandplay," *Humanistic Psychology Newsletter,* Apr., 1982, 14.

28. Ibid., 15.

29. Gary Gyjax is the founder and informing spirit of the game Dungeons and Dragons. See his *Advanced Dungeons and Dragons.*

30. Live Adventure Quest was begun in 1983 by Nick and Sue Hogan, Tim Shaw, and Bill Thorpe. It has been conducted once each year since then.

31. C. G. Jung and Wolfgang Pauli, "Synchronicity, an Acausal Connecting Principle," in Jung, *The Structure and Dynamics of the Psyche.* Also a more recent and excellent work on this subject: F. David Peat, *Synchronicity.*

32. David Eddings, *The Belgariad,* 7 vols.

33. *Adventure Quarterly* is published by Tim Shaw, P.O. Box 1471, Torrington, CT 06790. *The Quest Connection* is published by William and Kate Thorpe, 48 East Maine Road, Johnson City, NY, 13790.

CHAPTER 12: CREATIVE MYTHOLOGY EXERCISES

1. Ira Progoff should be credited with being the first modern psychologist to train people in keeping a systematic psychological journal. I studied with him in the early 1970s and later went on to develop my own simplified approach to journal keeping, with an

emphasis on the mythological. See also comprehensive personal mythology exercises in David Feinstein and Stanley Krippner, *Personal Mythology*.

2. In about 1969 I experienced an early version of this exercise by a student of Ed Steinbrecher, who had developed a guided imagery in which you go to meet the archetypes of your astrological chart. I found the exercise to be useful. Here the intent is somewhat different, the relationship to the guide may precede all of the other mythological encounters suggested in the exercises.

3. Harner teaches a very powerful version of this exercise in his workshops. See Harner, *The Way of the Shaman*.

4. This exercise is inspired by Stephen Gallegos's work on animals and the chakras. See Chapter 5.

5. This exercise is adapted from Roger and Jennifer Woolger's work. While this, like any form of guided imagery, may be used to explore the many rooms of the psyche, it is their (and my) recommendation that to explore deeply and with maximum effect, the reader should seek a trained past-life therapist or guide. See R. Woolger, *Other Lives, Other Selves*.

6. The original idea for this particular kind of clown was developed from a workshop conducted by the Australian teacher Heather Robb. Robb's method derives from her work with the French mime Jacques LeCoq.

Bibliography

Aaronson, Bernard. Psychosynthesis as System and Therapy. *American Journal of Clinical Hypnosis* 10(4).

Achterberg, Jean. *Imagery in Healing: Shamanism and Modern Medicine.* Boston: Shambhala. 1985.

Adorno, T. W., et al. *The Authoritarian Personality.* New York: Harper & Row. 1950.

Assagioli, Roberto. *Psychosynthesis: A Manual of Principles and Techniques.* New York: Viking. 1955.

Aubin, Nicolas. *Cruels effets de la vengeance du Cardinal Richelieu ou histoire des diables de Loudon.* Amsterdam: Aux dépens d'E. Roger. 1716.

Avalon, Arthur [Sir John Woodroffe]. *The Serpent Power.* Madras, India: Ganesh and Company. 1964.

Avens, Roberts. *Imaginal Body: Para-Jungian Reflections on Soul, Imagination, and Death.* Washington, DC: University Press of America. 1982.

Barthes, Roland. *Mythologies.* New York: Hill and Wang. 1957.

Bastian, Adolf. *Ethnische Elementargedanken in der Lehre vom Menshen,* Vol. 1. Berlin. 1895.

Baum, Frank. *The Wizard of Oz.* New York: Rand McNally. 1904.

Beckett, Samuel. *Waiting for Godot.* New York: Grove Press. 1954.

Bentley, Eric. *Theater of War.* New York: Viking. 1972.

Berne, Eric. *Games People Play: The Psychology of Human Relationships.* New York: Grove Press. 1964.

Black Elk. *The Sacred Pipe.* New York: Penguin. 1971.

Blake, William. *The Marriage of Heaven and Hell.* Miami, FL: University of Miami Press. 1963.

Bolen, Jean Shinoda. *The Tao of Psychology: Synchronicity and the Self.* New York: Harper & Row. 1979.

Bolen, Jean Shinoda. *Goddesses in Everywoman: A New Psychology of Women.* New York: Harper & Row. 1985.

Book of Verse, Childcraft. Vol. 1. Chicago: W. F. Quarrie. 1934.

Brand, Max. *The Untamed.* New York: Putnam's. 1919.

Brown, Barbara B. *New Mind, New Body: Biofeedback: New Directions for the Mind.* New York: Harper & Row. 1974.

Brown, Joseph Epes. The Wisdom of the Contrary. *Parabola* 4(1): 54ff. 1979.

Brown, Joseph Epes. The Bison and the Moth: Lakota Correspondences. *Parabola: Animals* 8(2): 6. 1983.

Bruner, Jerome S. Myth and Identity. In *Myth and Mythmaking,* edited by Henry Murray. Boston: Beacon Press. 1968.

Bruner, Jerome S. *Actual Minds, Possible Worlds.* Cambridge, MA: Harvard University Press. 1986.

Burney, Cecil. Exploring Personal Mythology through sandplay. *Association for Humanistic Psychology Newsletter* (April): 13–15. 1982.

Campbell, Joseph. *The Hero with a Thousand Faces.* Princeton, NJ: Princeton University Press. 1949.

Campbell, Joseph. *The Masks of God.* Vol. 1, *Primitive Mythology.* New York: Viking. 1959.

Campbell, Joseph. *The Flight of the Wild Gander.* New York: Viking. 1961.

Campbell, Joseph. *The Masks of God.* Vol. 3, *Occidental Mythology.* New York: Viking; Penguin, 1976.

Campbell, Joseph. *The Masks of God.* Vol. 4, *Creative Mythology.* New York: Viking. 1968.

Campbell, Joseph. *Myths to Live By.* New York: Viking. 1972.

Campbell, Joseph. *Historical Atlas of World Mythology.* Vol. 1, *The Way of the Animal Powers.* London: Summerfield Press. 1983.

Campbell, Joseph. *The Inner Reaches of Outer Space.* New York: Harper & Row. 1986.

Campbell, Joseph (with Bill Moyers). *The Power of Myth.* Edited by Betty Sue Flowers. New York: Doubleday. 1988.

Castaneda, Carlos. *A Separate Reality: Further Conversations with Don Juan.* New York: Simon & Schuster. 1971.

Castaneda, Carlos. *Tales of Power.* New York: Simon & Schuster. 1974.

Coleridge, Samuel Taylor. *Poems and Prose.* Selected by Kathleen Raine. Middlesex, UK: Penguin. 1957.

Corbin, Henry. *Spiritual Body and Celestial Earth.* Bollingen Series, no. 91. Princeton, NJ: Princeton University Press. 1977.

Covitz, Joel. The Jewish Myth of A-Priori Knowledge. *Spring.* 1971.

Crampton, Martha. The Use of Mental Imagery in Psychosynthesis. *Journal of Humanistic Psychology* (Fall). 1969.

Dante, *Divine Comedy.* Tr. Dorothy Sayers. Baltimore. Penguin Books. 1949.

Darwin, Charles. *Expression of the Emotions in Man and Animals.* New York: Philosophical Library. 1955.

Daumal, René. *Mount Analogue: An Authentic Narrative.* San Francisco: City Lights. 1968.

Davies, Robertson. *Fifth Business.* First book of *The Deptford Trilogy.* New York: Viking. 1970.

Davies, Robertson. *The Manticore.* Second book of *The Deptford Trilogy.* New York: Viking. 1972.

Davies, Robertson. *World of Wonders.* Third book of *The Deptford Trilogy.* New York: Viking. 1976.

Desoille, Robert. *Théorie et pratique du rêve éveillé dirigé.* Geneva: Ed. du Mont-Blanc. 1961.

Desoille, Robert. *The Directed Daydream.* New York: Psychosynthesis Research Foundation. 1966.

Donkin, William. *The Wayfarers: Meher Baba with the God-Intoxicated.* Ahmedragar, India: Adi K. Irani. 1948, 1969.

Dossey, Larry. *Recovering the Soul.* New York: Bantam. 1989.

Eddings, David. *The Belgariad,* 7 vols. New York: Random House.

Eliade, Mircea. *Shamanism: Archaic Techniques of Ecstasy.* Bollingen Series 76. Princeton, NJ: Princeton University Press. 1970.

Eliot, T. S. *Four Quartets.* London: Faber and Faber. 1944.

Ellenberger, Henri F. *The Discovery of the Unconscious: The History and Evolution of Dynamic Psychiatry.* New York: Basic Books. 1970.

Erdoes, Richard. *Lame Deer, Seeker of Visions: The Life of a Sioux Medicine Man.* New York: Simon & Schuster. 1972.

Evans-Wentz, W. Y. *Tibetan Book of the Great Liberation: Or the Method of Realizing Nirvana Through Knowing the Mind.* New York: Oxford University Press. Ed. 1954.

Evans-Wentz, W. Y. *The Tibetan Book of the Dead.* 3d ed. New York: Oxford University Press. Ed. 1957.

Evans-Wentz, W. Y. *Cuchama and Sacred Mountains.* Athens, OH: Ohio University Press, Swallow Press. 1982.

Feinstein, David. Personal Mythology as a Paradigm for a Holistic Public Psychology. *American Journal of Orthopsychiatry* 49(2). 1979.

Feinstein, David. Encountering Our Mythic Depths. *Association for Humanistic Psychology Newsletter* (April). 1982.

Feinstein, David, and Krippner, Stanley. *Personal Mythology.* Los Angeles: Tarcher. 1988.

Fenton, W. M. The Seneca Society of Faces. *Scientific American* 64. 1937.

Fenton, W. M. The Masked Medicine Societies. *Annual Report of the Smithsonian Institution*. Washington, DC). 1940.

Ford, Patrick K. *The Mabinogi and Other Medieval Welsh Tales*. Berkeley: University of California Press. 1977.

Fox, Jonathan. Moreno and His Theater. *Psychotherapy, Psychodrama and Sociometry* 31. 1978.

Fox, Jonathan. Playback Theater: The Community Sees Itself. In *Drama in Therapy*, edited by R. Courtney and G. Schattner. New York: Drama Book Specialists. 1981.

Fox, Michael. *Behavior of Wolves, Dogs, and Canids*. New York: Harper & Row. 1972.

Frank, Jerome David. *Persuasion and Healing: A Comparative Study of Psychotherapy*. Baltimore, MD: Johns Hopkins University Press. 1973.

Freud, Sigmund. *The Psychopathology of Everyday Life*. New York: Macmillan. 1914.

Freud, Sigmund. *Totem and Taboo: Some Points of Agreement between the Mental Lives of Savages and Neurotics*. New York: Norton. 1952.

Freud, Sigmund. *The Future of an Illusion*. New York: Doubleday. 1957.

Freud, Sigmund. *Collected Papers*, Vol. 5. New York: Basic Books. 1959.

Freud, Sigmund. The Psycho-Analytic Movement. In *Collected Papers*, Vol. 1. Translated under the supervision of Joan Riviere. International Psycho-Analytical Library, edited by Ernest Jones, no. 7. New York: Basic Books. 1959.

Freud, Sigmund. Dreams and Telepathy. In *Collected Papers*, Vol. 4. Translated under the supervision of Joan Riviere. International Psycho-Analytical Library, edited by Ernest Jones, no. 7. New York: Basic Books. 1959.

Freud, Sigmund. *A General Introduction to Psychoanalysis*. New York: Washington Square Press. 1968.

Frobenius, Leo. *The Voice of Africa*. 2 vols. New York and London: Benjamin Blom. 1913.

Frobenius, Leo. *Kulturgeschichte Afrikas*. Zurich: Phaidon. 1923.

Gallegos, Eligio Stephen. *The Personal Totem Pole*. Santa Fe: Moon Bear Press. 1987.

Garfield, Patricia. *Pathways to Ecstasy: The Way of the Dream Mandala*. New York: Holt, Rinehart & Winston. 1979.

Goleman, Daniel. New View of Mind Gives Unconscious Expanded Role. *New York Times*, Feb. 7, sec. C, 1. 1984.

Goslin, David A. *The Search for Ability: Standardized Testing in Social Perspective*. New York: Russell Sage Foundation. 1963.

Goslin, David A. *The School in Contemporary Society*. Glenview, IL: Scott, Foresman. 1965.

Goslin, David A. *Teachers and Testing*. New York: Russell Sage Foundation. 1967.

Goslin, David A., ed. *Handbook of Socialization Theory and Research*. Chicago: Rand McNally. 1969.

Graves, Robert. *Hercules, My Shipmate: A Novel*. New York: Creative Age Press. 1945.

Graves, Robert. *The Greek Myths*. Middlesex, UK: Penguin. 1955.

Graves, Robert. *The White Goddess: A Historical Grammar of Poetic Myth*. London: Faber and Faber. 1959.

Green, Hannah. *I Never Promised You a Rose Garden*. New York: New American Library. 1964.

Grof, Stanislav. Psycholytic and Psychedelic Therapy with LSD: Toward an Integration of Approaches. Paper presented at Conference of the European Association for Psycholytic Therapy, Frankfurt am Main, West Germany. 1969.

Grof, Stanislav. Theoretical and Empirical Basis of Transpersonal Psychology and Psychotherapy: Observations from LSD Research. *Journal of Transpersonal Psychology*. 1973.

Grof, Stanislav. *Realms of the Human Unconscious: Observations from LSD Research*. New York: Viking. 1975.

Grof, Stanislav. *LSD Psychotherapy*. Pomona, CA: Hunter House. 1980.

Grof, Stanislav. *Beyond the Brain: Birth, Death, and Transcendence in Psychotherapy*. Albany: State University of New York Press. 1985.

Grof, Stanislav, and Grof, Christina. *Beyond Death: The Gates of Consciousness*. London: Thames and Hudson. 1980.

Gurdjieff, G. I. *Beelzebub's Tales to His Grandson*. In *All and Everything: Ten Books in Three Series*. New York: Dutton. 1964.

Gyjax, Gary. *Advanced Dungeons and Dragons*. 4th ed. Lake Geneva: WI: TSR Games. 1977.

Hale, Nathan G., Jr., ed. *Psychotherapy and Multiple Personality: Selected Essays*. Cambridge, MA: Harvard University Press. 1975.

Hall, Calvin. What People Dream About. *Scientific American* 184. 1951.

Harner, Michael. *The Way of the Shaman*. New York: Harper & Row. 1980.

Hesse, Herman. *The Glass Bead Game (Magister Ludi)*. New York: Holt, Rinehart & Winston. 1969.

Hillman, James. *Revisioning Psychology*. New York: Harper & Row. 1975.

Hillman, James. On Peaks and Vales. In *On the Way to Self Knowledge,* edited by Jacob Needleman and Dennis Lewis. New York: Knopf. 1976.

Hillman, James. *The Dream and the Underworld.* New York: Harper & Row. 1979.

Huizinga, Johan. *Homo Ludens: A Study of the Play-Element in Culture.* Boston: Beacon Press. 1955.

Huxley, Aldous. *The Devils of Loudon.* New York: Harper & Row. 1952.

I Ching. Wilhelm Edition. New York: Bollingen. 1950.

James, William. *Principles of Psychology,* Vol. 2. New York: Dover. 1950.

James, William. *The Varieties of Religious Experience: A Study in Human Nature.* New York: New American Library. 1958.

Jaynes, Julian. *The Origin of Consciousness in the Breakdown of the Bicameral Mind.* Boston: Houghton Mifflin. 1976.

Jersted, Luther. *Mani Rimdu.* Seattle: University of Washington Press. 1969.

Johnson, Buffie. *The Lady of the Beasts.* New York: Harper & Row. 1988.

Johnston, Charles. *The Yoga Sutras of Patanjali: The Book of Spiritual Man.* London: John M. Watkins. 1964.

Jones, Gwyn, and Jones, Thomas, eds., Tr. *The Mabinogion.* New York; London: Everyman's Library. J. M. Dent & Sons. 1949.

Joyce, James. *The Portrait of the Artist as a Young Man.*

Joyce, James. *Finnegans Wake.* New York: Viking. 1947.

Joyce, James. *Ulysses.* New York: Vintage. 1961.

Jung, C. G. *Psychological Reflections: A New Anthology of His Writings, 1905–1961.* Bollingen Series XXXI. Princeton, NJ: Princeton University Press. 1953.

Jung, C. G. *Modern Man in Search of a Soul.* New York: Harcourt, Brace. 1955.

Jung, C. G. *The Archetypes and the Collective Unconscious.* Bollingen Series XX, vol. 9. New York: Pantheon Books. 1959.

Jung, C. G. *Memories, Dreams, Reflections.* Edited by Aniela Jaffe and translated by Richard Wilson and Clara Winston. New York: Pantheon Books. 1963.

Jung, C. G. *Mysterium Coniunctionis.* Bollingen Series XX, vol. 14. Princeton, NJ: Princeton University Press. 1963.

Jung, C. G. *The Practice of Psychotherapy.* 2d ed. Bollingen Series XX, vol. 18. Princeton, NJ: Princeton University Press. 1966.

Jung, C. G. The Practical Use of Dream-Analysis. In *The Practice of Psychotherapy.* Bollingen Seriex XX, vol. 16. Princeton, NJ: Princeton University Press. 1966.

Jung, C. G. *Symbols of Transformation*. 2 ed. Bollingen Series XX, vol. 5. 2nd ed. Princeton, NJ: Princeton University Press. 1967.

Jung, C. G. *Alchemical Studies*. Bollingen Series XX, vol. 13. Princeton, NJ: Princeton University Press. 1968.

Jung, C. G. Paracelsus as a Spiritual Phenomenon. In *Alchemical Studies*. Bollingen Series XX, vol. 13. Princeton, NJ: Princeton University Press. 1968.

Jung, C. G. *Psychology and Alchemy*. 2d ed. Bollingen Series XX, vol. 12. Princeton, NJ: Princeton University Press. 1968.

Jung, C. G. *The Structure and Dynamics of the Psyche*. Bollingen Series XX, vol. 8. Princeton, NJ: Princeton University Press. 1969.

Jung, C. G. On the Nature of the Psyche. In *The Structure and Dynamics of the Psyche*. Bollingen Series XX, vol. 8. Princeton, NJ: Princeton University Press. 1969.

Jung, C. G. *Experimental Researches*. Bollingen Series XX, vol. 2. Princeton, NJ: Princeton University Press. 1973.

Jung, C. G. *Word and Image*. Edited by Aniela Jaffe. Bollingen Series XCVII. Princeton, NJ: Princeton University Press. 1979.

Jung, C. G. *Seven Sermons to the Dead*. In *Memories, Dreams, Reflections*. Edited by Aniela Jaffe. New York: Pantheon Books.

Kagan, Jerome, ed. *Psychology: An Introduction*. 6th ed. New York: Harcourt, Brace. 1988.

Kaplan, Bert, ed. *The Inner World of Mental Illness: A Series of First-Person Accounts of What It Was Like*. New York: Harper & Row. 1964.

Kastenbaum, Richard, and Aisenberg, Ruth. *The Psychology of Death*. New York: Springer. 1972.

Kazin, Alfred, ed. *The Viking Portable Blake*. New York: Viking. 1946.

Keen, Sam, and Fox, Anne Valley. *Your Mythic Journey*. Los Angeles: Tarcher. 1989.

Keleman, Stanley. *Living Your Dying*. Berkeley, CA: Center Press. 1985.

Kelly, G. A. *The Psychology of Personal Constructs*. 2 vols. New York: Norton. 1955.

Kent, James Tyler. *Lectures on Homeopathic Materia Medica*. New Delhi: Jain. 1904.

Kerenyi, Carl. *Asklepios: Archetypal Image of the Physician's Existence*. New York: Pantheon. 1959.

Keyes, Margaret Frings. *The Inward Journey: Art as Therapy*. Rev. ed. Reality of the Psyche Series. Peru, IL: Open Court. 1985.

Kieffer, Gene, ed. *Kundalini for the New Age: Selected Writings of Gopi Krishna*. New York: Bantam. 1988.

Kirby, E. T. The Shamanistic Origins of Popular Entertainment. *Drama Review*.

Kluckhohn, Clyde. Recurrent Themes in Myths and Mythmaking. In *Myth and Mythmaking*, edited by Henry A. Murray. Boston: Beacon Press. 1988.

Kramer, S. N., and Wolkstein, D. *Inanna, Queen of Heaven and Earth: Her Stories and Hymns from Sumer*. New York: Harper & Row. 1983.

Kübler-Ross, Elisabeth. *On Death and Dying*. New York: Macmillan. 1969.

Kuhn, Thomas S. *The Structure of Scientific Revolutions*. Chicago: University of Chicago Press. 1962.

Laing, R. D. *The Divided Self: An Existential Study in Sanity and Madness*. Middlesex, UK: Penguin. 1965.

Laing, R. D. *The Politics of Experience*. New York: Ballantine. 1967.

Larsen, Robin. Spiritcatcher's Notebook, part 1. Ph.D. diss., Union Graduate School. 1977.

Larsen, Robin, ed. *Emanuel Swedenborg: A Continuing Vision*. New York: Swedenborg Foundation. 1988.

Larsen, Stephen. Myth and Consciousness. Ph.D. diss., Union Graduate School, 1975.

Larsen, Stephen. *The Shaman's Doorway*. New York: Harper & Row. 1976.

Larsen, Stephen. Swedenborg and the Visionary Tradition. *Studia Swedenborgiana* 3(4): 7. 1980.

Leuner, Hanscarl. Guided Affective Imagery (GAI): A Method of Intensive Psychotherapy. *American Journal of Psychotherapy* 10(4). 1969.

Levin, Harry. Some Meanings of Myth. In *Myth and Mythmaking*, edited by Henry A. Murray. Boston: Beacon Press. 1968.

Levinson, Daniel J. *The Seasons of a Man's Life*. New York: Knopf. 1978.

Lewis, C. S. *The Chronicles of Narnia*. New York: Macmillan. 1988.

Lommel, Andreas. *Masks: Their Meaning and Function*. London: Ferndale Editions. 1981.

Lopez, Barry. Renegotiating the Contracts. *Parabola: Animals* 8(2): 14. 1983.

McGuire, William, ed. *The Freud/Jung Letters*. Princeton, NJ: Princeton University Press. 1974.

Mann, Thomas. *The Magic Mountain (Der Zauberberg)*. New York: Knopf. 1927.

Marcuse, Herbert. *Eros and Civilization: A Philosophical Inquiry into Freud.* New York: Vintage. 1955.

Masson, Jeffrey. *The Assault on Truth.* Farrar Straus Giroux. 1984.

Masters, R. E. L. *The Goddess Sekhmet.* New York: Amity House. 1988.

Masters, Robert, and Houston, Jean. *The Varieties of Psychedelic Experience.* New York: Dell. 1966.

Matarasso, P. M., ed. *The Quest of the Holy Grail.* Middlesex, UK: Penguin. 1969.

Meher Baba. *Among the God-Intoxicated.* See Donkin.

Meier, C. A. *Ancient Incubation and Modern Psychotherapy.* Evanston, IL: Northwestern University Press. 1967.

Milgram, Stanley. Behavioral Study of Obedience and Disobedience to Authority. *Journal of Abnormal and Social Psychology.* 371–378. 1963, 1967.

Miller, David LeRoy. *The New Polytheism: Rebirth of the Gods and Goddesses.* New York: Harper & Row. 1974.

Moody, Raymond A. *Life after Life.* Saint Simons Island, GA: Mockingbird. 1981.

Moreno, J. L. *Theater of Spontaneity.* Boston: Beacon Press. 1973.

Murray, Margaret Alice. *The God of the Witches.* New York: Oxford University Press. 1970.

Mussen, P. H., Conger, J. J., and Kagan, J. Child Development and Personality. New York: Harper & Row. 1988.

Naranjo, Claudio, and Ornstein, Robert. *The Healing Journey.* New York: Ballantine, Walden Edition. 1972.

Needleman, Jacob, and Lewis, Dennis, eds. *On the Way to Self Knowledge.* New York: Knopf. 1976.

Neihardt, John G. *Black Elk Speaks.* Lincoln: University of Nebraska Press. 1961.

Neumann, Erich. *The Origins and History of Consciousness.* Bollingen Series 42. New York: Pantheon Books. 1964.

Nietzsche, Friedrich Wilhelm. *The Birth of Tragedy and the Genealogy of Morals.* Garden City, NY: Doubleday. 1956.

Oesterreich, T. K. *Possession, Demoniacal and Other.* New Hyde Park, NY: University Books. 1966.

Ornstein, Robert. *The Psychology of Consciousness.* New York: Harcourt, Brace. 1977.

Otto, Walter F. *Dionysus: Myth and Cult.* Bloomington: Indiana University Press. 1965.

Ouspensky, P. D. *In Search of the Miraculous: Fragments of an Unknown Teaching.* New York: Harcourt, Brace. 1949.

Ouspensky, P. D. *The Fourth Way: A Record of Talks and Answers to Questions Based on the Teaching of G. I. Gurdjieff.* New York: Knopf. 1957.

Pagels, Elaine H. *The Gnostic Gospels.* New York: Random House. 1979.

Paley, Morton D. *William Blake.* New York: Dutton. 1978.

Patai, Raphael. *The Hebrew Goddess.* New York: Ktav Publishing House. 1967.

Patterson, Francine. Conversations with a Gorilla. *National Geographic,* Oct., 483. 1978.

Peat, F. David. *Synchronicity: The Bridge Between Matter and Mind.* New York: Bantam. 1987.

Perera, Sylvia Brinton. *Descent to the Goddess: A Way of Initiation for Women.* Toronto: Inner City Books. 1981.

Perls, Frederick. *Gestalt Therapy Verbatim.* Lafayette: Real People Press. 1969.

Perry, John Weir. *The Lord of the Four Quarters: Myths of the Royal Father.* New York: Braziller. 1966.

Piaget, Jean, and Inhelder, B. *The Psychology of the Child.* New York: Basic Books. 1969.

Plotinus. *The Six Enneads.* Translated by S. Mackenna. Great Books of the Western World, vol. 17. Chicago: W. Benton. 1952.

Pound, Ezra. *The Cantos of Ezra Pound.* New York: New Directions. 1948.

Pribram, Karl. Problems Concerning the Structure of Consciousness. In *Consciousness and the Brain,* edited by G. Globus et al. New York: Plenum. 1976.

Prince, Morton. *Dissociation of a Personality: A Biographical Study in Abnormal Psychology.* Westport, CT: Greenwood Press. 1969.

Radin, Paul. *The Trickster: A Study in American Indian Mythology.* New York: Bell Publishing. 1956.

Ring, Kenneth. *Life at Death.* New York: Quill. 1982.

Ring, Kenneth. *Heading Toward Omega.* New York: Quill. 1984.

Robbins, Ronald. *The Rhythmic Cycle of Change.* Poughkeepsie, NY: Neshama Publications. 1988.

Robinson, James M., ed. *The Nag Hammadi Library.* New York: Harper & Row. 1982.

Rogers, Carl R., et al. *Person to Person: The Problems of Being Human.* Lafayette, CA: Real People Press. 1967.

Ross, Dorothy. *G. Stanley Hall: The Psychologist as Prophet.* Chicago: University of Chicago Press. 1972.

Rosten, Leo. *The Joys of Yiddish.* New York: Pocket Books. 1968.

Samuels, Mike, and Samuels, Nancy. *Seeing with the Mind's Eye.* New York: Random House. 1975.

Sandars, N. K., ed. *The Epic of Gilgamesh*. Middlesex, UK: Penguin. 1960.

Sanford, John. *Invisible Partners*. Ramsay, NJ: Paulist Press. 1980.

Sannella, Lee. *Kundalini: Psychosis or Transcendence*. San Francisco: H. S. Dakin. 1976.

Santayana, George. The Comic Mask. In *Theories of Comedy*, edited by Peter Lauter. Garden City, NY: Doubleday. 1964.

Schreiber, Flora Rheta. *Sybil*. New York: Warner Books. 1974.

Sechrist, Elsie. *Dreams, Your Magic Mirror: With Interpretations of Edgar Cayce*. New York: Warner Books. 1974.

Sheehy, Gail. *Passages: Predictable Crises of Adult Life*. New York: Bantam. 1977.

Sheldrake, Rupert. *The New Science of Life*. Los Angeles: Tarcher. 1981.

Sheldrake, Rupert. *The Presence of the Past: Morphic Resonance and the Memory of Nature*. New York: Times Books. 1988.

Shepard, Paul. The Ark of the Mind. *Parabola: Animals* 8(2): 54. 1983.

Shuttle, Penelope, and Redgrove, Peter. *The Wise Wound: Myths, Realities, and Meanings of Menstruation*. Rev. ed. New York: Grove. 1988.

Silberer, Herbert. Report on a Method of Eliciting and Observing Certain Hallucination Phenomena. In *Organization and Pathology of Thought*, edited by D. Rapaport. New York: Columbia University Press. 1951.

Simonton, Carl, and Simonton, Stephanie. *Getting Well Again: A Step-by-Step Self-Help Guide to Overcoming Cancer for Patients and Their Families*. Los Angeles: Tarcher. 1978.

Singer, Jerome. *The Inner World of Daydreaming*. New York: Harper & Row. 1975.

Sizemore, Chris C., and Pittillo, Ellen S. *I'm Eve*. New York: Jove. 1983.

Skinner, B. F. *Beyond Freedom and Dignity*. New York: Knopf. 1971.

Staudenmaeier, Ludwig. *Die Magie als Experimentelle Naturwissenschaft*. Leipzig. *See* Oesterreich. 1912.

Swedenborg, Emanuel. *Arcana Coelestia*. 8 vols. London: John Lewis, 1749–1756; New York: Swedenborg Foundation, 1949.

Swedenborg, Emanuel. *The Intercourse Between the Soul and Body*. Translated by J. J. G. Wilkinson. London: Swedenborg Society. 1769.

Swedenborg, Emanuel. *Spiritual Diary, 1747–1783*, 5 vols. Translated by A. W. Acton. London: Swedenborg Society. 1902.

Tart, Charles. *Altered States of Consciousness*. New York: Doubleday. 1969.

Tedlock, Barbara. Boundaries of Belief. *Parabola* 4(1): 70. 1979.

Thigpen, Cobett H., and Cleckley, Hervey M. *The Three Faces of Eve*. New York: McGraw-Hill. 1957.

Tolkien, J. R. R. *The Lord of the Rings*. New York: Ballantine. 1965.

Tolkien, J. R. R. *The Hobbit: Or There and Back Again*. Boston: Houghton Mifflin. 1966.

Tolkien, J. R. R. *The Fellowship of the Ring*. New York: Ballantine. 1973.

Tolkien, J. R. R. *The Silmarillion*. Boston: Houghton Mifflin; London: Allen & Unwin. 1977.

Tompkins, Peter, and Bird, Christopher. *The Secret Life of Plants*. New York: Harper & Row. 1973.

Towsen, John H. *Clowns*. New York: Hawthorn Books. 1976.

Trungpa, Chogyam. The Six Realms of Existence. In *Consciousness, Brain, States of Awareness, Mysticism*, edited by D. Goleman. New York: Harper & Row. 1979.

Van Dusen, Wilson. The Natural Depth in Man. In *Person to Person: The Problems of Being Human*, edited by Carl R. Rogers et al. Lafayette, CA: Real People Press. 1967.

Van Dusen, Wilson. *The Presence of Spirits in Madness*. New York: Swedenborg Foundation. 1968.

Van Dusen, Wilson. *The Natural Depth in Man*. New York: Harper & Row. 1972.

Van Dusen, Wilson. *The Presence of Other Worlds: The Psychological/ Spiritual Findings of Emanuel Swedenborg*. New York: Harper & Row. 1974.

Van Ehrenwald, Jan. *New Dimensions in Deep Analysis*. London: Allen & Unwin. 1954.

Von Eschenbach, Wolfram. *Parzival*. Translated by Helen M. Mustard and Charles E. Passeg. New York: Vintage. 1961.

Von Franz, Marie-Louise. *An Introduction to the Psychology of Fairytales*. New York: Spring. 1970.

Von Franz, Marie-Louise. *Interpretation of Fairytales*. New York: Spring. 1970.

Von Franz, Marie-Louise. *Shadow and Evil in Fairytales*. New York: Spring. 1974.

Wallace, A. F. C. Dreams and Wishes of the Soul. *American Anthropologist*. 1958.

Waters, Frank. Symbols and Sacred Mountains. *Phoenix: The Journal of Transpersonal Anthropology*, vol. VI nos. 1 and 2, p. 59.

Weaver, Rix. *The Old, Wise Woman: A Study of Active Imagination.* London: Vincent Stuart. 1964.

Werner, Heinz. *The Comparative Psychology of Mental Development.* New York: Science Editions. 1948.

Whitmont, Edward C. *The Return of the Goddess.* New York: Crossroad. 1982.

Whone, Herbert. *Church, Monastery, Cathedral: A Guide to the Symbolism of the Christian Tradition.* Tisbury, UK: Compton Russell. 1977.

Williams, Charles Allyn. *Oriental Affinities of the Legend of the Hairy Anchorite. Part One: Pre-Christian.* Chicago: University of Illinois. 1925.

Williams, Strephon Kaplan. *Jungian-Senoi Dreamwork Manual.* Rev. ed. Berkeley, CA: Journey Press. 1980.

Wirz, Paul. *Exorcism and the Art of Healing in Ceylon.* Leiden: Brill. 1954.

Wolfe, W. Thomas. *And the Sun Is Up: Kundalini Rises in the West.* Red Hook, NY: Academy Hill. 1978.

Woodroffe, John George. *The Serpent Power: Being the Shat-chakra-nirupana and Paduka-panchaka: Two Works on Laya Yoga.* Madras: Ganesh. 1964.

Woolger, Roger. Death and the hero. *Arche: Notes and Papers on Archaic Studies* 2. 1978.

Woolger, Roger. Imaginal techniques in Past-Life Therapy. *Journal of Regression Therapy* 1(1). 1986.

Woolger, Roger. *Other Lives, Other Selves.* New York: Doubleday. 1987.

Woolger, Roger, and Woolger, Jennifer. *The Goddess Within: A Guide to the Eternal Myths That Shape Women's Lives.* New York: Ballantine. 1989.

Worcester, John. *Correspondences of the Bible: The Animals.* Boston: Lockwood, Brooks. 1875.

Yeats, William Butler. *Essays and Introductions.* New York: Macmillan. 1965.

Yeats, William Butler. *A Vision.* London: Macmillan. 1969.

Zabriskie, Philip. Goddesses in our Midst. *Quadrant,* no. 17. 1974.

Zubek, John, ed. *Sensory Deprivation: Fifteen Years of Research.* New York: Appleton-Century-Crofts. 1969.

Index

Animals *(cont.)*
99; shape-changer, 73, 153–154;
spirit, 66, 149–150, 178; and
stereotypes, 157; swan, 286;
symbolism, 168–169, 172–174;
taboos, 153; theriogenic zone of
the psyche, 149; totemistic,
172–177, 182. *See also* Animism;
Finding One's Allies: Animal,
Vegetable, and Mineral; Horses;
Snakes; Theriomorphism
Animism, 32, 59, 71, 148–150,
242
Animus, 165, 188
ANS (automatic nervous system),
244
Anthropology, xxiii, 42
Anubis, 205
Anya-manas, 246
Aphrodite, 31, 76, 199, 201
Apocalypse, horsemen of, 168
Apollo, 202
Ares, 202
Archetypes, xxii, xxiv, 14, 28–29,
58–59, 65–66, 98, 100, 188,
195, 202–203, 268, 272; animal,
155, 160; coincidence, 181;
defined, xxiv, 328n; dream, 37,
38–39; feminine, 195, *195,*
201–202, 228; Great Man, xxxiii,
329n; Great Mother, 161;
hero, 105; hubris, 28; mandala,
282; male, 202; masculine
principle, 188; powers, 157, 182,
236, 258; in puberty rites, 33;
of psyche, 130, 197; psychodrama, 253; psychology, 46,
48–49, 58, 59, 91, 178, 216;
qualities, 133; virtues, 179;
wise old man, 210–214; witch,
194–196. *See also* Dream interpretation; Hillman; Jung
Ariadne, 106
Aristotle, xxxiv; logic of, 71, 262,
291
Ark, Noah's, 152, 155, 172
Ark of the Covenant, 152
Ars moriendi, 142

Art, xxvii, 47–48, 77–78, 357n;
therapy, 32
Artist, 47–48
Artemis, 76, 176, 199, 201
Arthur. *See* King Arthur
ASC (Altered State of Conscious-
ness), 81. *See also* Trance
Asclepius, 25, 130, 162, 222, 229,
243, 286; Asclepia at Epidaurus,
161, 229, 231, 233
Asia Minor, cults of, 152
Aslan, 173
Assimilation (cognitive), 62
Astrology, 199–201, 349n
Asura, 59
Atavistic behavior, xxviii
Athena, 201, 243
Atman, 205
Audience, 28, 30, 354n, 355n
Authoritarian personalities, 77
Autosymbolic function, 51
Avatar, 65
Avens, Robert, 46, 48, 71
Aztecs: comic performances, 264;
mythology, 123

B

Baba Yaga, 194
Baba, Meher, 60
Backster, Clever, 154
Balaam, 166–167
Barbera, Lucy, 278–284
Bardo plane, 59
Barfield, Owen, 48
Barry, Whistling Dan, 154
Barthes, Roland, 18
Bastian, Adolph, 28, 329n,
335n
Bathsheba, 78
Baucis, 213–214
Baudelaire, Charles, 232;
"Correspondences" (trans.),
352n–353n
Beastmaster, 154
Beauty and the Beast, 3
Beckett, Samuel, 183, 272

ABOUT THE AUTHOR

STEPHEN LARSEN, Ph.D., is a psychology professor and psychotherapist who lives in New Paltz, New York. Dr. Larsen is the author of *The Shaman's Doorway*. He gives lectures and workshops internationally on myth and the psychology of the visionary process. Dr. Larsen studied for years with the late mythologist Joseph Campbell and, with his wife, Robin Larsen, is currently writing Campbell's authorized biography.